Is it Genuine?

How to Collect Antiques with Confidence

Consultants

DANIEL AGNEW

DAVID BATTIE

JOHN BLY

SIMON BULL

GEORGE GLASTRIS

CHARLES HAJDAMACH

PETER HORNSBY

BRAND INGLIS

HILARY KAY

WILLIAM C. KETCHUM JR.

GORDON LANG

ANNE METCALFE

CHRISTOPHER PAYNE

DR. JOHN RICHARDSON

STELLA RUBIN

DONALD SACK

ERIC J. G. SMITH

PETER WALDRON

Acknowledgments

The Publisher would like to thank the following for their much-valued assistance with the production of this book:
Broadfield House Glass Museum, Peter Gould, Sharon Griggs, The Pewter Society, Derek Roberts Antiques, Robert Sack, Skinner Inc., Boston, Sotheby's Institute of Art, Southampton Institute, Roger Still, West Dean College, Robert Wren, The Worshipful Company of Pewterers.

Is it Genuine?

How to Collect Antiques with Confidence

GENERAL EDITOR JOHN BLY

Miller's Is it Genuine? How to Collect Antiques with Confidence
General Editor: **John Bly**

First published in Great Britain in 2002 by Miller's, a division of
Mitchell Beazley, imprints of Octopus Publishing Group Ltd.

This edition published 2003 by Chancellor Press,
an imprint of Bounty Books,
a division of Octopus Publishing Group Ltd
2-4 Heron Quays, London E14 4JP

Miller's is a registered trademark of Octopus Publishing Group Ltd

Commissioning Editor: **Anna Sanderson**
Executive Art Editor: **Rhonda Fisher**
Jacket design and styling: **Victoria Bevan**
Freelance Designer: **Gillian Andrews**
Editorial Assistant: **Rose Hudson**
Proofreader: **Miranda Stonor**
Indexer: **Sue Farr**
Picture Research: **Pernilla Pearce**
Production: **Angela Couchman**
Illustrations: **Amanda Patton**
Photography: **Steve Tanner**
Other photography: **Tim Ridley, Ian Booth, Chris Halton**

ISBN 0 7537 0858 2

A CIP catalogue record for this book is available from the British Library
Set in Stone Sans and Stone Serif
Produced by Toppan Printing Co., (HK) Ltd
Printed and bound in China

Jacket images from left to right
Front: A genuine Amos 'n' Andy toy (see page 212); a George III mahogany side table, c.1745; a
silver bowl with fake mark (see page 119); a copy of a Regency decanter, c.1880; a copy of a
Staffordshire figure group, c.1920
Back cover: A reproduction gateleg table, c.1930; a George II giltwood mirror

Contents

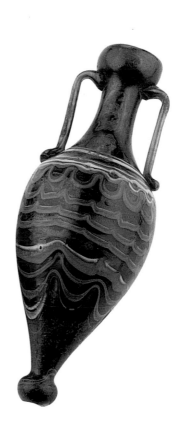

Introduction

▲ **A fake "Longquan" celadon vase, Song Dynasty**

The original vases are particularly sought-after by the Japanese, who call them *kinuta*. This is an extremely convincing copy, probably from Japan and made in the last 50 years.

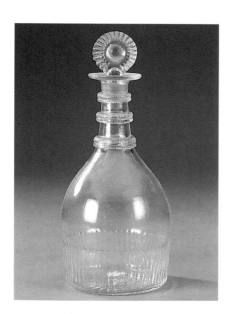

▲ **A fake Cork decanter**

Thinly-blown decanters such as this were probably made in the inter-war years. Many are marked on the base with "Cork Glass Co."

The genuine work of art has been perpetually copied. Over the years, domestic articles have been modified according to fashion trends or for the purpose of modernization. In recent times – that is, since the middle of the 19th century – antiques have been reproduced for a vast range of different reasons in varying degrees of accuracy, from the vague look-alike to the deceptively precise fake. This oft-neglected "why-factor" aspect of art history is very much at the heart of this book; it is understanding the reason, as much as the method, which enables us to answer the question: is it genuine?

Furniture is, without a doubt, the most problematic collectable antiques area. Unlike porcelain or glass, it alters with age. Even untampered with, it will have changed colour as the wood has oxidized or faded, and it will also have changed shape, albeit fractionally, as the timber has shrunk. Sadly, furniture has also been altered for fashion and use as well as pecuniary gain.

While the latter is immoral, it is not in itself illegal. But changing the character, use or appearance of a piece of hallmarked English silver certainly is. Here again, fashion was a force behind the existence of spurious pieces, but so too was a punitive tax system, and so we also gain an insight into economic factors.

Other metalwares were widely copied in the late 19th century, and after more than one hundred years' use, it can be a challenge recognizing the old from the not so old. Perusing manufacturers' catalogues of the 1890s can give an indication of how huge the brass and pewter reproduction industry was at that time.

Porcelain, too, can be a minefield for the novice collector, although here the main danger today is spotting the ingenious repair. Nevertheless, with an absence of marks on some wares and fake marks on others, the study of ceramics can become an all-absorbing passion, reflecting as it does the social history behind it.

There is no category of art or antique that has not at some time been copied, altered, improved, or in one way or another exists as less than genuine. The team of experts who contributed to this book are no strangers to such pieces, and their advice on how to detect them is as easy to follow as only instructions from dedicated tutors can be. Their love of their subject shines through. As any one of them will advise you: read the book, then handle the antique, then read the book again. Happy hunting!

JOHN BLY

WHAT DOES IT MEAN?

Genuine *adj.* not fake or counterfeit; original; real; authentic.

Fake *vb.* to cause (something inferior or not genuine) to appear more valuable, desirable or real by fraud or pretence.

Forgery *n.* the act of reproducing something for a deceitful or fraudulent purpose.

Reproduction *n.* an imitation or facsimile of a work of art.

Alteration *n.* an adjustment, change or modification.

Pastiche *n.* a work of art that mixes styles, materials, etc.

Collins English Dictionary

◄ The marriage

The base of this bureau is mostly 18th-century, but the rather odd proportions of the upper part show that it dates from the 20th century. The piece probably started life as a bureau, without any bookcase, and at the time the top was added the lower half was embellished with floral marquetry.

◄ How old are they?

The joint stool is the earliest form of stool commonly seen today. It was first popular in the 17th century (far left), but was reproduced in large numbers in the 1930s (near left). Signs of age you should look for include:

• A mellow sheen with variations in tone where the stool has been exposed to wear.

• Genuine wear on the stretchers. The modern version's stretchers have been artificially dipped in the centre.

• Irregular-shaped pegs standing proud – but beware of fakes left proud to give an impression of shrinkage.

• Dry appearance underneath.

Continental Furniture

▲ ▶ **A gilt bronze mounted ebonized cabinet typical of the French Napoleon III period, c.1860**
The overall "credenza" shape is also seen in England at the same time. However, in this instance some elements of the *pietre dure* marble inlay are from the 17th century; for example, the dromedary and the rather strange-looking buffalo.

FRENCH PERIODS & STYLES		
DATE	**PERIOD**	**STYLE**
1550	Renaissance	Renaissance Mannerist
1600		
	Louis XIII *1610–43*	Baroque
1650	Louis XIV *1643–1715*	
1700		Rococo
	Régence	
	Louis XV *1723–74*	
1750		
	Louis XVI *1774–93*	Neo-classical
	Directoire *1793–99*	
	Empire *1799–1815*	Empire
1800		
	Restauration *1815–30*	
	Louis Philippe *1830–48*	Eclectic
1850		
	2nd Empire *1852–70*	
	3rd Republic *1871–1940*	The Louis Revivals: Louis IV/V/VI
1900		Art Nouveau

The art of copying is as old as time itself, but in terms of European furniture it is practical to discuss only the 17th century through to the present day, quite simply because earlier pieces are rarely seen on the market or outside museums. It is as well, at this point, to bear in mind that the older the piece is, or is purported to be, the more likely that it has sustained alteration or at the very least repair.

It is necessary to distinguish between the fake and the reproduction, the deliberate forgery and the genuine copy, while at the same time bearing in mind allowable restoration or repair. The marriage is another, often unhappy, area of alteration that merits further examination.

Ultimately, nothing will replace hands-on experience – seize any opportunity to examine closely pieces of furniture of every date. It is only then that the theory will become clear.

The Copy

This is possibly the least contentious type of potentially deceptive furniture. Copies are mainly confined to the 19th and 20th centuries because the 17th, 18th and first quarter of the 19th centuries were mainly periods of progression. One style followed on from another, either as a natural evolution, such as the Rococo from the Régence, or as a direct conflict with and reaction against the former style, for example when the sophisticated Transitional style emerged out of the excesses of the Rococo about 1750. It is no accident that both these examples are taken from French, or, more correctly, Paris furniture, as Paris was the main disseminator if not the actual source of new material in these periods.

▼ **A Louis XVI-style table**
This is an adaptation of a table made by Jean-Henri Riesener in the 1770s by François Linke, c.1900. Linke has inserted a *fleur de pêche* marble top instead of a marquetry top, with two Muses representing the Arts and Sciences. He has also simplified the interior which now consists of one long breakfront drawer.

Copies of French Furniture

The 19th century, in its second quarter, saw a troubled Europe that had just emerged from a long and commercially damaging war. Restauration France experienced a brief and uncertain return to porcelain-mounted furniture, notably by A. L. Bellangé, inspired by the work supplied in the 1780s to Marie-Antoinette by the ébéniste Martin Carlin and the *marchands-merciers* Poirier and Daguerre. The advent of the Second Empire in 1848 saw a full-blooded return, the seeds of which had been sown in the two previous decades, to the styles of earlier centuries. Unfortunately this was not in any particular order – Gothic, Louis XV and Louis XVI were followed by Baroque and Renaissance.

The products of these revivals can be divided into two types. First, the exact copies of earlier, mainly Louis XV and Louis XVI pieces; and second, the eclectic pieces that either muddled up one or more styles or "improved" upon the golden years of the past.

"Improved" furniture styles were a result of the spirit of their age, which sought constantly to change and innovate, reflecting the massive changes in industrial, manufacturing and social organization since the early years of the Industrial Revolution. This was the age of the machine, of gas, iron and steam, which not only made more furniture available to more people more cheaply, but allowed ideas to travel faster as well. Fashion therefore became more international and was communicated at a speed unknown in earlier years.

▶ **This ormolu-mounted mahogany, parquetry and marquetry commode was commissioned in 1776 for King Louis XVI from Jean-Henri Riesener**
It was much copied, as can be seen below. The original is 95cm/38in tall and 165cm/65in wide, with a depth of 63cm/25in.

▶ **A late 19th-century commode after Jean-Henri Riesener**
This copy was made in the late 19th century. It is slightly smaller in height (93cm/37in) than the original, only 58cm/23in deep, and only 158cm/62in wide, a much more convenient size overall. The original has a more elaborate and pronounced breakfront; the mounts are finer and more elaborate. The copy is of good quality – it is only in direct comparison that the differences become apparent. The marble top is thick but not as thick as the original 18th century top – as marble became more expensive to quarry and as power saws became more available, slabs were cut thinner.

To a large extent eclectic or "improved" designs are not relevant to copies, or even to the fake or married piece. However, it is important to keep in mind an image of the pure earlier styles so that any obvious move away from the earlier period can be spotted quickly and identified. A knowledge of the development of styles is therefore useful, if not essential. So many collectors fall into the trap of buying a "Louis XV" piece that is clearly 19th century in origin and concept, not because of some highly technical construction details but because it simply does not follow the form of an 18th-century piece.

If the categorization of eclectic or improved pieces is at first daunting, the overall rule is to think of proportion. As the great houses of Europe were built smaller, so the scale of the furniture to go in them was proportionately reduced. Town houses in Paris and other capital cities followed this trend by the 19th century and, with the growth of the population and the emergence of a new middle class, the shortage of space for housing became more acute; families increasingly began to live in apartments rather than houses. The consequent reduced scale of a piece of furniture is an immediate tell-tale sign – sufficient at least to arouse suspicions and initiate a detailed examination of the article.

Proportion is the key, vital to the definition and distinction of a reproduction piece. The word "copy" implies an exact replica in size and detail. A "reproduction" implies a copy, but without necessarily keeping to the exact size and often skimping in detail, normally to keep costs down. The illustrations on the previous page are of two commodes, identical in form but very different in finish and quality. The first dates from the late 18th-century period, is larger and of better quality. The second dates from the late 19th century. The presumption that the smaller the piece and the less attention to quality, the later the date of manufacture, is a dangerous rule but a useful reminder.

The eclectic piece is often found distasteful, especially if it can be readily dismissed as "19th century": the purist is quick to recognize all the faults inherent in 19th-century revivals – at least if he has recognized the piece as being "late". Copies can sometimes be dismissed equally swiftly, often simply because their condition is superior to that of their models. It is surprising how the most sophisticated period royal commode can become

▶ **A Louis XV/XVI ormolu-mounted tulipwood amaranth and green stained parquetry commode, *c.1765***
This piece is of a similar style to that shown in the illustration right. It is stamped "P Denizot" three times and "JME" twice and also, although more indistinctly, with the mark of L. Boudin, who probably retailed the piece.

vulgar to modern taste when it is fully restored and cleaned. This vulgarity is often even more evident in the exact copy.

The exact copy, however, is often a superior work of art it its own right and in recent years is at last being recognized as such. The 19th-century craftsman was proud to copy what were considered the best of 18th-century pieces. Quite often these were royal items, but not always. It was comparatively rare, however, to copy pieces made prior to the 18th century: these were left to the "improvers". The usual reason is that earlier designs were quite simply too large for modern living.

There were approximately 2,000 *ébénistes, bronziers, sculpteurs, modeleurs, menuisiers* and *doreurs* in Paris by the 1880s working for the makers of the superior *meubles de luxe*. A large proportion of these fine-quality pieces were copies of either Louis XV or XVI examples. There were approximately 50 retail outlets for quality furniture at this time, underlining the popularity of the style that had worldwide and often royal patronage. The whole of Europe, including Britain, both North and South America, Imperial Russia, India and Egypt were customers of the Paris trade and the quantity that was produced is constantly seen, in ever-decreasing amounts as its popularity rises, in the world antiques market today.

One of the greatest of these copies must surely be that of the roll-top desk known as the "Bureau de Roi". The original was started by Jean-François Oeben in 1760 and finished by Jean-Henri Riesner in 1769. Copies of this desk are recorded by several of the great 19th-century makers, who by no

▼ Construction of a Louis XVI commode

These four scale drawings show exact details of a Louis XVI commode now in the Victoria & Albert Museum, London, and similar to the commode shown opposite. Taken from *Drawings of French Furniture*, printed in 1899 and drawn by W. G. Paulson Townsend, they are clearly intended for use. Certain significant details can be made out.

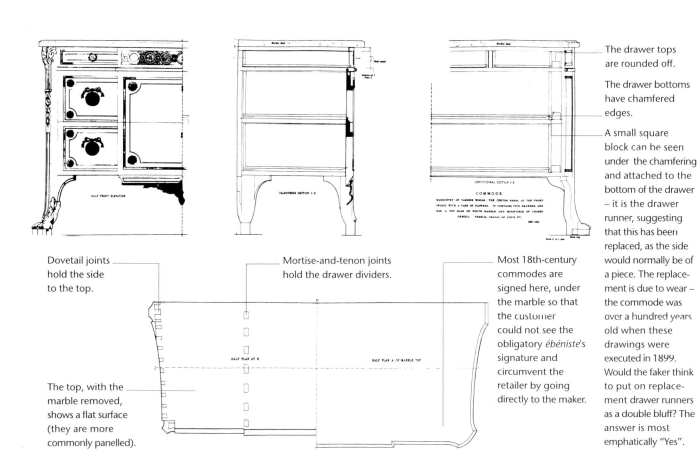

Dovetail joints hold the side to the top.

Mortise-and-tenon joints hold the drawer dividers.

Most 18th-century commodes are signed here, under the marble so that the customer could not see the obligatory *ébéniste*'s signature and circumvent the retailer by going directly to the maker.

The drawer tops are rounded off.

The drawer bottoms have chamfered edges.

A small square block can be seen under the chamfering and attached to the bottom of the drawer – it is the drawer runner, suggesting that this has been replaced, as the side would normally be of a piece. The replacement is due to wear – the commode was over a hundred years old when these drawings were executed in 1899. Would the faker think to put on replacement drawer runners as a double bluff? The answer is most emphatically "Yes".

The top, with the marble removed, shows a flat surface (they are more commonly panelled).

▲ **A copy of the "Bureau du Roi" of Louis XV, French, c.1855–60, now at the Wallace Collection, London**

It is interesting to note that the 19th-century example has incorporated a later Napoleonic amendment where the interlaced "L" ciphers representing Louis XVI have been replaced by Sèvres porcelain plaques of the Three Graces. The bronze plaque at the back with the head of Louis XVI was changed for a plaque incorporating Minerva.

It is possible that the rights to copy this desk where granted by Napoleon III to Lord Hertford who was a personal acquaintance, and the work was most likely carried out while the original desk was being restored after it had been removed to Versailles during the sacking of the Tuileries Palace.

means restricted themselves to pure copies. Examples are recorded by A. L. Beurdeley, François Linke (who made one for the 1878 Paris Exhibition when he was only 33), Zweiner and Henri Dasson. Dasson's example is the most accessible today in the Wallace Collection in London and was commissioned by Lord Hertford at a cost of 90,000 francs. This figure represents approximately £210,000–250,000/$305,000–360,000 converted to today's values, a staggering sum even when taking into consideration the far higher disposable income available to the rich of the time.

Permission to copy the piece from the original, which is now in the Louvre but at that time was in the *cabinet intérieur* of the Empress Eugénie at Saint-Cloud, was not difficult to obtain as Lord Hertford was well known to the Emperor Napoleon III. However (and incredibly), the stipulation was that no squeezes or moulds were to be taken from the original. Consequently all the bronzes, which are extremely elaborate, had to be measured and then sculpted in wood to match the originals. In sculpting the bronzes an allowance had to be made for the inevitable shrinkage during the casting process. Carving a piece of wood to the exact proportion of the required bronze was common practice at the time. However, to model it accurately from existing work required craftsmanship of extraordinary quality. This surely establishes that the 19th-century craftsman, forgetting for the moment the idiosyncrasies of design, was at least as accomplished as his forebears.

An 18th-century French *Table en Chiffonière*

A 19th-century English Copy of a French *Table en Chiffonière*

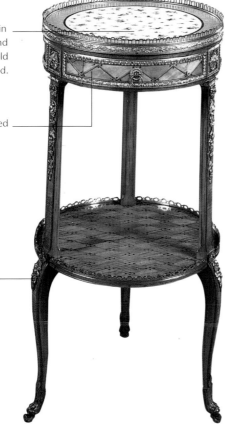

The Sèvres porcelain plaque is *c.*1782 and exactly as you would expect of this period.

The table is executed in amaranth and tulipwood, with fine dot-trellis parquetry ormolu.

The mounts are finely chased and detailed.

The porcelain plaque is a later French porcelain plate of Sèvres pattern, which is painted with a fake Sèvres mark (interlaced "L"s) on the underside.

The mounts, although probably cast from 18th-century originals, lack the finesse and quality of Carlin's mounts, with less meticulous chasing.

▲ Comparing two occasional tables

The *table en chiffonière*, above left, is by Martin Carlin (*d.*1785). The piece exemplifies the refined luxury of Louis XVI cabinet-making. The table above right, by the English firm of Town & Emmanuel (1830–40), which styled itself as "dealers and manufacturers in antique furniture", is clearly inspired by Carlin's prototype and is a response to the renewed enthusiasm for late 17th- and 18th-century French decorative arts, particularly in Britain. Numerous faithful copies of Louis XV and Louis XVI furniture abound – they are, however, considerably less valuable than the originals.

The exact date at which such items were copied is often uncertain. Certainly the Empress Eugénie had a love of Louis XIV classical furniture as early as 1850. The Board of Trade in London held an exhibition called "Specimens of Cabinet Work" at Gore House in 1853, showing 18th-century and earlier French masterpieces; a further important exhibition was held at the Manchester Art Gallery in 1857. The Marquess of Hertford was well into his career as a collector by the 1850s, commissioning John Webb, for example, to copy the Elector of Bavaria's desk made by André-Charles Boulle. Two copies were in fact made between 1855 and 1857.

The *Musée Retrospectif* exhibition, held in Paris in 1865, must have been a further impetus. Many items were lent by Lord Hertford, notably the Gaudreau commode made for Louis XV in 1739, with mounts by Jacques Cafficri (an Italian sculptor who worked in France at the royal palaces and was one of the finest Rococo craftsmen in any medium); this model was certainly copied several times in the 19th century (it is a little too lavish and complicated for the 20th-century copyist) and it would be logical to conclude that the copies were made after, possibly inspired by, the 1865 exhibition. Few if any of the copies of this model are signed and some could well be of English origin. There is documentary evidence to show that Lord Hertford sometimes commissioned more than one copy of an original piece already in his possession, as well as pieces he was unable to buy.

▲ **A table by the** *marqueteur*
Joseph Cremer
This is not a copy but a mid-19th-century
recreation of the Louis XV period. It should not
be mistaken for an original 18th-century table
as the form and shape did not exist in the
period. The inspiration is Rococo but the inlay
is too profuse and busy for the 18th century.

These exhibitions, together with important sales of great collections in England, gave rise to copies being made by both French and English craftsmen up to the First World War of 1914–18 and, to a lesser extent, during the inter-war years. It can be very difficult to tell the difference between English and French cabinet work of this period. London was certainly a great centre for this and its political stability was an incentive to many French craftsmen to settle in England in the mid-19th century.

There is constructive evidence to support the theory that French firms supplied mounts for English carcase work and there was a considerable to-ing and fro-ing of trade, especially from Paris to London. There is new evidence that Paris firms not only exported copies to New York but that they also exported "spare parts" and marquetry.

The psychology of buying or commissioning copies in the 19th century was altogether different – snobbery did not enter into it. Indeed, Francis Watson in the 1956 Wallace Collection catalogue points out that Lord Hertford was paying far more for a commissioned copy than he was for many of the original pieces he purchased for his collection. He paid £2,500 ($3,650) between 1853 and 1855 to John Webb for a jewel cabinet, now at Windsor; the cabinet had been lent to the Gore House exhibition of 1853 by Queen Victoria. This is a prime example of these early exhibitions inspiring fine copies, and the sum paid for the copy would now be roughly equivalent to £200,000/$290,000. Webb appears to have been used to commission copies of French furniture made in London and other pieces were made in Paris. This is an interesting point in that it appears to confirm the theory that English craftsmen of the period were equal to the French and that it was simply a question of expediency as to who made the copy.

The practice of commissioning fine copies had been a popular one throughout the 18th century, especially with paintings, so that the copy could be admired and discussed at home as the original had been admired on the Grand Tour. This trend continued well into the 19th century and the pieces were seen as complementary to existing collections. The copies were in no respect intended to deceive – indeed, Francis Watson states that "Each of Lord Hertford's copies varies slightly from the original. Possibly Lord Hertford did this to prevent the perpetrations of frauds, should his copies ever fall into the hands of dealers".

It is difficult to obtain a clear picture of the quantity of 18th-century furniture that was copied exactly in the 19th. However the proportion of chair frames made as exact copies of Louis XV and Louis XVI models is high compared with that of cabinet work. As an approximate guide, possibly as many as one in five pieces available on the market today would fall into this category.

The main discussion inevitably centres on French copies and their English counterparts. Other European countries, however, were quite capable of making copies but rarely on such a grand scale as the French. There were fewer royal items of an international flavour and access to royal pieces was possibly restricted. What had started out in France as copying the finest pieces of the Louis era with a sincere desire to emulate their sophisticated forms became in other countries a race to produce copies of sometimes quite ordinary items. As the rapid development of the 19th century progressed, each country chose to copy the very best that it had produced, whatever the period. Whereas the French had only to go back to the monarchies of the 18th century, the Dutch, for example, looked back to the 17th.

Copies of Dutch and Spanish Furniture

The period of the greatest flower paintings of the Dutch masters, the floral marquetry work of Amsterdam and the Hague and the incredible work of Jan van Merkeren, was recaptured from the middle of the 19th century, either in a purely 18th-century form but with 17th-century-style marquetry, or by simply taking one of the many plain and unadorned 18th-century walnut or mahogany pieces and inlaying it. The Flemish draw-leaf table, one of the earliest types of extending dining table, is a common subject for reproduction; the copies, mainly dating to the early part of the 20th century, realize about half the value of 17th-century pieces.

▶ **A Dutch walnut bureau dating from the early part of the 18th century**
All of the inlay on this piece has been added in the second half of the 19th century – the coat of arms suggesting the alterations were by a *nouveau riche* family with pretensions to noble ancestry. The whole bureau is very similar to the English style of the early 18th century and it can be difficult to tell the difference; however, the bracket feet are English and almost certainly have been changed in the 20th century.

Spain, too, recaptured its golden era – this time the 16th century. The early 16th-century Mudéjar style of Moorish geometric ivory and coloured woods became popular, especially as French and, to a lesser extent, English taste turned towards the Middle East and Arabia for exotic inspiration.

Spanish craftsmen seem to have been able to produce copies of earlier work easily. They were looking back 300 years, but neither the standard of work nor the materials had changed much. This can make it very difficult to distinguish copies from the originals or fakes from copies. Only with experience and careful study can you tell a late 18th-century drawer lining from an earlier one. Examples from the 19th century inconveniently seem to slip back to the earliest period: possibly these really were made to deceive.

▲ An Italian ivory-inlaid walnut commode, mid-18th century
In common with Dutch furniture Italian furniture was also often "improved" by adding inlay, in this instance profuse decoration of flowers and birds. Sometimes the work would be in bone; but for more expensive items it was often in ivory.

▶ A Hispano-Moresque cabinet-on-stand
This unusual bone-inlaid, parquetry, ebony and metal marquetry cabinet is 17th century in style and probably Hispano-Moresque in origin. The geometric architectural form and decoration, mixing different woods with inlaid ivory, is typical of the Moorish style which became popular again 300 years after it was first seen in Europe.

Collectors and Collections

It is important at this stage to understand the strength of the English furniture industry of the 19th century in relation to copies of earlier pieces. The whole of Europe saw a vogue for the Romantic and Britain was no exception – indeed, Britain was responsible for a huge production of furniture in 18th-century styles, especially those of the Louis. Alongside this manufacture many of the Bond Street dealers, such as Edward Holmes Baldock, were buying antique pieces direct from France; a lot of these items, some branded with Baldock's initials, were "improved" and additions were made to cater for contemporary taste.

The great 19th-century collectors such as Lord Hertford, the Duke of Hamilton, the Rothschilds and John Jones bought such pieces. Their taste was reflected in the shops selling both contemporary and antique furniture and, when their collections were eventually dispersed, they in turn renewed the enthusiasm for the Louis styles. Many pieces were copied; for example after the Hamilton Palace sale of 1882, and likewise on the bequest of the Jones Collection to the Victoria and Albert Museum in the same year.

The great 19th-century collections consisted, therefore, partly of authentic antique furniture in its original state, partly of antique furniture altered to contemporary taste and partly of copies. More and more interest is being focused on these copies. They are to be seen at most of the better museums in Europe. (American museums have had to concentrate more on period or contemporary innovative design. They have not had large quantities of excess furniture at their disposal and have therefore spent their resources on "purer" examples.) Though there is a tendency today to dislike or even scorn the copy, this will pass as they and the background that fostered their manufacture become better understood.

▶ **A Louis XV ormolu-mounted amaranth, *bois satiné* and parquetry *bombé* commode by François Mondon**
The commode is correctly stamped twice by the maker Mondon and once "JME" – the mark of the *Jurer Maître Ébéniste* which was a guild requirement until the law was repealed in 1791. This commode has the added brand mark "EHB". The brand "EHB" was employed by the famous dealer and entrepreneur Edward Holmes Baldock, whose business in Hanway Street, London, flourished between 1805 and 1843. Baldock effectively acted as a *marchand-mercier* and specialized in the sale of 18th-century French furniture and Sèvres porcelain. He also altered furniture and remounted porcelain to accommodate the tastes of his aristocratic English clientele. In the past when there was only an "EHB" stamp, both collectors and dealers assumed this referred to some unknown French maker. It is important to remember that Baldock also stamped pieces that he altered in his own workshops.

The Marriage

A huge amount of two-part Continental furniture has been "married": a piece has been borrowed from one period source to be allied with another.

This is easy to imagine in the example of an 18th-century bureau that has had a bookcase added to it at a later date. The bookcase could either be contemporary, taken from another piece of furniture, or made up for the purpose. The bookcase has little value in its own right and the bureau has its value, or at least its practicality, enhanced by the addition. A quick look at the back of the whole piece should decide whether the panelling matches as it should if both parts are of the same date. A look at the sides will show whether the decoration, if any, or veneer is compatible. Lift the top part away from the bureau – is the top of the bureau veneered or decorated? Does it have good-quality wood hidden away? Few cabinetmakers would spend money or time on materials that were never to be seen. The faker certainly would not.

Few stands survive with their cabinets today. This is because they were often itinerant pieces that travelled from house to house in the 16th and 17th centuries. Larger, static cabinets have also lost their stands, some of which make very nice pier tables. It is unusual these days to find an original stand, so be very suspicious; aim to prove the stand belongs, or at least that it is of the period.

Alongside marriages of independent or quasi-independent pieces, a great many items of furniture were made up to reuse fine old parts – panels in particular. The cabinet illustrated opposite is an example of the type that was made up, seemingly in great numbers, during the second quarter of the 19th century. The inspiration for these pieces was the contemporary love of antiquity, which frequently manifested itself in Gothic and medieval artefacts. The demand produced many married pieces and possibly some of the earliest fakes. A powerful source for the Romantic vision in France was Alexandre du Sommerard. He owned the Hôtel de Cluny, which, with its medieval and Renaissance contents, was presented to the nation on the owner's death. The collection was not conscientiously catalogued until the 1920s and many of du Sommerard's pieces of furniture were then judged to be fakes, or at least made up from old carving and panelling.

The cabinet opposite (bottom), from the Soulages Collection, is another victim of 19th-century lack of expertise. The acquisition of the collection from France was, at the time, a great coup for Henry Cole, supported by Prince Albert. The collection went on display in the Victoria and Albert Museum in the 1860s.

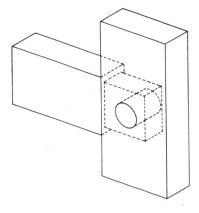

◀ **French mortise-and-tenon joint**
An exploded view showing a simple French mortise-and-tenon joint with a pin (*goujon*) inserted for added strength. After a few years, as the surrounding wood shrinks, the pin will stick out by one or two millimetres, cracking the decoration (see page 65).

▼ **A large walnut cabinet of architectural form purporting to be from the Henri II period in France, *c*.1560**

This cabinet forms part of the Soulages Collection bought by the Victoria and Albert Museum in the 1860s and bears all the allegorical hallmarks so popular in the 16th century (and revived in the 19th). The centre panel of David and Goliath is flanked by Justice and Fortitude, Judith and Holofernes.

At the time of acquisition the carving was attributed to Bachelier of Toulouse. The main panels may well be by him, but they are the only parts that date to the 16th century. This is an early example of 19th-century Romantic makers devising pieces in an imaginative Renaissance style, using important old panels. In recent years it has become common practice for dealers to buy the whole piece at auction simply for the early panels and to leave the carcase behind. It is open to question whether this piece should be described as a fake, a marriage or a Romantic copy.

▲ **A print taken from a book of designs, *c*.1560, by Jacques Androuet du Cerceau (*c*.1510–85), reprinted in Paris by E. Baldus, *c*.1880**

The print shows the typical balance of 16th-century furniture, which was not observed in the eclectic piece shown left. Quite clearly the maker of the cabinet, probably from the Toulouse area, had seen the du Cerceau prints and took one of the winged squatting female griffins directly from the 16th-century source.

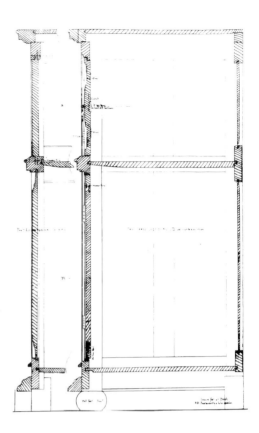

▲ **A design from *Drawings of French Furniture*, 1899**

This shows the authentic construction of cabinets similar to that below left, as made in France throughout the 16th century. Note the wooden pins (*goujons*) used at this time and the sophisticated chamfering on the back and front (carved) panels and the middle and lower shelves. The front ball feet and the rear block feet are later additions or replacements, but are stylistically in keeping.

This figure was probably taken directly from the 16th-century du Cerceau print above left.

Many other pieces in this collection were dubious and most of them now lie unseen in the museum's stores. But the display of both the Cluny and the Soulages collections led to copying and this may explain the wealth of eclectic pieces that came onto the market from the 1870s onwards, when the Renaissance style gathered commercial momentum.

Alterations

A popular alteration was to reduce the size of a piece to accommodate it to contemporary apartments. Taller pieces were especially vulnerable. In a commode a drawer can be removed easily and neatly, though a loss of proportion may give the game away. Look at the drawers – is the graduation even? Are the drawers numbered on the back by an earlier repairer and if so, are the numbers now consecutive? Reducing in width or depth is both far more complicated to do and much easier to spot.

Hinges

▲ Alterations due to a change of use

This little Italian commode, one of a pair, was made in the mid-18th century and was originally from the estate of a member of the Royal House of Savoy, by descent from King Vittorio Emanuele III. Such commodes make perfect bedside tables, and to make them more practical for this purpose they were altered, probably in the 20th century, to have cupboard doors instead of the three original drawers. The cupboards have hinges on opposite sides to allow for the bed in the centre. When altered, the use of cupboard doors probably made the pieces more valuable, but as connoisseurship has improved in recent years, they would be worth less today.

Certain items were altered in the 19th century for a specific use and are now being converted back to their original state. The Louis XV and Louis XVI *petite commode* or *table en chiffonière* is a very popular item in today's small apartments. In the 19th century, these were often altered into the delicately-named "night tables". The three small drawers were taken out to make a cupboard for a chamber pot. Today they are very popular, either as bedside tables or drawing-room furniture, and so the drawer linings are put back. Do not therefore be puzzled by an old-looking carcase with new drawer linings.

Another common alteration was to remove the end cupboards from French commodes and make them into corner cupboards; this is, however, rarely satisfactory to the eye. The remaining chest of drawers can be veneered at the sides – though again the proportions would be unsatisfactory. Fine 18th-century commodes have also been altered to accommodate wash basins. No one would even consider making such a drastic alteration to an expensive piece today but similar alterations, on a lesser scale, must be being made to pieces that are considered of little value in today's market.

Reducing the Size of a Drawer

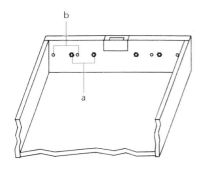

▲ **Tell-tale signs of the reduction in width of an 18th-century drawer**
When the drawer is reduced in width, the original handles (in position b) will be too close to the sides. They have to be moved to position a – if indeed the original handles are being used again, rather than updates. Then check the face of the drawer: if there are no filled holes to correspond, the drawer has either been re-veneered or veneered later. (See page 36 for more on handles).

▲ **Clear signs of a drawer that has been reduced in depth**
The dovetails have been cut through and the joint has been remade, crudely, with modern nails. On an 18th-century chest such as this the alteration stands out a mile, but only if the drawer is taken right out and checked.

The Fake

"Fake" (a word shunned by most experts), when applied to furniture, means an item made in an earlier style with intent to deceive. The dictionary definition also includes: "to rob or attack", "to doctor" or "counterfeit". In the context of furniture, "to doctor" includes the arrangement of marriages and "to rob" is certainly a result of successfully passing off a fake as a genuine article. "To counterfeit" underlines the intention to deceive but is further defined, *inter alia*, as "to copy without authority". This can be seriously misleading. No authority is needed to copy an old piece of furniture, save for permission of access. To take the example of the Marquis of Hertford, it was his friendship with the Emperor Napoleon III that procured access for Mr Webb of Bond Street to take measurements in order to make a copy. Nobody today thinks of Webb's work as a fake – there was no intent to deceive.

The fact that no permission is necessary means that any competent cabinetmaker can set himself up to fake furniture (I do not intend to be sexist, but there is no reason to believe that there were ever female cabinet fakers).

Locks: Genuine, Fake and Modern

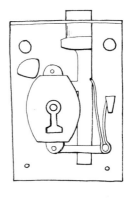

▶ **This artwork shows the style of lock typical of the Louis XIV period, c.1700**
The steel on locks such as this would have rusted and the edges would show traces of hand filing. Note that the upper screw holes are considerably larger than the lower ones – this does not help with dating but no copyist ever makes them like that and few fakers would think of it. This a typical French double-throw lock and the tongue is shown half out.

▲ **A small fake modern lock**
About 30 years old, this is a determined effort at faking, but is far too small to be of the 1730–50 period it tries to simulate. The steel has the robustness of a tin can compared to an original lock. The tongue has only a single throw – an elementary mistake.

▲ **A late 19th to 20th-century French lock**
A straightforward lock of the type used in France from the mid-19th to the early 20th century. It still has a double throw (here fully extended) but is made of brass and is much smaller than its predecessors.

There is little evidence to suggest that furniture faking was ever done much before the latter years of the 19th century. Major museum collections contain fakes of works of art from earlier dates, but little or no faked furniture. Is it that furniture was too difficult to fake? Is the reverse true – that it was so easy to counterfeit that modern expertise has not yet advanced enough to detect untold pieces of fake furniture in the galleries of the world? Is it not profitable enough? Is there insufficient demand for fine furniture? The answer to all of these questions must be a resounding no. Furniture is certainly difficult to fake but by no means impossible. Modern expertise has advanced a long way and is so analytical that fakes can surely, by now, be identified. Even given the high costs of labour today it is always possible to make the more sought-after pieces at a cost sufficiently below the market price to enable the perpetrator to make his profit. And the demand for furniture over the last hundred years has always been high enough to stimulate the art of the faker.

It is this last point that needs the closest examination – there are unlikely to be fakes until the market demand is strong enough for the originals. Then the faker can step in, as often as not trading not only on his skills as a craftsman but on the greed and covetousness of the buyer, be he the end user – the collector – or the intermediary – the dealer. Certainly one point must ring clear: a fake is only good if the judgment that approves it is poor. A copy may be good – very good – but, for example, the sophisticated French reproductions made in the second half of the 19th century were not intended to deceive – above all, many were signed by their makers. It is frightening to think of the consequences if a craftsman of this calibre were to become a rogue maker.

The Skills Required

Demand for French furniture rose in the early part of the 20th century. Britain wanted good 18th-century furniture as much as it wanted Queen Anne in the pre- and inter-war periods; the United States had the same requirements. French taste, always somewhat patriotic, meant an even greater demand for the Louis styles. Other European countries, without an international following for their domestic styles, produced fakes of their own earlier work.

It may be a dangerous assumption but it is probably fair to say that any good fake would have to be made a) in the country from which the piece to be faked originates, and b) with only slightly less conviction, that the faker should be a native of that country. A piece of furniture has many components and several skills are needed to create it. For example, to make a "Louis XV" commode one would need to:

 1. find wood of sufficient age;
 2. cut it to the required thickness of veneer – approximately 1.1 mm/⅛in;
 3. ensure the thickness is not too even;
 4. make the carcase – worth several points in its own right, especially when it comes to the dowels;
 5. make the drawers correctly – one of the most obvious areas, but one that consistently lets down the fake;
 6. cast the bronzes and handles;
 7. gild or lacquer the bronzes and handles;
 8. cut and colour the marquetry and/or stringing;
 9. apply the veneer and let in the marquetry;
10. decide how much age or patination to apply.

Construction

1 Hand-cut dovetails

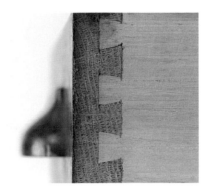

2 Machine-made dovetails

3 Fake Régence dovetails

▲ Dovetails

From the latter part of the 17th century, dovetail joints were used in case furniture, such as chests of drawers and cupboards. Initially quite crude, with the influence of Dutch craftsmen they became finer, especially on top-quality pieces.

(1) On hand-cut dovetails the scribing line is often quite visible, as here. These dovetails have nice narrow pins. Late 17th-century drawers are often pinned with handmade nails, not dovetailed.

(2) By the 20th century, the more sophisticated workshops were using machinery to produce dovetails. Note how the prongs on machine-cut dovetails such as this are the same size as the insets. There is also never any scribing line.

(3) Dovetails from an out-and-out fake commode made in the 1970s. This drawer is pine-lined, but the sides are not smooth enough and the dovetails are appalling, filled with dust and glue. There is no comparison with the quality of workmanship seen left, in the genuine article.

If the faker has not selected his timbers carefully, the wood itself will give the game away. If it is from another piece of the period he is imitating, there is the possibility that there will be old joint marks or holes, albeit carefully covered up. This applies especially where drawer handles are concerned.

One of the easiest ways to tell the difference between a piece of 18th- and a piece of 19th-century furniture is to look at the drawers, not necessarily at the dovetails, but at the standard of finish. The drawers of many 18th-century commodes are poorly finished – they were not intended to be seen by contemporary owners. The interior of most 19th-century pieces by contrast is well finished – often veneered and frequently polished.

Then look at the dovetails. Handmade dovetails have a narrower tail attached to the drawer facing than the receiving joint at the side of the drawer. Machine dovetails have an even-sized positive and negative tail or fan. If the joints are machine-made then the piece has to be after the 1880s and was more probably made in the 1920s.

A further check is that sides of 18th-century French drawer linings very commonly had rounded tops. Copyists often omit this detail (except M. Millet of Paris in the second half of the 19th century) and so do fakers. However, do not be led into the trap that every piece that lacks this detail is a fake – the guideline is not a rule.

Patination often makes or breaks the fake. Too much dirt is easily spotted, too little becomes immediately suspicious. Dirt applied in the wrong place(s) is a certain giveaway, so is wear in places that would not normally be subject to use. This is especially so with chair and stretcher rails of the Régence period – chair legs are often quite wrongly distressed on the inside. In the same manner veneer is aged and distressed in places that would never normally be affected by everyday wear (though very occasionally this is a result of restoration with old veneer).

Examine the dirt. On a piece of dubious parentage it may be no more than old sawdust and glue – both in plentiful supply in a cabinet workshop. Nibble away at the dirt with a small blade: if it breaks sharply away it may well be mainly glue. Also be on the lookout for long runs of fresh glue – they may indicate that a piece is not very old, though of course they may simply indicate that it has been freshly repaired. However, the clever faker may even build in "repairs" to his work as a double bluff.

The colour of the timbers used must be even all the way through if it is old wood, traditionally seasoned for seven years. Kiln-dried wood will have no depth of colour. The faker makes up for this by applying colour liberally to show the wood, but there is a sharpness, freshness and lack of depth to fake colour.

Modern taste, however, has done the faker a great favour. In many European countries, France and Germany especially, the vogue is for everything to look brand new. This view is not shared by the British collector, who admires patination more than most and abhors repolishing. American collectors share both attitudes: some repolish, some don't. But in a large part of the market it is as if the faker himself had dictated fashion to suit his own ends.

Signatures and Stamps

Signatures are a constant problem on European furniture, especially on French pieces. A would-be cabinetmaker in Paris in the 18th century had to spend a total of nine years in training before he was allowed to call himself *maître*, and from 1741 onwards every master was obliged to stamp his work with his name. This practice continued until it was abolished by the Revolutionary Council in 1791. With the Restoration in 1815 some of the better makers stamped their furniture again, although this was not a requirement. The practice spread until it was comparatively common by the third quarter of the century. However, it was not until 1882 that there was any publicized study of the use of the stamp in 18th-century France. In that year another exhibition devoted to the glories of the previous century was mounted by the *Union Centrale des Arts Decoratifs*, at which the use and advantages of the marks was aired. This corresponds to the period from which fakes of 18th-century furniture began to arise.

▶ **Looking back for inspiration**
This highly carved cabinet was probably made in Malines, Belgium, where huge quantities of 17th-century-style carved oak furniture were made in the late 19th and early 20th centuries.

▲ A genuine château stamp, 18th century

A genuine example from the Château d'Anet, built by Diane de Poitiers and subsequently belonging in the 18th century to the Duchesse de Maine, Louis XV and Louis XVI. It became the property of the Duc de Penthièvre in 1775. Louis-Jean-Marie de Bourbon, Duc de Penthièvre (1725–93) was the grandson of Louis XVI and Madame de Montespan. The distinctive inventory brand of an anchor symbolized his role as Grand Amiral de France and would have been applied during his lifetime. These marks can often be difficult to trace and, as a result, in the 19th century fake or imaginary marks were used to give the piece added prestige. Genuine marks were stamped and never carved.

▲ A 20th-century gilt metal table

Furniture made of bronze should always be regarded as suspect until carefully examined. This table was made in the second half of the 20th century and copies exactly a highly sophisticated Louis XVI design. There have been many small tables of similar or varying design on the market since c.1950.

It is fairly common to find false stamps on French furniture. Sometimes the piece is a perfectly genuine 18th-century example that was for some reason unsigned originally; or the signature of a lesser-known cabinetmaker may have been replaced by that of someone more saleable. Pieces with replaced signatures are quite often "improved" – embellished with *bronze doré* mounts, either taken from another piece of the period or cast at the time the work was carried out. Mounts are very often difficult to date but at least they give the appraiser a sporting chance – added 18th-century mounts often look stylistically wrong, for example. Also, it is always important with French veneered furniture to look for evidence that old mounts have been removed. Often the small pin holes can be seen, carefully filled in with dirt and glue, and if the faker has not done his job too thoroughly there may be slight variations of colour around the replaced mounts. Unfortunately, it was common practice in the 18th century to have mounts regilded or relacquered, and therefore they may have been taken off. If they have been returned to exactly the correct places then suspicion is not aroused, but if there are different pin holes alarms may sound for the wrong reasons.

Stamps may also be removed. Certain dealers in the post-war period are known to have taken the signatures off English 19th-century pieces in the Louis styles. Today an item in the French style with an English maker's stamp – for example, that of Edwards & Roberts – would be just as saleable as a French piece or even more so. Thirty years ago it would have been to the detriment of an item not to have been French, so the stamps were removed.

Château marks are also falsely applied. A perfectly genuine piece by a good maker will be easier to sell and will fetch more with a good provenance. If the "improver" knows his business he will use the mark of a château to which the existing maker is known to have supplied furniture. Both makers' and château marks are well documented, but it is surprising how often the faker will apply stamps that are implausible.

Modern Fakes

There is a tendency for people to write off automatically any piece that reproduces an 18th-century or earlier style as "19th century". Undoubtedly, fraudulent imitations and replicas were produced in the late 19th century, but the greatest period of deception has been since 1918.

With the dramatic increase in the value of furniture of all nations in recent years, there are many more dubious pieces on the market. Workshops in the backstreets of many capital cities are still being asked to alter furniture to suit market trends and requirements. However, it is difficult to believe that today there are many people actually producing fakes. "Improvements", yes – constantly; but actually faking furniture is usually too difficult. Continental workshops are, however, making very sophisticated modern copies that reproduce older pieces with uncanny accuracy, even down to poor-quality drawer linings. These would not begin to deceive an expert, and the amateur must learn to look beyond the sales talk to the true character of his purchase. The deception is more likely to be in the description than in the piece.

Nevertheless, informed opinion is well aware that there is considerably more Continental furniture on the market today than can possibly have been made for the 18th-century market. Care, thought and specialist advice should be taken with every step and every purchase.

Woods, Inlays and Surface Treatments

One of the easiest ways to tell that something is wrong with a piece is to recognize that it incorporates a material that had not been introduced in the period from which it purports to come. Once a material had been introduced, it could, of course, be revived at any time, but fashion kept quite a tight hold on the standard items of furniture and there is reason to double-check if a piece of expected form includes an unexpected wood or type of decoration. The chart is necessarily only approximate, but is designed to show which materials you would expect to see used period by period in the main Continental furniture-producing countries.

	17th CENTURY			18th CENTURY			19th CENTURY	
	1600	1650	1700	1750	1800		1850	1900

FRANCE
- Walnut
- Oak
- Mahogany
- Tulipwood
- Kingwood
- Beech (chair frames)
- Lacquer
- Japanning
- Bois clair
- Gilt-bronze
- Giltwood
- Marquetry
- Parquetry
- Porcelain

LOW COUNTRIES
- Oak
- Walnut
- Boulle
- Mahogany
- Marquetry
- Giltwood
- Ivory
- Satinwood
- Lacquer
- Ebony
- Bois clair
- Tortoiseshell

GERMANY/AUSTRIA
- Walnut
- Oak
- Giltwood
- Tortoiseshell
- Boulle
- Painted

ITALY
- Walnut
- Giltwood
- Lacquer
- Mahogany
- Stone inlay
- Marquetry
- Painted
- Japanning
- Gilt-bronze

IBERIA
- Tortoiseshell
- Ebony (Port.)
- Rosewood (Port.)
- Marquetry
- Parcel-gilding
- Painting
- Poplar
- Mahogany
- Walnut

▲ **A 20th-century scagliola top**
The base of this table is in carved and gilt wood made in Italy c.1880, following a vaguely early 18th-century style; the top is a later replacement in marble that could have been made in Italy or as far afield as India.

Identifying Wood Types

Kingwood

Mahogany

Flame Mahogany

Oak

Rosewood

Satinwood

Tulipwood

Walnut

Decorative Treatments

Marquetry

Seaweed Marquetry

Parquetry

Gilding **Gilt-bronze**

Japanning

Brass Inlay

Bone Inlay **Painted Furniture**

Tortoiseshell

English Furniture

There are, beyond any doubt, numerous pieces of deceptive English furniture on the market among the mass of good honest pieces. But provided you are aware of exactly what a piece is, can use it, will enjoy it and can afford it, there is no reason not to buy. Problems arise only when a piece that is not genuine is passed off as the authentic article – and at the price of the authentic article.

A great many pieces that are not quite genuine took on their present form with no trace of fraud and no motive of greed. Cutting down a large piece of furniture to make it fit in a room smaller than it was designed for is a perfect example. The ignorant repair of a badly damaged piece of furniture with wrong materials is another.

Fashion, too, is of the utmost significance. We may scorn the ignorance of our forebears who chose to update old-fashioned furniture by reshaping or redecorating it, but we change our styles too.

Furniture, however stylish, always has a practical purpose. If that purpose becomes redundant – as with the thousands of washstands that were made before modern plumbing – do we simply throw away a mountain of furniture? Or should we adapt it?

Thus if we combine the triple motives of economy, fashion and practicality it is not difficult to see the reasons why so many antique pieces exist that are not quite what they seem or are not quite as they were made.

For complex reasons, attitudes to furniture were changing by the 1830s. Throughout the 18th century one new style had followed another, but by the end of the Regency the taste for older things which the dilettanti of the late 18th century had fostered in élitist seclusion was becoming the public taste. The prices of Queen Anne, Georgian and earlier items started their erratic rise, the cost of manufacture fell with mechanization and a margin appeared in which the faker, reproducer and pasticheur could operate.

◢▶ Adapted pieces

Some pieces of furniture are altered for perfectly genuine reasons – the most common being because the item is now redundant due to changing fashions or developments in modern plumbing! This simple walnut stool, right, started off life c.1730 as a commode. The deep sides of such stools enclosed the chamber pot, and were later cut and shaped as this one has been, to disguise its original purpose. A commode stool is worth a fraction of the value of an ordinary stool – three figures rather than four. Many commodes, such as the one above, have been altered by having the pull-out seat and chamber compartment converted to a drawer.

▶ **Hand- and machine-cut veneers**
Here, the difference in thickness is clear between the 18th-century veneer on the right and the much thinner, machine-cut veneer on the left.

Fakes

There are few examples of the out-and-out fake, that is, a piece of furniture made from scratch and purporting in every detail to be from an earlier period.

Faking can be undertaken only by those workshops with access to materials of the right sort – old and seasoned timber, hand-cut veneers, handmade steel locks and screws, clout nails and hand-forged hinges, handles and even castors. Such furniture was made by men of considerable skill, and pride in their craft rarely allowed them to resist leaving some trace, almost like a signature, that would give away the identity of the piece to a trained eye. However, in the 1920s and '30s, when walnut furniture was fashionable, several skilled makers were constructing furniture that was true in almost all its details to its William and Mary or Queen Anne models. Whether or not they intended to deceive is a moot point. They reused old drawer linings for example, but frequently used thin machine-cut veneers.

Classics of these makers are more often in the William and Mary and Queen Anne styles, with the small fall-front bureau on an open stand with turned legs and joined stretchers being particularly popular; so too were card tables and glazed-door china cabinets. Any such piece on the market should therefore be looked at with considerable care. For example, the mouldings on the originals were applied in small sections with the grain running across the moulding rather than along its length. The timber naturally shrunk across the grain, opening up gaps between the sections. These 20th-century makers applied their cross-grain moulding in exact replica, spaced the sections to simulate contraction and even made the edges curl slightly away from the carcase – a refined touch. The thin veneers, plus signs of wear which are not entirely credible, often betray these pieces.

◀ **A George III-style commode**
This British commode was made c.1910 in the George III style. The ribbon-tied scrolling foliage, anthemia and floral sprays with urns at the sides are all common motifs of the style, but its over-slender proportions and general delicacy are just a little too feminine for an 18th-century piece.

Pastiches

A pastiche can be more difficult to identify than an outright fake. It is a piece that started life as one kind of furniture and was altered to quite another. It will retain a substantial proportion of its original bodywork or carcase – perhaps 25 or 30 per cent – and so old timbers will be visible and proportions are likely to be convincing. A cursory inspection may indicate that the item is genuine – it is only if you know that such items have been prone to alteration that you are likely to examine more thoroughly.

The chest of drawers of modest merit turned into the highly desirable kneehole desk or dressing table is a typical example of the profitable and deceptive pastiche (see page 47). Another is the lower part of an 18th-century tallboy with open base turned into a fashionable writing table. Or the scrambled set of chairs, in which perhaps six original chairs have been disassembled, some new parts made and eight chairs made up, all of which consist of a majority of antique parts (see pages 42–3).

Reproductions

The reproduction, a copy of an earlier style, is by no means new; nor is it necessarily not respectable.

During the 18th and 19th centuries, when large estates were split up and the contents of grand houses dispersed, it was common for sets of furniture to be divided. The recipient of, say, 12 from a set of 24 chairs might wish to recreate the original set and would commission a chairmaker to produce a dozen duplicates. These would be honest copies, not pastiches, but inevitably the materials would be slightly different from those of the

▶ **A fine walnut chest-on-stand of the George II period**
It is most unlikely that anyone would now divide such a piece, given the high price it would fetch as it stands, but at various times since it was made its constituent parts, suitably amended, would have fetched more than the whole. It is a relatively simple matter to lift off the top of a tallboy, add bracket feet and be left with a chest of drawers (see top far right). These are usually readily identifiable: they are unusually tall, they have three drawers rather than the customary two in the top tier, and the cornice is much too substantial for an authentic piece. When the chest part is removed, one is left with a highly desirable writing table (see bottom far right).

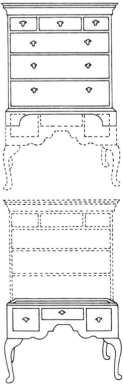

▲ A George II period walnut tallboy

A fine example of an early George II period walnut tallboy, also known as a chest-on-chest or highboy, just perfect to make into two separate pieces of furniture at any time since it was first created in the 1730s. The same rules of adaptation and detection applying to the chest shown on page 30 are equally appropriate here.

▶ A secretaire bookcase, c.1790

The secretaire bookcase, which was also made with solid or 'blind' doors instead of glazed, was introduced to English society in the last quarter of the 18th century. The secretaire part is the deep top drawer which is hinged at the bottom edge to fall forward when open in order to form a large writing area and afford room for the knees of the sitter. However, it is important to remember that occasionally such a fitment was built into a walnut chest-on-chest of the George I and II periods, but the difference is that such early examples are as shallow as the normal drawer, thus providing a much smaller writing area when open. Again the secretaire bookcase was ideal for conversion for either innocent or guilty reasons and the same rules apply as on page 30.

◀ A bureau-bookcase, c.1745

Another fine example of two-piece cabinet furniture, the bureau-bookcase. At the time this was made, solid wooden panels were an alternative to the glazed doors. The term bureau-cabinet is an equally correct description of both types. In either case a separated bureau will be seen to have a deeper top to accommodate the cabinet than one made to stand alone. Also, as a general rule, this part was left without veneer if meant to take an upper part. However, this, like many other guides and rules, is rarely sufficient evidence on its own to damn the piece.

originals and the workmanship would be by a different hand. The period from which the best of these "out of period" pieces come is approximately 1830–60. They are therefore antiques in their own right and can be expected to show signs of ageing. Several factors conspire to make this period the best for reproduction, especially of George II and George III fine mahogany furniture. First, the tradition of craftsmanship at the highest level was by no means dead. Second, the advent of mechanization meant that some pieces could be produced relatively cheaply in multiples. And third, "antique" furniture was beginning to be appreciated in its own right.

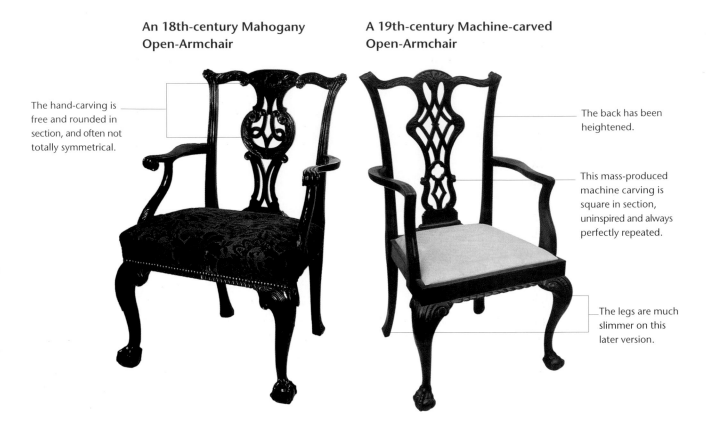

An 18th-century Mahogany Open-Armchair

A 19th-century Machine-carved Open-Armchair

The hand-carving is free and rounded in section, and often not totally symmetrical.

The back has been heightened.

This mass-produced machine carving is square in section, uninspired and always perfectly repeated.

The legs are much slimmer on this later version.

▲ **Comparing two chairs of similar style**

On the left is the archetypal mid-18th-century mahogany open armchair in the style which has become synonymous with Thomas Chippendale. Note how the stance of the chair personifies our idea of the good solid Georgian gentleman, a mahogany Dr. Johnson. It also shows how chairs of the middle and upper classes reflect the style and demeanour of the people from any given period. The importance of this observation here is that not all genuine antique furniture is necessarily elegant; it is very much of its time. Thus the later revival pieces, such as this good example of a late 19th-century machine-carved open-armchair in the Chippendale revival style, combine the design and decorative elements of the 18th century with the feigned sophistication of this later period.

During the latter part of the 19th century, and particularly in the Edwardian period at the beginning of the 20th, a different kind of reproduction became commonplace. There was a great revival of most of the later 18th-century styles: Chippendale, Adam, Hepplewhite and Sheraton. The resulting furniture was not so much reproduction as pieces made "in the style of", and neither proportions, materials or methods of manufacture were wholly true to their models. Reproductions of this period are rarely deceptive and should usually be taken at face value.

Separations, Marriages and Alterations

The alteration is a most intriguing phenomenon that accounts for many dubious pieces on the market. There are two principal types: the structural adaptation of a piece, for which the reasons can be either honestly practical or dishonestly commercial, and the later decoration of pieces to make them more acceptable to fashionable tastes; again, the motive varied from the pure to the profitable.

Separations

Imagine a farmer requiring extra cupboard or drawer space in his bedroom. He travels to a country-house sale, and acquires one or perhaps two magnificent tallboys which he takes home. But even if they will go up the stairs they are too tall, when put back together, to stand in his low-ceilinged room. What more natural than to have the local carpenter fill in the open top of the bottom part to make a chest of drawers, and put some new bracket feet on the top part for another chest or cabinet. Since the latter part of the 17th

▲ Alterations

The size of a chest affects value; small chests are particularly desirable today, but sometimes larger chests are reduced in size to make them more valuable or convenient. Most of this chest dates from c.1720 and it looks to have been lowered and raised by those strange add-on fee. There also is a marked difference in the depth of the two long drawers which suggests there may once have been a third.

century, two-part furniture has been part of the cabinetmaker's repertoire. The chest-on-stand, the chest-on-chest (also known as the tallboy or highboy), the bureau-bookcase or bureau cabinet (the latter has solid wood rather than glazed doors) and the secretaire cabinet (shown on pages 30–31), have been the subjects of both separation and marriage since the 18th century. Early examples can be harder to detect because several generations of use can hide the more obvious differences in colour and timber. However, once pointed out, the elements of proportion should be sufficient to arouse suspicion.

Marriages

Just as two-part pieces of furniture such as bureaux, cabinets and bookcases were split up during the 18th and 19th centuries, so it became inevitable that there would one day be a demand for their reunion. Unfortunately, it was a rare occurrence when the original partners found each other again. More often such a union was of items that had never seen a partner before – writing bureaux, for example, were made more desirable by having a bookcase added. The secretaire chest with drawers or cupboards underneath was accorded the same treatment, as were plain low cupboards and chests of drawers.

Always look closely at all two-part pieces, however handsome, to see if they have been married off. Provided both parts are of the same period and as long as they are sold today as a marriage no harm is done. The price difference however between such a piece and an original is considerable.

Proportion, colour, quality and the similarity of timber used are general things to look for, and if all seems right there are three specific points at which to check the initial impression. First, when a cabinet was designed to sit upon a cupboard or desk base, it was made narrower and shallower than the base in order that it might fit within a retaining moulding. The retaining moulding is nearly always fixed to the base rather than to the bookcase or cabinet top. Second, and more important, is the veneering to the top surface of the base part. When the upper part is moved, the top surface of the base should show carcase timber. Veneering was always expensive and the cost was unjustified if the surface was not to be seen in ordinary use. The presence of veneer does not necessarily mean that the two parts have been married, but the absence of veneer is always a good sign.

The backboards are the third place to look. Whatever their quality – very best panelled or rough-hewn planks – ideally, they should be the same on both parts. If both backs have been treated similarly it is still no guarantee of original association, but if they are different it is not a good sign and more detailed examination of the piece is called for.

Alterations

In the mid-19th century a minor industry established itself in the structural alteration of Tudor and Elizabethan furniture. The public taste for this kind of furniture followed a sentimental view of Elizabethan England as a place of honest good cheer, chivalry and bold initiative; unfortunately, few citizens had houses of knightly dimensions. As the population had grown and more people found themselves living in terraced houses of increasingly modest size, original Elizabethan furniture simply did not fit in without being dismembered and then reassembled on a smaller scale.

HIDDEN CARVING

From time to time a hidden part – the back of a side table or the lining of a drawer – is found partly or fully carved. The explanation is that carving was done by the batch for application to rooms that were being panelled. Surplus pieces were taken by the joiners and used, rather than waste the timber, in places where they would not show. The value of the piece of furniture is neither augmented nor diminished by the presence of hidden carving, but its interest is enhanced.

▶ **An oak sideboard typical of the Warwick School, c.1865**
The carving on this piece owes something to the example of Grinling Gibbons and something to Neo-classical taste, finished with a generous sprinkling of sporting motifs.

Decorative Alterations
Carving

Nineteenth-century enthusiasm for Tudor, Elizabethan and generally "Gothic" furniture did not stop at reusing old carved parts in new settings. Carving was a minor rage – and not just for humble artisans, but as a pastime for the genteel. During the 1850s Warwick became a centre for carving of the most elaborate kind. The ornamentation ranged from fruit and clusters of flowers through to warriors in Tarzan-like fur drapes brandishing anything from a trident to a club; martial and hunting trophies, hunting scenes and musical instruments were meat and drink to the carver, whose imagination was the only factor limiting what might appear on one of these extraordinary pieces of furniture. While its popularity meant the style was much copied elsewhere, the finest examples are still referred to as being of the Warwick School.

Unfortunately, when requiring something upon which to practise, many an untalented amateur was let loose upon a plain piece of 16th- or early 17th-century furniture. It is for this reason that so many panelled or boarded blanket chests of that period should be viewed with some caution when they are elaborately carved. The finest would have received lavish attention when made, but the majority, being modest domestic items, were left undecorated save for a chipped carved edge or moulded border.

The reassembly and recarving of oak furniture from the 16th and 17th centuries, done largely during the 1850s and '60s, was perpetrated in the main for innocent reasons. This, of course, does not make any difference to commercial values today: the article in question is not genuine; it is not as it started life. However, somehow this kind of alteration does not seem quite

▲ The carved tripod base of an 18th-century mahogany tea table

The fact that the edge of the top, the column, the knees and the feet are all carved suggests that this is a table of particularly fine quality. However, if you look closely at the profile of the carving you will see that it is confined within the lines of the parts – it does not stand proud. This table therefore started life plain and has been carved later.

as bad as an alteration done solely to increase value, which is so often the case where mahogany furniture of the 18th century has been recarved.

Although 18th-century furniture was rarely attacked by the vicar's amateur carving class imitating the Warwick School, it was certainly done commercially in furniture workshops. Good mid-18th century mahogany furniture in the curvilinear style, elegant and full of shape but perfectly plain, went in one end of the workshop to come out carved with the most elaborate Rococo and Baroque designs at the other. And of course the value of a carved piece of 18th-century furniture, created as a work of art, is vastly higher than that of the plain and ordinary item.

Much of this later carving was done in the early 1900s, following the passion for furniture in the manner of the 18th-century high-style Rococo and Baroque designers such as William Kent, Thomas and Batty Langley and Thomas Chippendale. The work is now some 60–80 years old; decades of wax, dirt and handling have all added depth of colour to the new carving.

So how do you tell? When a piece of furniture was to be carved, the maker allowed sufficient timber for the carver to create his designs in high relief. When the job was finished the carving appeared encrusted, as if the scrolls, or other motifs, had been applied. When the piece of furniture was to be plain, no such extra timber was required or allowed, so that any carving that was added subsequently would have to be incised below the outline of the existing surface. Flat carving of this type can easily be seen.

Carving is unfortunately only one kind of potentially deceptive surface decoration; by far the most taxing deception to detect is later veneering.

The profile of the leg showing how clearly original carving stands proud of the lines of the member.

The curls terminating the splat and those ornamenting its sides are neither perfectly identical nor perfectly symmetrical (see far right), indicating that they were hand-carved. No 19th-century machine would have tolerated this imperfection.

The quality of the carving to the crest rail is excellent, and it stands well proud of the outline, suggesting that it is original.

▲ A fine George II period walnut side chair

This clearly shows signs of authenticity in the high-relief carving and the slight variations to the back, as described.

Handles: Are They Original?

Handles can provide useful clues to dating a piece of furniture because styles changed from period to period. However, as always, one cannot rely on dating by style alone. Handles can easily be replaced and this was often done to update the look of a piece. It is common to find replaced handles; this is not serious as long as there are no bad scars on the front and they are both stylistically correct for the period and of good quality.

Original 18th-century handles
From the outside these swan-neck handles look original. There are no tell-tale signs of other handles visible from the outside to suggest they could have been replaced at any time. Further inspection inside the drawer confirms this view as there are no plugged holes or other signs of interference. In the 17th century, and into Queen Anne, handles were fixed with split-pins. After about 1710 they were secured by pommels and nuts (see right). The nuts used to attach handles in the 18th century were circular and slightly irregular as above – modern nuts are regular and hexagonal.

A positive mark of authenticity
Look for visible signs of wear – here you can see where the drop handles have "bruised" the drawer over time; a reassuring sign.

Ideally, all the drawer furniture should be in a similar style
The style of this escutcheon clearly reflects that of the handles, which is a good sign.

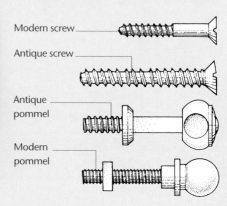

Modern screw

Antique screw

Antique pommel

Modern pommel

Antique screws usually have an irregular and open thread often running the entire length of the shank, unlike modern screws (see above). The groove also tends to be off-centre.
Antique pommels were hand-cast in a single piece of brass. The thread goes halfway up and the remainder of the shank is square-shaped. Modern pommels have brass heads with steel shanks and the thread runs the whole length.

Identifying New Handles

Look for clues to replacement handles inside and outside the drawer.

Check and double-check before drawing any conclusions
At first glance there are no obvious signs of interference on this drawer. The style of the handle is in keeping with the piece and there are no variations in the patina – everything looks exactly as it should. However, a quick look inside the drawer reveals a single redundant hole which immediately reveals that the current handles are later replacements. Remember that original handles will have built up a layer of dirt and grease over time on the front of the drawer, causing dark shading around the edges and in the crevices (see above). Take another look at the front of these handles and compare them with the originals above. The area around the replacement handles looks different; it is clean and there is no evidence of a build-up of dirt.

External scars are clues to replacement
These handles are in style with the piece but the cuts in the timber in the frieze drawers indicate where earlier handles were placed.

Look for visible differences in patina
These handles are replacements. The pale "shadow" of the larger earlier handles can be seen where the wood has oxidized at a slower rate due to earlier lack of exposure to air.

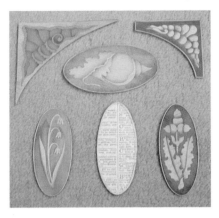

► **A collection of 19th-century panels of inlay in the manner of the late 18th century**

These were used in great quantity for the revival of Sheraton-style furniture in the last quarter of the 19th century and on into the 20th. Made by specialist inlay cutters, they were supplied to cabinetmakers ready for use.

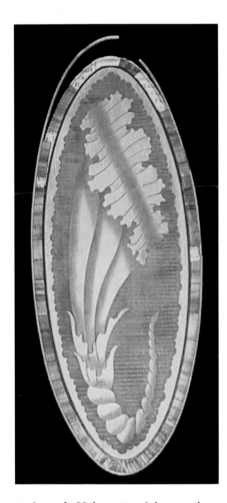

▲ **An early 20th-century inlay panel made for reproduction furniture**

Its back gives it away. Traces of the backing paper, which was usually made of contemporary newspapers, may be found where the veneer has chipped away or been removed.

Later Veneering

The commonest example of later veneering is when a modest piece of early 18th-century oak furniture – say a chest of drawers or a small bureau – is taken into the workshop and its surface decorated with walnut veneer, to enhance its status and its value. The piece, because of its thoroughly genuine carcase, will have pleasing proportions, and when you turn it up to view the underside, all the proper signs of age and wear will be visible. It appears to be genuine. But pull out a drawer. An English 18th-century drawer made for an oak piece will necessarily have its front made of oak; if the drawer was made to fit in a walnut-veneered piece the situation is different. The drawer lining may be made of oak, but the drawer front will not be – or not entirely. The face of the drawer front was to be veneered, so it was a waste of money to use more expensive oak when cheaper pine would do as well. Yet when the drawer was opened one did not want to see a bare pine surface at the top of the front. The solution was to place a slip of oak along the top of the drawer front. The depth of this slip varied enormously, but below the oak some pine or other cheaper wood will show if the piece was made to be veneered (see page 58). Solid oak on the inside therefore almost certainly indicates a piece that was not intended by its maker to be veneered, or one of foreign provenance.

More evidence of later veneering can be found on drawer fronts. It was quite common practice to update chests of drawers from time to time by changing their handles (and it is perfectly acceptable – even desirable – to change them back to handles of the original pattern though of later manufacture). The handles were secured by drilling through the drawer front and fastening them at the back, the earliest with split pins and later ones with pommels. In the 19th century, when turned wooden knobs were fashionable, quite large holes had to be bored, often with a screw thread.

If a piece has had its handles changed at some time, there will almost certainly be two sets of holes visible on the inside of the drawer front – more, if there has been more than one change. Yet the perpetrator of later veneering is trying to produce a handsome article, and he will hardly drill through his new veneer to create matching holes. It may be necessary to remove a handle to make sure, because perfectly genuine holes might be hidden under the handle's backplate, but if the holes on the face do not correspond with those on the inside you can be sure that the veneer is not original. But do note that what you are looking at might be the result of reveneering in the course of restoration. Check the other drawers in the same way. If there are none, the next test – the thickness of the veneers – may prove conclusive.

All 18th- and early 19th-century veneers were cut by hand, the sawyers often using multi-bladed saws. It is impossible to cut by hand a veneer noticeably thinner than 1½mm/¹⁄₁₆in, but the veneer-cutting machines used from the early 19th century could cut it almost paper thin (see page 29).

WALNUT VENEERS LAID ON OAK
Exceptions to the guide that walnut veneer laid on solid oak indicates later veneering include the doors of the longcase clocks.

Because the inside of a door was seen every time it was opened it had to be of quality timber, and therefore it is standard to find solid oak doors on walnut-veneered clock cases.

The manufacturer could get at least twice as much veneer from a given plank as before, though it was more fragile and therefore less serviceable. If you can find an edge or a chip in the veneer of any piece purporting to be 18th-century, you can tell from the thickness whether that piece of veneer is compatible with the date of the carcase. Even allowing for wear at the edges, a uniform thickness will be apparent if it is of the machine age.

Also, a veneer "bubble", more common on highly-figured timbers, can be a guide. If the raised area is thin enough to be depressed easily the veneer is machine-cut or the surface has been sanded down to remove damage.

Marquetry

English marquetry appears in three main periods: the late 17th to early 18th centuries; the late 18th to early 19th centuries and the late 19th to early 20th centuries.

In the 17th century, marquetry showed a definite influence from the Continent and was fashioned in two main styles: arabesque or seaweed, and floral. Arabesque marquetry was made with two timbers – boxwood or holly and walnut – and the style was what one would expect from the name: fine, intertwining scrolls of the most complicated patterns. The best examples are so fine as to suggest movement. Floral marquetry used holly, boxwood, most fruitwoods, walnut, ebony and any woods that would successfully take a dye. The colours of floral marquetry when new were astounding in their brilliance and range – greens, blues, reds, yellows, black and white – but over the last 300 years they have faded (see page 27).

Details on 17th-century marquetry, such as the veins of leaves and petals, were cut through, which is the most laborious way of producing the effect. In marquetry of the Classic period, however, from 1775 through to the end of the 18th century, such details were etched on once the marquetry had been cut and laid. Late 18th-century marquetry that shows fine detail created with a saw rather than by engraving will not be English but Continental. If it is found on a piece of furniture purporting to be English there is every reason to be suspicious. Marquetry from the late 19th and early 20th centuries, when so much of the work was done by machine stamping, will also show engraved, not saw-cut, detail.

Given the appreciating values of good-quality late 18th-century furniture in the early 20th century, it was inevitable that some plain pieces would be fitted with marquetry panels to lift them into a higher price bracket.

▼ **A late 17th-century piece of English marquetry with appropriate signs of age**

Note the raised grain effect where glue has squeezed through and solidified – a good test of the panel's authenticity.

▲ A detail of a Queen Anne brass-mounted figured walnut bureau-cabinet

This bureau cabinet has an eight-drawer section (see below) which can be removed to reveal a secret well (above). You can clearly see the difference in colour between the wood which has been exposed to air, and is consequently much darker, to the paler internal areas which have been protected by the drawers.

▼ The eight-drawer section from the same bureau as above

Again, all the differences in colour you would expect in a genuine piece are there. Also evident are the signs of wear on the top where the section has been pushed back and forth into the well above. All these are good signs of authenticity.

However, it is difficult to set in panels of marquetry and leave the surface as flat and perfect as it would have been in the original. The way it is done is to set the new work to stand proud and then polish it down flush. However, over the ensuing three or four years the glue contracts and the let-in piece sinks – a fault easy to spot when the surface is viewed obliquely against the light. You can also feel the dip if you stroke the surface lightly.

On a genuine article there will be raised grain or glue ridges. These arise where tiny crevices in the grain were first oiled or waxed, causing them to swell. When the wood shrank, it squeezed out excessive oil, grain filler and polish from the pores. Over the years this debris catches minute particles of dust and solidifies to create a ridged effect. The lines created by the saw cuts in a marquetry pattern cause a similar result as they allow the glue to squeeze gently through to the top surface. The patterns therefore can not only be seen, but also felt. This is something the faker of marquetry has not yet managed to achieve.

Distressing

A considerable amount of rubbish is talked about distressing; some of it is highly imaginative – for example, thrashing a table top with chains – and some of it is downright ridiculous, such as firing a shotgun at a chair frame to create the appearance of woodworm.

If a piece is distressed to deceive, the activity is plainly reprehensible, but if it is done to tone in a legitimate restoration, it is arguably respectable – if a chair has to be restored with a new leg, or part of a top needs repair on a chest of drawers or a table, the new part can spoil the look of the whole unless it is harmonized. A skilful polisher can simulate virtually any surface, colour and condition. Simple staining will tone in restored pieces, but large surfaces – the top of a period chest, for example – may sometimes be given the mellowness of age by bruising with a clinker, staining and polishing.

You can clearly see the scraping marks where the drawers have rubbed against the wood as they have been opened and closed. Signs of wear should always correspond to practical use and if it does not, it is more than likely that it has been faked.

The drawers are numbered individually and the numbers correspond to the drawer wells left. You can see at a glance whether any have been replaced. The style of lettering on all the sections is identical, indicating they were carved by one person at the same time.

► **Unnatural distressing**
This 18th-century style walnut chest was made *c.*1930 and the distressing on the drawer fronts is just too regular to be 200 years of genuine wear.

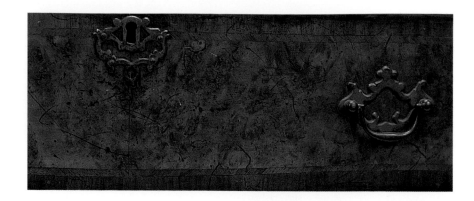

No genuinely old piece will be evenly worn, but the faker has often proved himself incapable of self-restraint, and instead of simulating wear only on those parts that should be worn with use, he has also treated surfaces that would, if the piece were genuine, be in near-pristine condition. Wear in improbable places is a very bad sign. For this reason it is always worth looking at how you naturally handle a piece you are appraising. You will put your hands where countless others have put theirs, each time leaving a minute trace of oil from the skin. Over the course of a century or two, this will result in darker patches; if you do not see them you should be very wary.

(1) The William and Mary bun foot of the late 17th century varied considerably in detail: this is the archetypal shape, much revived in the 19th century.

(2) One of the popular variants on the bun foot shape. Bun feet could be ornamented with rings and some of the finest were carved with foliate motifs.

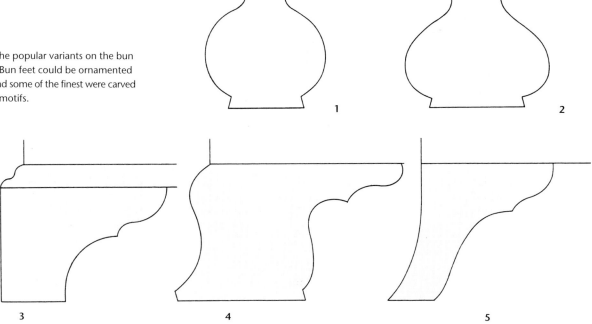

(3) The plain bracket foot, used on middle-quality furniture from *c.*1720 to *c.*1780.

(4) The typical shape of an ogee bracket foot as used on fine-quality chest and cabinet furniture from *c.*1740 to *c.*1775.

(5) The splay of the French foot, which appears on fashionable chest and cabinet furniture from *c.*1810. The more generous the sweep, the more luxurious the piece.

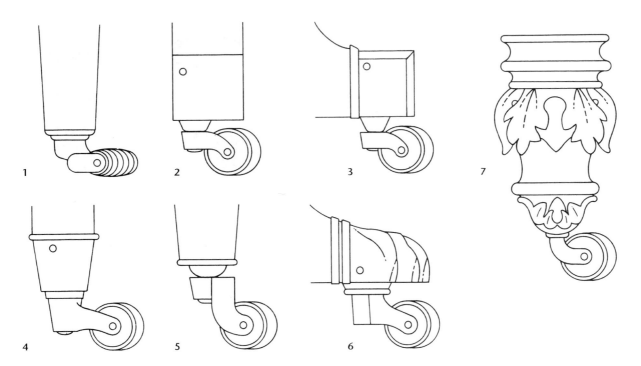

(1) The type of castor – the wheel made of leather discs – used c.1740–60 and completely concealed beneath claw-and-ball feet or square, untapered legs.

(2) The square cup castor, c.1760–75; by now the wheel is likely to be brass.

(3) Plain toe castor used on 18th-century splay-leg furniture; if it tapers it is likely to be post-1790.

(4) The tapered cup castor: from about 1785.

(5) The simple brass castor used on small pieces of furniture in the last quarter of the 18th century.

(6) The lion's paw castor, used on splay-leg furniture 1800–20 and on much reproduction furniture since.

(7) Cast gilt-metal castor of the late Regency period – after 1825. The decoration of the castor now reflects the ornamented foot.

Note that polished surfaces present far less of a problem to the faker than unpolished surfaces. Polished surfaces can be doctored, but plain wood is much more difficult to treat. The interiors of drawers, for example, should never appear stained or greasy; it is extremely unlikely that anything could have happened to them to create such an effect legitimately. On finer pieces of furniture the interiors of small drawers (for example, those in bureaux) will look almost brand new, as they will have had little or no exposure to circulating air (see page 39).

Bureau-bookcases

Slant-front writing desks with drawers below were made to stand on their own as well as to form bases for bureau-bookcases, and can be found dating from the late 17th century. An early example of the two-part form has for some time been so desirable that it is both tempting and profitable to arrange a marriage.

A bureau made to stand alone will differ slightly in shape from one that was intended to support a bookcase – it will have a shallow top and a gentle slope. The bureau made to receive a cupboard over it will have a deeper top and therefore a steeper fall. It is also unlikely that the top of the bureau will be veneered if it is then to be hidden by a cupboard, though this is not an absolute rule. It is preferable to find the retaining moulding where the two pieces join fixed to the bureau rather than to the underside of the cupboard, since that is the logical place to put it if it is to be more than mere ornament.

Another useful clue to a mismatch is that many cabinets made to sit on bureaux and secretaire chests were fitted with a row of small drawers at the bottom. These will properly be of the same quality of construction and of the same timber as the small drawers in the fitted part of the bureau or in the secretaire drawer. As with all two-part furniture, check overall for compatibility of quality, timber and backboards.

▶ **Comparing a carver and a side chair**
Two examples from a set of fruitwood dining
chairs, *c.*1800. Notice the difference in seat
width: the carver to any set of late 18th- or
early 19th-century dining chairs will always
have a wider seat than the single.

There is a tremendous demand for sets of
six or eight chairs that include at least one, if
not a pair, of carvers. As there were only one
or two in original sets of 12 or more chairs
there has been an obvious temptation to add
arms to singles to meet demand. Therefore,
put a carver face-to-face with a single, compare
seat widths and you will see immediately if
this deception has been practised.

Chairs

In the 18th century, the average upper-middle-class household would
probably have had a set of 24 chairs – certainly a minimum of 12. Over the
years, these sets have been divided by inheritance and it is now rare to find
a set of 12 or even 10 dining chairs from the late 18th or early 19th
centuries. In the 1950s and '60s long sets were not in demand – sixes were
what the market wanted, made up of six singles, five singles with one carver
or four singles with two carvers. At that time carvers, highly valued today,
bore only a small premium over singles, and all were relatively cheap.

But demand has changed in the last ten years. As large pedestal dining
tables have come back into fashion, longer sets of chairs are required to
accompany them.

Scrambled Sets

The simplest solution would be to copy up to the number required, but this
is relatively expensive in materials and labour and the result is not as
authentic-looking as the alternative: to scramble the set.

The easiest sets to scramble are those with stuff-over seats and a
minimum of carving. Drop-in seats of course leave all the seat rails exposed,
and remaking them is more expensive in materials and finishing. Carving,
too, is expensive, but the overstuffed seat is upholstered onto beech rails,
which have often become weakened through several reupholsterings and,
quite possibly, through woodworm as well. They therefore need replacing,
and to do this you must take the chair to pieces. At this stage the opportunity
presents itself to increase the size of the set.

If a couple of copies are taken of each component you have enough parts
to make two reproduction chairs. But if, when the chairs are reassembled,
one or two copied parts are introduced into each old chair you get two
extra chairs identical with the others – all of them are in the main made

▶ **Scrambled sets**

The Regency mahogany dining chair with stuffed-over seat (far right) is a favourite candidate for scrambling.

The effect of scrambling a set of chairs. The tinted areas show the new parts on each chair; the majority of each remains original.

from original, authentic parts. None of the chairs is wholly authentic, none is a copy, all are identical and if the job is well done it is extremely difficult to discover.

To recognize a scrambled set you have to look for the incongruities. If, on a given chair, one leg is original and one newly made, check for a plausible match of the scuff marks at the bottom. Remember also that although differences in timber would have been well concealed when the set left the workshop, a very few years' use may have revealed new stain and polish.

The scrambled set of chairs is a good example of the opening comments to this chapter: providing you are made aware of any alterations, and the chairs are priced accordingly, there is no reason not to buy.

18th-century Drop-in Seat

19th-century Sprung Upholstery

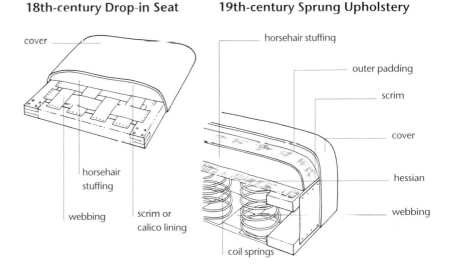

▶ **What is inside a chair seat?**

Before *c.*1830 the upholstery on chairs was made from thin layers of horsehair and padding supported by webbing covered with fabric. Upholstery using coiled metal springs covered with padding and webbing was made *c.*1830.

Seating and the Importance of Structure

The structure of an any piece of furniture is highly informative, and it is important to look at it carefully. Close examination of the undersides of upholstered seat furniture will reveal if repairs have been made or whether a piece has been put together with assorted genuine parts cannibalized from other items of furniture. Corner reinforcing blocks, in particular, can reveal worthwhile information, as these photographs demonstrate.

▲ **The expected underside of an 18th-century window seat**
In order to strengthen an overstuffed upholstered seat frame, the rail was cut before upholstering to receive a strut dropped in from the top at an angle of 45 degrees across the joint.

▲ **Typical 19th-century corner blocks**
The shaped angle blocks shown here are typically 19th century, used consistently from the 1850s onwards. They have the advantage that it was not necessary to strip off the upholstery to fit them, as they were screwed on from underneath. But at no time in the 18th century were such blocks used on English seat furniture. If found on a piece of apparently 18th-century make they should indicate innocent 19th-century restoration (as here) but the piece ought to be checked carefully to make sure it is not of Victorian manufacture.

The strengthening of corners on drop-in seat furniture was quite different. Corner struts were less commonly used; instead, makers applied corner blocks of quadrant form made up of two pieces of wood. These blocks were extremely effective and should still be in place.

▲ **A Hepplewhite window seat, c.1775**
A charming example of a Hepplewhite period window seat retaining some of its original upholstery, the best condition to buy such a piece if you get the chance, for the original construction can be more easily seen and "read". As it is vastly more valuable than a similar-style chair of the same period, it is important to make sure that an antique window seat is not a 20th-century pastiche made up from four genuine chair legs and some old bits of frame.

◄ **Underneath the window seat**
The underside shows a discrepancy in the braces of the frame. If the style of joints varies from one end or on one side of a piece to the other, it is likely that at the very least rails have been replaced, and at worse that the piece is made up.

Dating Mirrors

Do not confuse 18th-century carved giltwood mirrors with later gilded composition ones. The latter are often catalogued as 19th century even though they could be as late as 20th century, and will only be a fraction of the price of an 18th-century original. Elements such as undercut decoration and thickness of glass can provide vital clues as to the date.

A carved giltwood oval looking-glass
This looking-glass, *c.*1770, dates from the reign of King George III.

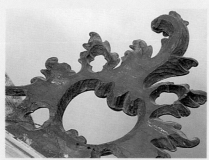

Georgian undercutting
The detail above, from the back of a Georgian carved giltwood mirror, shows how the back of the carved decoration was tapered inwards (undercut) so that the decoration appeared lighter when viewed from the front or side. Few later copies have such attention to detail. The accumulation of dirt that you can see here is difficult to simulate and is a reassuring sign of age. Undercutting is a term that applies to all carving, whether on a mirror or the back of a chair splat.

Composition
During the Victorian era less expensive mirrors were made from plaster reinforced with wire, known as composition. A tell-tale sign is the cold, hard feel of the cement-like substance over a wire frame on any undecorated areas, as opposed to the warmer, softer feel of carved wood. The damage to this *c.*1860 mirror above shows the vulnerability of plaster to breakage. Composition frames are much less expensive than giltwood ones so do not buy a damaged one.

Dating Glass

A simple test with a coin can give you an idea of the age of the glass.

Georgian glass, such as this 18th-century mirror, is relatively thin, so the reflection of the coin appears quite close. Bevelling should be attractively shallow and the cutting may be slightly uneven.

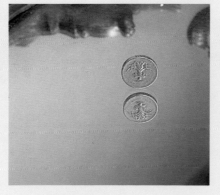

By the mid-19th century glass was made much thicker, and the reflection of the coin here is noticeably further away. Bevelling is cut at a more acute angle and there is no variation in cutting.

This is a modern imitation "antique" glass, made in Italy. The impurities are completely regular and the closeness of the coin's reflection shows the glass is even thinner than that made in the 18th century.

When the cupboard doors are opened, turned columns can be seen in the corners.

Conclusive evidence – the underside reveals a stretcher that bears no relationship to the cupboard.

▲ ▶ Checking for alterations

Alterations are usually executed for aggrandizement, but by no means always. The heavy glazing bars of this cabinet, forming plain rectangular panels, suggest an early date, though the style of the early cupboard doors is more that of the mid-18th century. The disparity could well be the result of provincial manufacture, particularly if the piece was made on a large estate where so often the rules of construction were confounded by the restrictions placed on the maker by the materials to hand. More questions are raised on further inspection, revealing all is not what it first seems.

Finally, right, as it was meant to be: an attractive oak cabinet-on-stand of provincial manufacture dating from between 1700 and 1710. We must assume that the cupboard has been added for utilitarian reasons.

Cupboards

It is usually possible to tell by looking at the doors when a large cupboard has been reduced in height. Glazed doors, provided that the panes are rectangular, can be reduced by removing one tier of panes; blind doors can be cut down at will. But in either case an unconvincing proportion may result, and unless the doors are trimmed both top and bottom, the keyhole will be out of place (it should be about central or a little below if the piece is really tall), and the hinges will be out of alignment. A further guide is that the tenons of the cross members should pass right though the door stiles.

Kneehole Desks

One of the classic alterations to enhance value is the transformation of a chest of drawers into a kneehole desk. Examples of this particular deception are more likely to date from early in the 20th century – good-quality chests of drawers have become expensive now in their own right and the craftsmanship required to do this job well is of a high and therefore expensive order.

Kneehole desks (also known as dressing tables) appear only in the better examples of 18th-century furniture. The best type, dating from the mid-century up to the 1780s, have six bracket feet, but large numbers were made with four feet only, one at each corner, leaving the kneehole apparently without visible means of support.

It is the four-footed type that it is easier to make out of a chest for it saves having to effect two old bracket feet in the centre. Even then, it is no mean task. When the drawers are cut to accommodate the knee-space, old drawer linings are required to make the extra inner sides. The dovetails at both front and back of the new drawer sides have to match the original joints (see page 23 for more on dovetails).

Be aware of, but not overly concerned by, the common practice of wiping the joints and edges of drawers with a "rubber" or quick brush of stain, as though attempting to disguise inadequate joinery. It may well be something sinister but it could indicate nothing more serious than a replaced cockbead.

A surer sign will be the effects of wear on the inside of the carcase where the drawers slide – generally around the drawer opening and more especially on the bottom (see page 48 for typical wear). Marks of wear should always be compatible with any moving parts.

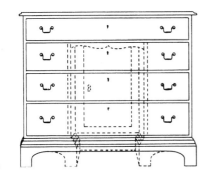

▲ The tinted area highlights what needs to be done to a relatively commonplace 18th-century chest of drawers to make it into a much more expensive kneehole desk with either four or six feet.

▶ **The perfect piece – an early George III period kneehole desk**
This is what is being strived for with the kind of work undertaken above.

Sideboards

Sideboards in the 18th- and 19th centuries were practical, working pieces of furniture as well as being objects upon which to lavish ornamentation according to the wealth of the owners. They had to be large enough to hold food and drink, plates and glasses as well as give room to serve. Elegant as proper period sideboards are, they have proved rather large for modern homes and for some periods of 20th-century taste.

It is not uncommon to come across unnaturally shallow sideboards with altogether authentic fronts and timbers and an otherwise convincing appearance. There are two easy ways to tell if a sideboard has been reduced in depth. Remove a drawer and look at the runners. You should see some wear and particularly a dip towards the back (see below). The last 1cm/½in should show no signs of wear at all, as the drawer would not run that far, being stopped so that it would not hit the backboard and stress its joints. If the runner is still dipping when it meets the backboard you probably have a reduced piece: the back has been brought nearer the front.

If the runners have been replaced – as they all must be, sooner or later – there is another test. Look at the back corners, beyond where the drawers reach. You should see a darker area – the result of oxidization and the accumulation of dirt. Again, if the sideboard has been reduced in depth this part will have been cut off and you will see only clean wood right to the back.

One of the more serious alterations to sideboards is replacing good, honest, turned legs by those of the square tapered variety. This is because the square tapering leg is of an earlier period, and therefore, up to the present anyway, more valuable than the turned leg. The first turned legs were plain and elegant and continued the spirit of their predecessors. The main part of the column was tapering and terminated in a spade or flared foot. Gradually, the turner added more and more ring decoration to the legs, making it possible to date

▼ **The interior of a sideboard carcase with a drawer removed**
The details all suggest authenticity.

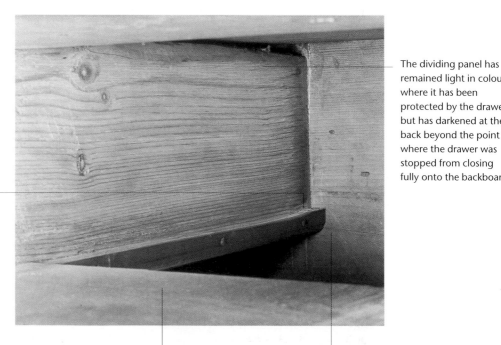

This is the panel that divides this drawer cavity from the next. At the base of this panel is the drawer runner fixed with handmade nails. The wear to the runner is exactly compatible – dipping towards the back, then rising again where the darkening of the divider occurs and where the drawer never ran. If the runner does not rise again at the back, and if the back 1cm/½in of the dividing panel is not darkened, the piece has probably been reduced in depth.

The dividing panel has remained light in colour where it has been protected by the drawer, but has darkened at the back beyond the point where the drawer was stopped from closing fully onto the backboard.

front rail   backboard

► **A fine example of a Hepplewhite period mahogany sideboard, *c.*1790, decorated with carving and inlay, all original except for the handles**

At the point where legs and carcase meet, there may be an applied strip of the astragal moulding. Check that this does not conceal a join where turned legs have been cut off and replaced with square tapering ones. Remove one of the lower drawers, look into the corner and ensure that the stile continuing into the leg is one piece of timber.

▲ **A Regency turned-leg sideboard**

This later sideboard is now slightly heavier than its predecessors. This is material for the "improver", who would replace the legs with square tapering ones and disguise the joint with applied moulding to create something similar to the piece above. However, if this had occurred the black line inlay to the drawer fronts would be a giveaway – this indicates a post-1800 date and would be quite incompatible with any amount of alteration that creates the appearance of a sideboard of the Hepplewhite period.

Regency turned-leg furniture quite accurately by the complexity of the patterns of rings as well as by increasing heaviness as the period progressed.

A sideboard's leg is the extended stile of the carcase – it is not added on. If the leg is cut off at the bottom of the carcase and another one joined to it, there must be a means of disguising the join. This was done by applying a band of stringing or line inlay, or by attaching a thin astragal moulding. The stringing could comprise any combination of popular veneers such as satinwood, kingwood, rosewood, boxwood or, particularly after 1800, an inlay of ebony or ebonized timber. One would expect to find this black line inlay rather more on turned-leg sideboards, when it was also quite common to find some of the ring turnings of the legs ebonized. If, therefore, you find a line of stringing or a line of cross-banding on a sideboard with square tapering legs at the point where leg and carcase meet, check that the grain of the wood is consistent above the inlay and below it.

An original square-legged sideboard is more likely to have applied astragal moulding at the top of the leg rather than inlay, but such a moulding was nearly always applied to other parts of the sideboard as well – typically to the drawer fronts and the panels on the upper parts of the legs. Line inlay superseded applied decoration but followed the same patterns.

Breakfast Tables

Just as the huge dining tables of the 18th century were cut down and remodelled in the 20th century, many breakfast tables were similarly adapted. Often the alteration was simply to improve their appearance but, more frequently, the larger breakfast tables were reduced in seating capacity at the same time as sets of six or, at the most, eight chairs were in vogue.

The most desirable breakfast tables are still those of the late 18th century in the Sheraton style. Oval versions are more highly prized than rectangular. The key features are a top without a frieze and a fine four-splay base, each leg sweeping down and out in an unbroken curve from a "gun barrel" centre stem.

Breakfast tables of the early 19th century tended to become heavier, with the addition of a frieze to the top and a more cumbersome column. These tables were sometimes made with the top divided and extendable: a single leaf could be dropped in to allow two more place settings or two small leaves could be added to the outer edges, supported on lopers. The lopers passed through holes cut in the frieze and the leaves were attached with brass U-shaped clips.

A Late 18th-century Oval Breakfast Table

▲ **A late 18th-century oval breakfast table, the top cross-banded and inlaid, on a finely turned column and four splay legs**
These tables became fashionable again during the 1950s, and consequently a number of rogues appeared on the market.

Note both the high-quality fitments and the lack of oxidation where the supporting block fitted the top closely. Neither of these signs of authenticity is conclusive, but it is wise to be wary if either is missing.

There are signs of handling in the darkening at the edge. This is the sort of detail that "improvers" rarely bother with.

The line of inlaid stringing is original. This is a rare but not unique feature and it confirms that the table has been oval-shaped since it was made and not later cut down.

BRITISH PERIODS & STYLES		
DATE	BRITISH PERIOD	STYLE
1558–1603	Elizabethan	Italian
1603–25	Jacobean	Renaissance
1625–49	Carolean	Gothic
1649–60	Cromwellian	1st Chinoiserie
1660–88	Restoration	Baroque
1688–1702	William & Mary	Baroque
1702–14	Queen Anne	Rococo, Gothic
1714–60	Early Georgian	2nd Chinoiserie Architectural
1760–1811	Georgian	Neo-classical French Empire Graeco-Roman 3rd Chinoiserie
1812–30	Regency	Egyptian French Revival
1830–37	William IV	Eclectic
1837–1901	Victorian	International Influence Arts & Crafts Japanese Rococo Revival Classic Revival
1901–10	Edwardian	Art Nouveau International Influence Arts & Crafts Japanese Rococo Revival Classic Revival

There was no point in adapting 18th-century examples, except when they were huge. It is generally the 19th-century versions that have been tampered with. Ten-seaters have been reduced to a more manageable six-seater size, rectangles have been cut to ovals or rounds, friezes have been removed to simulate the delicate appearance of Sheraton models and columns and legs have been trimmed to a graceful George III sweep. The result is that early 19th-century tables seating eight or ten are now scarce, but there is an abundance of not-quite-genuine smaller tables of deceptive elegance.

Cutting a rectangular table into an oval is not as easy as it sounds: it is surprisingly difficult to draw an oval that is thoroughly pleasing. If a table has been cut down either to an oval or to a round, it is usually not too difficult to tell. The original, in normal use, will show signs of darkening round the underside edges where it has been handled, and these signs will be approximately uniform. A table that does not show this patina of handling at all has either not been used (rare indeed) or has been cut out a distinctly larger one. If it shows darkening in some places – especially at its widest points – but not in others, the chances are that it has been cut down but has retained one or more of its maximum dimensions. The adapter will rarely have bothered to simulate handmarks on his new edges, and even if he has tried, the result is rarely convincing.

Another useful check for cutting down is the presence of a series of small dents to the edge of the underside. These are the marks left by the small wooden clamps that ladies used to hold needlework, painting frames and so on, for breakfast tables were likely to be used throughout the day and not just for meals. Again, it is unlikely that an improver will have bothered to add these marks, for they are not a requirement of the form but merely an attractive confirmation of an otherwise wholly authentic table.

The presence of reeding on a table's edge is no guide at all to authenticity, because, when it was cut down, it was standard practice to reed the edge to finish it off. Table edges are, however, rather vulnerable, and a reeded edge that is largely free of cuts, dents and scratches – or one that is uniformly distressed – should be viewed with caution.

The removal of the frieze to a breakfast table usually leaves traces, unless it is done in conjunction with substantial cutting down. Whereas the rest of the underside (except for the part covered by the block) will have been exposed to the air and will have darkened accordingly, the thick line near the edge where the apron was screwed to the top will be of unexposed and therefore lighter wood. The screw holes can be filled and the marks polished over, but it is almost impossible to disguise the alteration completely; the unexposed timber is and will remain slightly different, and there will be an abrupt end to the haphazard ring of handmarks. The only way to avoid this problem is to cut the table within the line of the apron – but then it will not show handmarks at all.

A tilting top to a breakfast table is no guarantee of originality. Some pedestal-base or two- or three-part dining tables had this tilting feature to each main segment. Look for signs of any previous attachments on the underside of the edges and check that the reeding or moulding to the lip does not conceal places where the small rectangular tongues protruded or fitted into the leaves of a dining table.

Altering the Legs

As the 19th century progressed the legs of pedestal tables became more ponderous. The simple downward sweep of the Sheraton style was more and more interrupted by a knee. Earlier in the 20th century this was an unfashionable feature and it sat ill with an "improved" top. It therefore became standard practice to shave off the knees until the legs showed the sweeping form of the finest exemplars. The legs could then be reeded to add conviction. This is a difficult alteration to distinguish, and perhaps the best guide is proportion. A good 18th-century pedestal table always has a very substantial support – it will be gracefully executed but there will be plenty of it. If the legs look delicate and short rather than handsome, they may have been redrawn.

The column too might be reworked. The block and legs would be taken off, the column put on a lathe and turned to a gun-barrel stem. Only the freshness of its appearance and the marks of the chisel (which should not appear on an original piece) will reveal this refinement.

If a breakfast table shows no signs of these alterations it should still be checked for the compatibility of its parts. The block should have left a precisely matching pale area where it fits the underside, for example, and the catch or catches should not have been moved. Bear in mind, too, that breakfast tables of quality have always been expensive and therefore the catch, casters and any clips should be of the finest manufacture.

Dining Tables

Early 18th-century dining tables were formed as though a row of drop-leaf tables had been attached to each other. By the 1770s two D-shaped ends were added. These were free standing, each being supported on four legs matching those of the centre drop-leaf. A frieze rail set back slightly from the edge secured the legs to the top. Additional leaves could be inserted between the centre table and the D-ends and a further refinement was to make the leaves of the centre part detachable, so the table could be reduced.

▼ **An extending dining-table, *c.*1860**
This round burr walnut table divides to accommodate up to four extra leaves, forming a long top with half circle ends when extended. Note how the extension has a good strong colour which is original, whereas the the main body is much paler after being exposed to the sunlight.

▲ A pedestal dining-table, c.1820
This table is exactly right and the pedestal legs finish within the edge of the table. The legs should never extend beyond the edge of the table, as this suggests that the top has been reshaped or made narrower and, as a result, the proportions will be wrong.

Its versatile nature has meant that this type of table has been prone to alteration; the centre drop-leaf, useful but unfashionable in its rectangular form, can be cut to a more desirable oval, and the two D-ends can be used as side tables or joined with an odd leaf to make a small dining table.

The dining table of a wealthy man in the late 18th century would have been up to six feet wide, supported on as many as six pedestals and with extra leaves. A more ordinary household would have a table with three pedestals, the centre one probably having four splay legs, the two ends having three such legs and the top with a minimum of two extra leaves. Large dining tables were made through much of the 19th century, but as great houses were demolished and families split up, leaves and tables were dispersed.

In the early 20th century, large multi-pedestal tables were virtually unsaleable and even the smaller sizes – two or three pedestals with a three- or four-part top – were cut up for timber. Alternatively, many a pedestal table had its top removed, which was then given a frieze and set on 18th-century style legs to augment the supply of 14-leg tables, which remained in demand. Regency tables of this type were built with turned legs, often being decorated to match the chairs of the same period. It is this model that went out of fashion early in the 20th century to make another reversal. Turned leg tables 3.5m/12ft long make a fraction of the price of their fellows supported on pedestals. Inevitably, there are a number of pedestal tables on the market that have been amalgamated from several tables to meet this demand.

There are some guides to spotting the made-up dining table. The undersides of the tops and leaves will show where earlier fixings have been removed, look for paler strips and disguised screw holes from previous runners or lopers; make sure the fixings for leaf clips are all compatible, and that the small rectangular tongues, or, later, the round pegs that secured leaf to leaf are matching and original.

To see if a fine oval drop-leaf table has been reduced from a rectangle check that when the leaves are up the supporting legs are not too close to the outer edge. Generally the overhang should not be less than 5cm/2in.

A Mahogany Kettle Stand on Tripod Base with Baluster Stem and Dished Top, *c.*1750

The fine turning of the column and the proportions of the piece in general are good quality.

The patina here is also general, the colour rich and deep.

The pillar is joined to the top with a separate turned disc made of oak, which implies good-quality manufacture. Some junction discs are made of ash, beech or other less important timbers, and are prone to woodworm and warping. They may have been legitimately replaced, but a new block could also indicate a marriage.

The undersurface of the top shows a fine all-over patina, carried on to the block where countless hands have picked up the table. There are no scratches, dents or bruises, such as would have been caused if the top had once been used as a tray.

The iron strengthening bracket appears to be of the right date and may therefore be considered original.

⊿ The demand for small tripod tables has led inevitably to the adaptation of tripod pole screen bases into tables by adding tray tops. During the first decades of the 20th century it was possible to find 18th-century drinks trays quite easily. They were made in mahogany as well as cheaper wood, and could be any size from 20cm/8in up to 76cm/30in in diameter. But the bottoms of such trays always show signs of wear and use, and it is therefore advisable to inspect the underside of tripod tables of this sort.

As this stand is examined in detail, everything points towards authenticity. Though none of these points on their own would be conclusive, taking all the elements together we may safely assume this is an original piece.

Kettle Stands

Many of the finest quality kettle stands are made with a turned spindle or fretted gallery round the top. In the 18th century fretted galleries were made of three-ply mahogany, but this detail was normally neglected in the profusion of early 20th-century copies. If the fret was cut in the 19th century it will probably be coarser as the machine-saw bands tended to be thicker. Also, if there is a fault in the machining of one of the sections in the gallery it will be repeated identically in the other sections – this is particularly evident on octagonal or hexagonal kettle stands.

The natural way to pick up a kettle stand is as with a tray, and so an authentic 18th-century example would show a darkening all round the rim of the underside from repeated handling, but the wood should be paler towards the centre where the hands do not reach. The block that fixes the column to the top may be of oak, with the grain running counter to that of the top.

If a kettle stand has been made up with a period tray adapted to make the top there will be tell-tale signs. A tray that has seen any wear will show signs of its use on the underside – the sort of wear that comes from setting it down on a stone sink or standing it on edge against a wall. This kind of wear is completely inappropriate for the underside of a table, which should show signs of handling but not of any other kind of damage.

If you find a kettle stand that appears to have a former tray for its top, it is quite likely that it is one of the legion of kettle stands/wine tables whose bases are adapted from pole screens. Pole screens were commonplace in Georgian and Regency drawing rooms, but had fallen out of favour by the end of the 19th century. As the kettle stand soared in popularity and price, it was a relatively easy matter to cut down a pole screen on proper tripod base to provide the column, add a slightly turned extension to it, conceal the joint with a turned ring and fit a tray top. Well done, these adapted pole-screen column supports are very difficult to discover. Look for compatibility of grain throughout the column.

Somewhat easier to notice are conversions of pole screens into wine tables, but using the screen as the table top. In the Regency and Victorian periods, pole-screen banners became smaller. They were often panels of needlework and beadwork, glazed and fitted in a rosewood or walnut frame carved in the Rococo Revival manner. Many of them were removed from their poles, the poles were taken away from their bases and the tops were fixed back to the bases to make small drinks tables. But banners and screen panels were made to slide up and down their poles by means of two hoops screwed to the back of the panel. If the pole screen has been adapted into a table, signs of these fixings will probably be visible. There are also likely to be signs of abrasion at the outer edges of the screen where the poles would have rubbed against the frame.

▲ A modern, 18th-century-style reproduction kettle stand
The broad striations are the marks of a band saw, made even more prominent by the application of polish. There is no point in polishing the underside unless to simulate patina. The underside of the top shows no handling marks, confirming this view.

◄ A fine example of an early George III period pole screen with needlework banner and tripod base.
The tripod is so similar in form to the base of the much more desirable wine table or kettle stand of the same period that countless numbers have lost their poles and banners to be replaced by a small turned tray top. The increase in value is phenomenal, on average a ten-times multiplication. This has been the case since the 1920s, with the last half of the 20th century up to the present day seeing the most activity in this particular element of faking. Some guides to spotting such alterations are featured on page 59.

Sofa Tables

Sofa tables dating from the late 18th century are perennial favourites. Of rectangular form and with two small hinged leaves, early designs were supported on standard ends so that they could be pulled over sofas or daybeds. This was essentially a weak structure and it was not long before a stretcher was introduced. Some stretchers were of rectangular sections, some were turned and tapering or even scrolled in the heavy Regency form, but whichever the decoration, a stretcher precluded the table's use for its original purpose. They were, however, delicate and attractive pieces of furniture, and so they remained in production.

During the Regency period the centre column supported on a platform base with legs or bun feet became fashionable and remained so for much of the 19th century, until the standard-end variety, with its more elegant, swept legs and a high- or medium-placed stretcher, returned to favour.

Adapted Dressing Tables

Early in the 20th century demand led to the adaptation of much later pieces of furniture into apparently antique sofa tables. The classic case is the alteration of a Victorian dressing table and its union with a late 18th-century, but until recently unsaleable, cheval mirror. Tables of the type shown on the left were generally made in pairs. One, the washstand, had holes cut in the top to receive the various fitments, such as the jug, basin and soap dish. The other was made with a solid top as the companion dressing table.

The thumb moulding from the edges of three sides of the top of such a dressing table was removed and the edge was either cross-banded or reeded. The leaves were taken from a small Pembroke table of the correct period (until the 1960s these were cheap and plentiful). The standard ends of a cheval mirror were then cut down to table height and joined by means of tenons (the correct method) into the underframe of the top. If the table was wider than the cheval mirror the original turned stretcher of the mirror could be extended by inserting a section, turned and perhaps ebonized, to fit. Alternatively, the standard ends would have the stretcher removed and the holes it left disguised with turned paterae, thus reproducing the first type of sofa table.

Where the legs on the washstand were cut off the end grain of the table frame was constructed. So, apart from polishing and checking that all the screws and hinges used were old, little more needed to be done.

This kind of alteration would hardly be a worthwhile commercial proposition now that Pembroke tables and cheval mirrors command respectable prices. But sofa tables contrived some 20 years ago exist, often with the benefit of waxing, polishing and two decades of loving care. It can therefore be difficult to recognize one of these fraudulent pieces, even if you know what to look for.

However, after a quarter of a century there will probably be signs of staining and stained polish being used in certain places; when it was applied it blended in, but now it may stand out plainly. If signs of tampering or restoration appear at places where an alteration might have occurred – such as the junction of the legs to the frame or the edge of the top – or if the leaves do not match in quality (which may be visible under strong light or

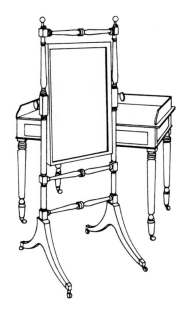

▲ **A Victorian dressing table of the type often remade into a much more saleable sofa table (see opposite page), together with a cheval mirror, which provides the legs and stretcher**
To create a sofa table the back, sides and legs of the table were discarded, leaving the top, to which flaps were added from a Pembroke table. The ends of the mirror are cut down and the stretcher may need lengthening.

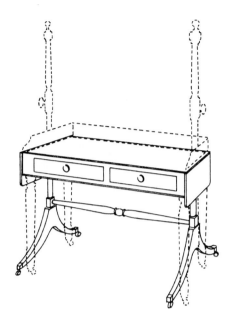

▼ ▶ **Below, how a dressing table (with flaps added) and a cheval glass fit together to make a sofa table (right)**

sunlight) and if the rule joints between top and leaves look unnaturally raw or unnaturally dirty, then the piece could well be a modern contrivance, and should be priced accordingly.

A complication arises from a design fault in this type of table. If the grain runs across the top the veneer may have shrunk and cracked. To repair this the restorer would loosen and refix the top, having closed up the split. This makes the top too short to allow the leaves to hang vertically. Easing the position of the hinges is one remedy, but the problem may be so bad that extra fillets of wood have to be inserted into the top. This is a necessary repair and does not of itself indicate any lack of authenticity.

Chests of Drawers

Apart from the later veneered chests of drawers whose oak is dressed up as walnut, which are dealt with under "Later Veneering" on page 37, the most characterful chests that are not quite genuine are those that result from dividing a tallboy. Honest alterations that they almost always are, they betray their origins quite easily by their improbable proportions.

The proportions of a chest made by dividing a tallboy are never as fine as those of a chest made as such. The 18th-century furniture makers had a great ability to build furniture of even the humblest sort with the correct dimensions; any disproportion may be a warning sign. If you take the top part from a tallboy it leaves the bottom with drawers too deep and cumbersome to sit beneath a filled-in top – or at least, to do so with conviction.

An 18th-century chest of drawers will have an overhanging top or, more rarely, one which bears what is called a caddy moulding to the edge (a quarter-round moulding setting the top back no more than 1cm/½in. The bottom half of a tallboy, however, has a deep retaining moulding in which the top part sits. Merely filling in the top results in a stepped-back effect too pronounced for it to be original, and it is also most unusual to find one where the top has been filled in with the correct timber.

Because of its height the top part of a tallboy is allowed a wide, deeply moulded cornice, often further decorated with a dentil moulding or even blind fretwork in the Chinese or Gothic manner. Such a heavy moulding was never applied to something below eye level – while it looks fine seen from below it is ponderous and bizarre when you look down on it. Also it was fairly common, particularly in the walnut period, to put three short drawers along the top row surmounting three long drawers of graduating depth. Three drawers along the top of an 18th-century chest of drawers are an indication that the piece is the upper part of a tallboy, particularly if there is a wide over-hanging moulding as well. A close look at the feet will then almost certainly show whether or not all is as it should be.

The exception to this is the tall chest of five long drawers below two or three short ones – a type that was produced in the North of England after the mid-18th century, usually in oak. Its intermediate height – 150–180cm/5–6ft – obviates the possibility of its being converted from anything else.

A Walnut Chest of Drawers, *c*.1710–20

▶ The drawer fronts and top are decorated with panels of marquetry. This is apparently a quality item and should be checked carefully. Only then do the findings confirm that this is a sound piece, not entirely in its original condition but fully restorable. Its faults (replaced handles and feet) are so typical of its age that they are in themslves reassuring.

The bracket feet are the only parts of this chest that are obviously wrong – they are too late for the carcase, which should, if it is authentic 1710–20, originally have been fitted with bun feet. The plugged hole revealed by removing the bottom drawer is typical of such feet having been fitted and then removed, either because they were damaged or to update the chest.

On the drawer front it is possible to see old holes that have been camouflaged adjacent to the handles. These, then, are not the first or original handles. This is by no means sinister – much worse to find evidence of such handles on the inside of a drawer but not on the outside. Restoration of this sort on a fine piece of this period is, in general, reassuring.

The lining paper in the drawers covers up the evidence of several sets of handles, but just enough is torn away to reveal an oak slip above an otherwise pine drawer front – exactly as one would expect. Had the front been of solid oak then the chest would have been either Continental in origin or veneered later.

▶ **A really good example of a well-drawn tripod table base with what is now a rare rectangular top, *c*.1750**
Many were made in this form but were subsequently cut to the round for utility reasons. Hence the present rarity.

The "birdcage" mechanism underneath which enables the top to turn as well as tilt to the vertical when not in use.

Compare the wonderful bold claw-and-ball foot to the small, inferior version on page 35.

Note where the columns of the birdcage have bruised the underside of the top correspondingly. This is another good sign.

The perfect sight when the table top is tilted. The area where the top has been closed for most of its life onto the supporting block is paler than the outer area. This is because the air will have oxidized and darkened the surrounding timber.

▲ **A mahogany tripod base, tray-top table, *c*.1765**
This attractive piece of furniture is constructed from a period tripod base and a contemporary drinks tray. It is a little too low for its width; a table of these dimensions would have stood at a normal table height, that is approximately 74cm/29in.

Tripod Tea Tables

One of the most altered pieces of furniture is the tripod-base tea table. These were made in enormous numbers and in every range of quality from the 1740s onwards. The finest had dished or tray tops, the edges of which, during the period 1755–70, were carved and shaped in "piecrust" fashion. Alternatively they had a simple raised lip to form a tray top, the upper edge of which might be inlaid with a stringing of contrasting timber or even a brass line. The main surface of the top was sometimes brass inlaid but this is rare – the commonest form was plain and solid.

The tops were supported on single columns, the best of which were carved in classical or architectural forms with Rococo, leaf-capped and scrolling motifs. The legs would be carved at the knee, and the most desirable have claw-and-ball feet. All the carving will appear to stand proud of the outline and the claw-and-ball foot (representing the Sacred Pearl of Wisdom being held by the dragon's claw) should always appear as a good round ball seized by life-like claws.

Slightly lower down the social scale a finely carved base would support a perfectly plain, flat top. This would be fairly thick, approximately 2cm/1in at the centre, but chamfered on the underside of the outer edge to give the appearance of thinness. On tables of lesser quality there is less carving or none at all, but there is nothing wrong with a finely drawn plain table of this type, and good examples should not be undervalued.

Nevertheless, a plain top table will make only a fraction of the price accorded to a dished top, and it soon became evident to furniture makers and dealers that the old plain tops were sufficiently thick to give room for "improvement". Fortunately, there are some very clear guides to indicate when such a table has been upgraded.

A "Dished" Tripod-base Tea Table, c.1750

▲ Although this table is quite plain, it would still be well above average if it had been in its original form. Sadly, the top has been dished to make it into a tray top, which has always been more desirable than the plain version, and the edge has been carved to a "pie-crust", a pattern popular on the most luxurious models in the second half of the 18th century.

Detection is comparatively easy: firstly, when made to be a tray top, the timber was thick enough to withstand the reduction, but when done later the top becomes too thin and any fixing screws for the underside rail will be exposed (see above middle). Also the top will be light in weight, which is another bad sign. The fact that the underside of the top has been cut to allow room for the screw heads suggests that many of the alterations were done some time ago and indeed done so badly that they are, if you like, honest repairs. So the top itself was aggrandized some time in the 1920s, but the reduced timber was unstable to the extent that it cracked and had to be mended and moved.

This can be put to rights to make it once again a most attractive piece of antique furniture but it should never command more than a tenth of the price of its role model.

The fixing screws for the underside rail have been exposed.

Here is what you do not want to see: replaced rails, evidence of a variety of previous fixings and positions for the rails and the latch, and a most alarming metal plate on the top platform.

Nearly always, tripod tables were made to tip. This was done by pivoting the top on one side of the square supporting block that was fixed to the top of the column. Two runners were fixed to the underside of the top, precisely parallel and fitting close against the block. Two rounded sections like thick dowels were carved from the block to extend into two holes in the runners cut to receive them, forming the hinge. The top was fastened with a metal latch.

A sophisticated variation was the birdcage, which enables the top to turn as well as tip. This was made of two blocks of exactly the same size, approximately 10cm/4in apart and joined by (usually) four turned columns. The lower block had a large hole cut in its centre and the upper block a much smaller hole, again in the centre. The top of the column was turned to form a large spindle, which passed through the lower block. The top of the spindle was turned to a much smaller diameter to pass through the smaller hole in the top block, forming a column around which the two blocks would swivel without wobbling. To fasten the block or birdcage to the column, a wooden wedge was slipped through a hole cut in the column.

All these features can point towards – or away from – authenticity. First the runners are fixed to the underside of the table top with screws (originally, of course, hand-filed screws). An original tray top was made thick enough for these screws to be turned home without coming through the upper side. But when an "improver" dishes the top he has to take out a sufficient depth over most of the surface to leave a pronounced rim, and he must go as close as he dares to the ends of the screws to achieve this. Even if the original screws are removed and cut short, the holes stopped and the screws replaced, the holes themselves will still show or there will be small bumps in the tray's new surface. So, to ensure that a tray top is original, look carefully across the top along lines corresponding to the runners below, and see if there are any regular marks. They may be disguised by distressing, scratches or stains, but once you know where to look, they are easy to spot.

Dishing a top is done on a lathe. The result, therefore, will be perfectly circular, but an 18th-century top will never be perfectly circular, for the wood will have shrunk across the grain and there may be as much as 1cm/½in difference between the diameter measured along the grain and the same dimension across the grain.

Some piecrust borders have been added to table tops by simply gluing on sections of wood and then carving them into the correct patterns. The joints, however well disguised with carving and hard wax, can usually be discovered, and a strong light will reveal the grain of the timber not running in perfect accord with the rest of the top; tray tops and piecrust edges were not made like this in the 18th century. It might just be an innocent repair, but beware.

Wood's behaviour gives us another guide. Turn the table up to make sure the top does in fact belong to the bottom. When wood is exposed to the air it darkens gradually; and if a top has been in place upon its block for some considerable time this area will have been less exposed and will be lighter than the rest of the underside. If all is exactly as it should be, the area of light timber will match precisely the block which has protected it. While signs of more than one latch are acceptable, as latches do break, all should have been fixed approximately in the same place; old holes and associated marks should be around the central position, not to one side.

Birdcages provide excellent guides to authenticity. Not only should there be a pale patch corresponding with the block, but period blocks will by now have shrunk. The columns, however, will not have shrunk in height (only in diameter) and so should protrude very slightly above the top of the upper block, where over the years they will have left perceptible bruises in exactly corresponding positions (see page 59). These bruises, along with the patch of paler wood, are things the faker rarely achieves.

▲ **An elegant oak George II side table, often "improved" in the 1920s with the addition of walnut veneer**
Its style and workmanship are perfect, but the fact that it is made of oak suggests that it was a provincial piece. Had it been later veneered, the drawer front – if not the veneers – would have given it away, as part at least of the front would have been made of softwood.

▲ **A George I walnut lowboy**
A deception in reverse. Whereas all walnut furniture should be examined closely for signs of later veneering or even 20th-century manufacture, this piece demands inspection because of its lines. It is in fact a perfectly genuine George I walnut lowboy, but the curve of the legs is understated to a significant degree. At first sight, one might well suspect that this was a later piece of slightly inferior design subsequently dressed up.

▶ **An authentic George II period mahogany fold-over card table of considerable style**
This is exactly the kind of piece that was "improved" in the early 1900s to enhance its value. Tables such as this were carved at the knee, given shells and scrolls at the feet and their tops were finished with ribbon or Chinese motifs around the edges.

American Furniture

At the top end of the market, fine examples of authentic American antique furniture now command very high prices, reflecting their quality, beauty and authenticity. The danger area for many collectors, unable to afford these top-quality items, is the mass of furniture that has perhaps the right form, but lacks both the detail and conviction that any authentic work of art must possess. Such pieces, looking not unlike – in some cases very like – the exemplars are rarely if ever the bargains they purport to be. It is always better to buy a genuine item of a humbler form than to pay for a dubious example of a desirable form.

Would-be collectors must realize that for every piece that has come down to us intact there are many more pieces that have suffered some kind of alteration or restoration over the years. These pieces were not always looked upon as antiques, but as old or used furniture to be put aside or perhaps altered to fit the owner's needs. As interest in collecting American antiques has developed during this century, these wrecks or altered pieces have drifted into the marketplace to be reprocessed into "original" high-priced forms by unscrupulous people.

In addition to reprocessing there was always the matter of "improving" – making a more valuable form out of a genuine piece. Fully trained restorers must, of necessity, have all the skills required to make any part of a period item, and these skills can be subverted on occasion into "improvement" rather than legitimate restoration.

Before and After: An "Improved" Piece Restored

Near right, a block-and-shell Connecticut secretary as it appeared on an auction flyer. The piece has later Victorian carving on the bonnet, the feet and along the base, a serious but not fatal addition which could be remedied. Far right, the same secretary after the carving was removed and the piece restored to its original state. It is still only one of nine known and worth just as much as if the work had never had to have been done.

▼ An exploded view of a Queen Anne chair
This picture clearly shows the mortise-and-tenon construction of a genuine 18th-century piece of American furniture.

To make the situation even more confusing, during the Centennial period in America (the last quarter of the 19th century), cabinetmakers were legitimately making copies of 18th-century forms. Although similar in appearance (carving style and proportion excepted), one major difference is that Centennial furniture was constructed with dowels instead of the mortise-and-tenon joints of the 18th century. In addition, machines were used in the Centennial period, and the tell-tale marks of those machines are very much in evidence.

Seven years after the Centennial Celebration in America an article under the title *Faking Antique Furniture in New York – 1883* by Ian H. G. Quimby appeared in *The Decorator and Furnisher* for November 1883. "It has been strongly hinted that a large house in this city actively and extensively engaged in the manufacture of antique furniture, is about to be 'shown up' by certain irate customers. It appears that absolute relics of the time of Louis XIV, or even Charlemagne if so desired, are made in an uptown factory, fired full of buckshot, treated to a dose of acid and sold at ridiculously extravagant figures to the amateur collector. There is a marvellous amount of credulity displayed by customers of these dealers in ancient relics."

During the same period, New York cabinetmakers such as Ernest Hagen were making exact copies of Duncan Phyfe furniture. Even today, pieces made by Hagan are often mistakenly catalogued as originals, since they were made exactly the same way Phyfe and his contemporaries made them. These pieces were not made as fakes but as superb reproductions using the same techniques and materials that the early 19th-century craftsmen would have used, but they can muddy the waters of collecting.

► A Centennial Baltimore Hepplewhite chair, c.1875
A piece of this type will have the characteristic dowel construction of Centennial furniture.

Boston and Philadelphia Fakes

In the 1920s, when collecting and interest in American antique furniture began in earnest, fakers in Boston were busy making pieces from old parts, creating rare butterfly tables from plain tavern tables (see page 66), blockfront bureaux from straight front ones, veneering over solid fronts, adding inlaid eagles, fans and bellflowers to plain tables, clocks and chests. They were also recreating fine Federal pieces such as Hepplewhite and Sheraton sewing tables, tambour desks, card tables and veneered bureaux.

In Philadelphia at the same time, dishonest cabinetmakers were making elaborately carved scrolled-top highboys and chests-on-chests from plain flat top ones. They carved the pedestals and legs of plain tripod tea tables, added English mahogany trays as tops and made more valuable piecrust tea tables, or they made similar tables by using the bases of fine pole screens and adding birdcage supports and piecrust tops. See pages 59–60 for ways to identify these illegitimate pieces.

The Categories of Antique Furniture

To arm himself against these deceptions the collector needs to be aware of what makes an antique genuine, and of the background of restoration. He needs to know what the expert or dealer looks for in an antique, how restoration occurs and how it is graded.

Pieces can be allotted to five categories from perfect items in their original state to outright fakes made to deceive. Within these categories there are various degrees of restoration, from minor to major.

▼ Below left, an original Chippendale New York armchair, *c.*1760–80; below right, a later Centennial New York armchair, *c.*1876–90

▲ A genuine 18th-century stool
Note how an original mortise pin stands
proud as the surrounding wood shrinks. The
colour of the head of the pin is almost identical
with that of the leg. Although a craftsman can
fake the "popping out" effect by leaving it
long, it is very hard to match the colour of
the surrounding wood.

THE GENTLE ART

Over 60 years ago Herbert Cescinsky
wrote *The Gentle Art of Faking
Furniture*. In it he said: "There is more
English antique furniture exported to
America in one year than could have
been made in the whole 18th century."
American cabinetmakers were no
more principled than their English
counterparts. In 1845 an article
appeared in the Portland, Maine
Transcript, concerning the faking
of Mayflower furniture. The faker
describes how he is going to cut
down an overly large bed to one that
is a more saleable size. "He says we
have no idea of the enlightened
interest which the ladies take in
everything antique, and he feels
quite certain that he could sell it [the
bed] at a very handsome price,
especially if he adds a little carving to
one corner and breaks off the top of
one of the posts."

The Perfect Piece

This is a piece with all its structural parts intact and glue, blocks, inlay,
surface, edges, finish, etc in a perfect state of preservation. It retains its
original brasses, finials and decorative carving. The genuine antique radiates
its own authenticity and shows the following features:

- patina – the surface quality of the piece, a natural glow that develops
  after many years of care and shines out to the observer;
- erosion of edges – this natural erosion develops after generations of
  waxing, polishing and handling;
- shrinkage – wood shrinks across the grain and this causes irregularities
  where elements are joined: after 200 years mortise pins become compressed
  and pop out; a chair's splat with its vertical grain shrinks from side to
  side, while the crest, with its horizontal grain, shrinks from top to
  bottom, causing a minor break in the flow of design where they meet;
- colour of structural elements due to oxidization – these structural
  elements were left untreated and therefore oxidized naturally over the
  centuries, turning various shades of brown; to simulate this natural
  colour the faker must stain the altered pieces of wood, but this produces
  an artificial colour that can be spotted easily by the experienced eye;
- contrast of structural colour depending upon exposure – structural
  elements that are more exposed to the air will oxidize more and turn a
  darker brown than protected elements; for instance, the undersides of
  the bottom drawers of a highboy will be much darker than those of the
  upper drawers.

All of these points reflect the natural ageing of the object over the centuries
and can be seen by the naked eye – as long as it is a trained eye.

Minor Restoration

The basically intact genuine piece with a few missing blocks, a possible
crack in a bracket foot or a small missing segment, some chewed-off edges
on a drawer lip, a segment of moulding broken or missing, a chipped toe,
finials or pendants restored, some or all brasses replaced, drawer runners
replaced, cracks filled in, and so on. These are still fine pieces: they are just
showing the normal wear and tear of everyday use for 200 years.

Major Restoration (Back to its Original Design)

This is a piece with greatly restored areas of inlay, or with a new foot or feet,
a new drawer front, new base, a case piece with new bonnet mouldings or a
partially restored bonnet, or a piece restored a generation ago but with a
family background that might give it a false promise of authenticity.

All these restorations are part of the preservation process and restore a
piece to its original form; they may or may not seriously devalue the item.
Unfortunately, many of these restorations are poorly done, sometimes by
amateurs but often by inexperienced cabinetmakers. In this area the loudest
differences of opinion occur and do, to a great degree, depend on the
importance and rarity of the piece in question. Defining these restorations
requires experience and judgment, and a piece in this category may be
misunderstood or go unrecognized by inexperienced collectors and dealers.

An attempt to outline here what would be considered acceptable by
people of good will encompasses too many variables to be feasible.

It is perhaps enough to state that the general principle of acceptability based on rarity and importance should temper the judgment employed.

Major Restoration (to Create a More Valuable Form)

This is a piece that has been altered to increase its price, and is the area of fraud: value is being created where it did not exist before. These pieces have been altered to deceive and, no matter how beautiful, are misrepresentations and false bargains. They may appear in a private or public sale with a wonderful provenance which may be true to the original form, but the provenance of the altered section is obviously not going to be revealed in the catalogue. The seasoned expert knows what to look for because over the years he has accumulated his list of likely alterations, and he therefore examines a piece with these things in mind. Some typical alterations are listed here but it is by no means an exhaustive list:

- a butterfly table from a more common tavern table by cutting the sides of the top, hinging them, and adding butterfly wings for support;
- adding arms to a side chair (in this case the chair will usually be narrower in the seat than a true armchair – see page 42);
- cutting down large pieces (sideboards or sofas) to make them smaller and more desirable (see page 48);
- adding feet to the top sections of a highboy or a chest-on-chest when the two sections have been separated (see page 30);
- adding a top to the lower section of a highboy or chest-on-chest to create a lowboy or a chest;
- marrying highboys, chests-on-chests and secretaries (joining the top of one piece to the base of another);
- making more desirable round-leaf tables from square-leaf tables (see page 50);

▼ **A fake butterfly table converted from a genuine tavern table, c.1720–1810**

All the parts have been cannibalized, the top cut and hinged, and butterfly wings added. If the piece was original, the hinges would be attached with rose-headed nails.

• carving a shell or fan on the lid of a desk where one did not exist or replacing the plain interior of a desk with one that has blocked drawers and fan carving;

• replacing bonnet or scrolled tops on highboys, secretaries and chests-on-chests which had been cut off to fit them into low-ceilinged rooms, or adding bonnet or scrolled tops to pieces that originally had flat tops;

• putting new or recarved legs on chairs, tables, highboys and lowboys;

• adding ball-and-claw feet or ogee bracket feet to pieces with plain bracket feet or whose feet were missing;

• switching clock works from one case to another;

• adding a label of a famous maker to an unmarked piece;

• adding legs to highboys, lowboys, chairs and tables with cut legs; these are called "amputees".

The Complete Fake

A piece that has no roots in history but has been created with the intention of deceiving. This, without a doubt, is the most vicious of all the crimes perpetrated upon the collecting public. Important forms are made from scratch, sometimes with the aid of old parts, but more often with new wood, by a skilled craftsman with knowledge of regional motifs, forms and woods. Today, with many pieces of American antique furniture bringing hundreds of thousands of dollars, the incentive to fake is considerable.

▼ **A genuine Hepplewhite card table, c.1790–1810**

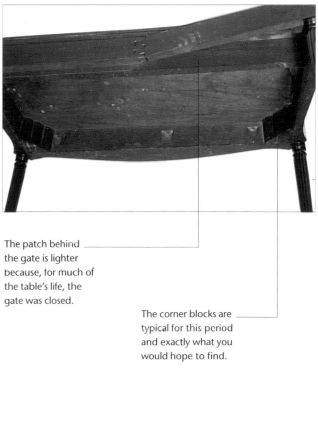

The overall colour on the underside is a natural golden-brown.

The patch behind the gate is lighter because, for much of the table's life, the gate was closed.

The corner blocks are typical for this period and exactly what you would hope to find.

Any staining to make
new wood look like
old should ring
alarm bells.

The faker has no
knowledge of
genuine structural
detail.

▲ **A fake Hepplewhite card table with Chippendale-type top and reeded legs**
The faker has no knowledge of period design or form.

Demand decrees what fakers will supply – it has been this way for generations. Even before the great Philadelphia pie-crust tea table was sold in January 1986 for more than $1,000,000 (£690,000), fakers were making and selling this desirable form along with rare corner chairs, bombé bureaux, block-and-shell Rhode Island bureaux and kneehole desks. Now that the million dollar mark has been reached, the collector can be sure another rash of fakes will appear on the market.

This is where the dealer has a tremendous responsibility. Like a doctor or an attorney, if he hangs out his shingle he should be an expert; but many are not. Of course, if a dealer makes a mistake it won't be fatal, but it can certainly be expensive, and if he continues to make the same mistake or worse, it can and will have a long-lasting effect upon his or her reputation and on dealers in general.

Collectors have a responsibility too – a responsibility to exercise self-restraint, to resist temptation, and to use common sense. Why would a rare form be offered at a very advantageous price? Is it the collector's lucky day? Probably not, but it may be the faker's.

Clocks

▼ **Parts of a simple clock**

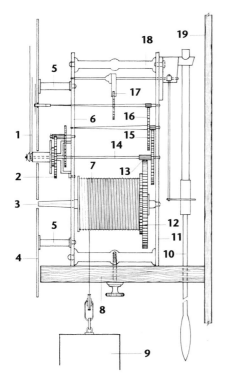

(1) Hands
(2) Motion work
(3) Winding arbor
(4) Dial plate
(5) Dial feet
(6) Front plate
(7) Barrel
(8) Seatboard
(9) Weight
(10) Pendulum

(11) Back plate
(12) Main wheel
(13) Pinions
(14) Centre arbor
(15) Centre wheel
(16) Third wheel
(17) Anchor escapement
(18) Pillars
(19) Backboard

This chapter is not intended to describe the variety of antique clocks most frequently found or how to go about buying them: its purpose is to alert collectors to the more common alterations or deceptions which, if they go unnoticed, can cost the buyer dearly.

Most clocks have the following elements: the dial and its fittings, the movement and the escapement. We shall look at each in turn, before considering particular points about certain familiar types of clock.

Dials and Their Fittings

Dials fall into the following categories: painted metal, painted wood, enamel on metal, and engraved metal.

Painted Metal Dials

This was a popular form of decoration for bracket, longcase and wall clocks of the late 18th and throughout the 19th centuries. It was relatively cheap and is therefore found particularly on provincial clocks. Iron was the metal most commonly used, for reasons of cost.

An authentic example will almost certainly show crazing, similar to that found on old oil paintings. If the dial has been cleaned or restored the crazing will be less obvious, but will show as hairline cracks or small indentations respectively.

▼ **Parts of the dial**

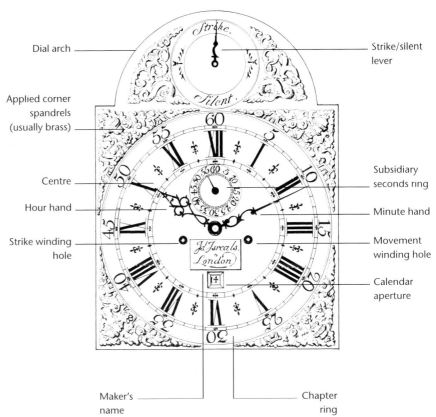

Dial arch

Strike/silent lever

Applied corner spandrels (usually brass)

Centre

Hour hand

Strike winding hole

Subsidiary seconds ring

Minute hand

Movement winding hole

Calendar aperture

Maker's name

Chapter ring

Minute and hour hands are of blued steel.

This is a classic early dial with original ground.

Typical crazing for a dial of this date.

The centre sweep date hand is of gilded brass.

The chapter ring employs Roman numerals for the hours and Arabics for the minutes. The latter disappeared from clock design at the end of the 18th century.

The maker's signature is present.

DAMAGE AND RESTORATION
Enamelled dials: slight chipping around the winding holes and some fine crazing over the dial surface is acceptable.
Painted metal dials: repainted figures and signature are acceptable.
Crazing on the dial surface is a sign of age and authenticity.
Silvered brass dials: the silvering compound can wear off revealing the plain brass finish underneath. Resilvering is acceptable.

Most dials bear a signature (probably that of the clock seller, rather than that of the maker) and it is quite possible to alter these to more famous names. The test here is that the quality of the clock, in all its parts, should match the importance of the signature. Local interest can add a premium and so it is not unknown for an appropriate signature to be contrived.

Painted Wooden Dials
The quality and signature criteria applicable to painted metal dials are equally relevant here. Further, the wood of an authentic dial will certainly have contracted and cracks would show. If they appear on the back of the dial, but not on the face, the dial has been restored.

Enamelled Metal Dials
Make sure that the dial is original to the clock by checking that the dial feet fit into their original fixing holes and that the winding squares are properly centred in the winding holes.

The signature will usually be underneath the glaze and will not therefore show signs of wear. However, certain clocks, especially those of the later 19th century, were retailed by jewellers and large stores, who painted their names on top of the enamel. The presence of such a signature does not add to the value nor does wear to the signature detract from it.

Engraved Dials
Throughout the 18th century the standard form of dial for better-quality longcase and bracket clocks was engraved brass, often enhanced with applied spandrels and a separate chapter ring. The backs of metal dials are generally brownish, partly because of oxidization and partly because they were not highly finished. This appearance can be simulated chemically – a deception that is very difficult to spot if it has been done well.

Simple brass dials have sometimes been later engraved with scrollwork or flowers, for example, to enhance their charm or value. If the style of the added decoration is compatible with the period of the clock, this too can be difficult to tell. A good general rule for initial assessment is that a plain dial goes with a plain-looking case and one would expect to find an elaborate dial ornately cased. Similarly, the spandrels should balance the rest of the engraving and the size of the dial plate. For example, the more elaborate the half-hour marks on the chapter ring, the more ornate the spandrels should be.

It is also important to examine the mounts of brass dials with applied decoration and chapter rings. The back of the dial should show no signs of additional or blocked holes indicating that the screw fixings have been changed.

From about 1700 to about 1740 winding apertures were often ringed. However, rings have sometimes been added later to cover up damage caused by clumsy winding and, more seriously, they may have been applied to disguise minor movement of the winding holes. When a dial has been transferred from one clock to another and the apertures do not coincide exactly with the winding squares, new holes have to be bored and the old openings blocked or partly blocked (see opposite page for an example of plugged holes). The metal is then matted flush with a punch and finished off with rings to complete the disguise.

▲ The back of a late 17th-century longcase dial
There are extra open holes for mounting the chapter ring which suggests this is not the original and the dial has been replaced.

SIGNATURES
To check whether a fake signature has been added to an unsigned clock, feel the engraving; old engraving feels smooth, whereas new work can feel sharp.

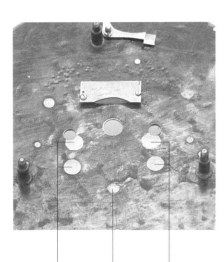

Plugged holes

▲ Back of a wall clock dial
There are plugged holes where the previous winding arbors had been showing, indicating that the dial had been fitted to different movements.

It is very difficult to spot a signature that has been added to a previously unsigned clock. If it conforms in style to the period of the clock the only test is that for later engraving. The only way to alter an existing signature, however, is to file it away and hammer fresh metal forward from the back for re-engraving. When a dial has been signed at the base the back can be examined and signs of hammer marks or thinning will probably show. If the original signature was on the chapter ring the only sure way of checking is to remove it.

Chapter Rings

Engraved chapter rings were normally silvered, though the silvering may have worn away in part or in whole. Some rings, therefore, are now found polished. Resilvering is a normal part of restoration, but it can disguise a blocked hole. It is therefore important to examine the back of the ring if at all possible, as it is much more difficult to disguise a blocked hole from the reverse.

Chapter rings vary enormously both in the size of the numerals and the decoration of the half-hour marks. The guide is that the decoration should be of the ring form and style for the period of the clock, and to determine this there is no substitute for looking at as many clocks and reading as much about them as you can.

Chapter rings are fixed to the clock by feet that pass through the dial plate, where they are pinned. The feet should be in their original holes and should fill them adequately.

Calendar Rings

Many longcase and some bracket clocks are fitted with calendar rings that show the date through an aperture. The ring is usually designed to run in rollers, but friction has often taken its toll and the wheel that carries the advancing pin has been removed or had the pin cut off.

Hands

Replaced hands do not necessarily detract from the value of a clock. If the hands are of the correct style for the period and of a matching quality with the rest of the clock there should be little cause for concern except on the most elaborate and costly pieces.

Movements

It is not often that one finds a movement which has had the planting of the trains altered to fit another dial. However, if the clock has not been cleaned and polished recently it is often possible to detect blocked holes by looking at the back plate. Blocked holes are warning signs, but do not automatically indicate a transferred movement. A clockmaker is unlikely to scrap an entire movement just because he made a small mistake in planting a wheel.

Although a clever restorer will use contemporary brass to make a plug so that there is no (or virtually no) disparity in the colour of the metal, it is possible to see small circles of slight discoloration where the plugs have been inserted. If modern brass has been used the discontinuity in colour will be obvious.

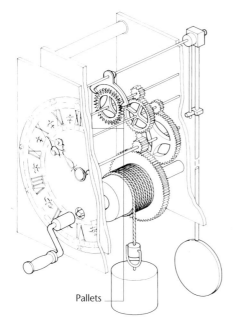

▲ **Anchor escapement**
Developed from c.1665, this movement was first used in longcase clocks with a seconds-beating long pendulum. From c.1800 it was used in bracket clocks with a half-second-beating shorter pendulum. The pendulum used in conjunction with an anchor escapement swings in a narrower arc than that fitted with a verge escapement; it also has a disc-shaped rather than a bulbous bob.

Pallets

It has a new, square back cock.

▲ **A high-quality early 18th-century French striking clock converted to anchor escapement**

The back plates of bracket clocks made in the 17th and 18th centuries are often engraved (those of longcase clocks are almost invariably plain), so jobbers' repairs and bad hammering become more difficult to remove. Blowing very hard on the back plate will often reveal signs of damage or blocked holes.

Spare holes are another matter. Bracket clocks often had repeating trains which, when they became worn, were sometimes removed rather than repaired. Removal leaves a series of spare (but legitimate) holes down one side of the plate.

Uniformity in the colour of the parts of a movement is a useful guide to originality, though one must be prepared for the replacement of those parts that move the most or the fastest – the fly pinion (or regulator) on the striking train and the escapement. Similarity in style of pillars, arbors and collets can also point towards or away from originality.

Signs of Wear

Certain types of repair, which may have been carried out a long time ago, should be treated with care. In particular there is the clock jobbers' tendency to try and close worn pivot holes with a punch (see below left, page 73) – the proper technique is to use a bush – but it is often possible to cover up this form of bad workmanship by restoring with a bush.

Bushing of holes, particularly of those whose wheels turn rapidly, is to be expected. Another good sign is a certain degree of ovalizing of the barrel arbor holes – a result of the considerable pull exercised by the weights.

Always examine pinions for signs of wear. This is to be expected as dust and oil become impacted into the teeth, where they form an abrasive sludge which wears away the steel of the pinions. Some wear is a good sign of age, but excessive wear can be very expensive to repair.

Bells can crack and need replacement. Old bells have a silvery colour, a sweet sound and they resonate after the strike. The metal of modern bells tends to have a pinkish tinge and the ring is more strident.

Escapements

Longcase Clocks

The escapement on a longcase clock will almost certainly be one of two types – anchor or dead beat. The anchor escapement was introduced in the third quarter of the 17th century and continued in general use through to the decline of the longcase clock in the mid-19th century. As it is continually in motion, the steel pallets wear and have often been replaced. The simplest way to identify a replacement is to look at the brass collet on which the anchor is fixed – in most cases it will be in a different style to the other collets in the clock. One way of replacing worn pallets was to solder slips of spring steel to the faces, but it may not be possible, once these have been removed, for the original pallets to be kept.

Dead beat (or Graham) escapements are more rarely found, being generally reserved for regulators and precision time-keepers. Dead beat escapements should always be examined carefully for wear as the cost of restoration will be high.

It is always desirable to have original weights and pendulum, but many have gone astray, quite legitimately, and their absence does not immediately imply that a clock is "wrong".

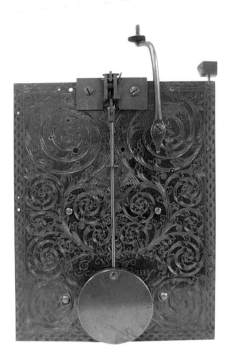

▲ **Rear view of an 18th-century bracket clock by Jacob Massey**
Note the empty holes in the upper left sector where the quarter repeating has been removed and a late Victorian conversion to anchor escapement with over-sized pendulum has been made.

▲ **Back plate of a late 18th-century longcase clock**
Note the heavy punch or hammer marks bottom left. This is a poor attempt at closing a worn pivot hole.

▼ **Verge escapement with fusee**
Until c.1800 clocks were regulated by a verge wheel escapement with a short bob pendulum and as such was most often fitted in portable bracket clocks. English spring-driven bracket clocks were generally fitted with a fusee, attached by gut or a chain to the spring barrel, to equalize the force of the spring as it ran down.

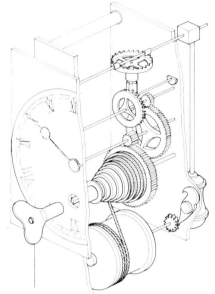

▲ **An ebonized inverted bell-top bracket clock with verge escapement by James Fenton, London, c.1770**
The clock still has its verge escapement and original small bob.

Bracket Clocks

The standard form of escapement for bracket clocks throughout the 17th and 18th centuries was the verge, although in the latter part of the 18th century precision clocks tended to use the anchor with a short pendulum. It was common practice in the 19th century for clockmakers to replace a worn verge escapement with an anchor, which could be bought off the shelf and fitted easily. This is a perfectly genuine alteration and the argument has raged for years as to whether one should reconvert or leave the modified escapement as part of the clock's history. Many experts now accept that the returning of a clock to a verge escapement is a permissible, even desirable, restoration, justified by the softer "tick" and the aesthetic improvement.

Conversion from verge to anchor is easy to spot. The anchor escapement requires a large, flattish bob which, in the case of a clock with an engraved back plate, will cover a considerable portion of the engraving as it swings. By contrast, the small bob of the verge balances the design and shape of the back plate much more closely.

The verge requires a top and bottom block (potence) to fix the crown wheel. These blocks are removed when the escapement is converted and the holes they occupied are left open or may still be visible if they have been blocked. On original verge-escapement clocks the pendulum bob was normally drilled out so that a plug of wood could be inserted into which the pendulum rod was screwed. This made a tight fit for the threads of the rod, lessening the likelihood that it would unscrew itself with the motion of the pendulum. Restorers frequently forget this detail.

If a clock has been reconverted recently, there will be little wear to the crown wheel and pallets. Another sign may be that the back cock or keeper, which on an original escapement would have been engraved, does not have decoration of a quality to match the backplate.

Most bracket clocks made during the 19th century are fitted with fusees to compensate for the varying force of the main spring as the clock runs down. The cord connecting the fusee to the main spring was usually of gut; less frequently it was a chain, constructed like a miniature bicycle chain. If the clock was designed for gut lines, the grooves will be semicircular – chains ran in square-section grooves. If broken chains have been replaced with gut the wrong shape of the groove will be obvious.

Recently, gut has begun to be replaced by wire, but this tends to scratch or cut the barrels and it is always worth checking for this carefully. Nylon-coated fishing line is a more satisfactory replacement. Badly worn gut in a fusee train should always be replaced immediately: if a cord breaks it will release massive power from the mainspring and this could result in serious damage to the movement.

Longcase Clocks

The cases of longcase clocks were made by cabinetmakers, and therefore should be assessed as antique furniture. What particularly concerns us here, however, is establishing whether the clock belongs with the case.

In a small group of exceptionally rare and valuable 17th-century clocks, the hood was originally of the rising type, but due to the inconvenience of this design, they were often converted to a conventional opening door. Signs of this conversion will not appear on any modestly priced longcase clock.

The dial should be an adequate fit inside the mask of the hood door, which should neither conceal the decoration of the dial nor reveal its edge. When you remove the hood, examine the seatboard on which the movement rests. Ideally the seatboard will be original, showing age in the timber compatible with the rest of the case, but seatboards do have a heavy weight to carry and some have broken and therefore been replaced, quite legitimately. However, any indication of a non-original seatboard should immediately raise suspicions.

The movement of a long case clock is usually secured to the seatboard by hooks that pass over the bottom pillars of the movement or by bolts drilled up through the seatboard into the pillars. If the movement and the seatboard belong together there should be only one set of aligning holes, whichever fixing method was used.

A seatboard should be neither clumsily thick nor apparently too thin to support the weight of the movement. If the board is raised on blocks it is possible that there has been an alteration. Seatboards were normally nailed or screwed straight down into the cheeks; therefore any holes in the seatboard should have corresponding holes in the trunk side panels below. A line was often scored across the backboard when the original seatboard was fitted. If the existing seatboard does not conceal or coincide with this line, it is quite possible that it has been moved to accommodate a transferred movement.

The backboard can be revealing in another way. The one-second pendulum

▲ A Charles II walnut longcase clock by Joseph Knibb, London, c.1680
Although the bun feet are replaced they follow the original style. The flat top and plinth are all as you would expect on a piece of this date. These are often replaced or altered.

has a virtually standard length of 1m/39½in. If the pendulum has knocked against the back or the sides for any length of time, there will be scrape marks. If these marks do not correspond with the present position of the bob the likelihood is that the seat board has been moved up or down to accommodate a transferred movement.

Wall Clocks

The earliest form of English wall clock is the lantern, dating from c.1620. Their age, simple construction and desirability mean that they are one of the most faked types of clock.

Early lantern clocks were fitted with balance wheel escapements, but surviving examples are almost unknown. In general, any lantern clock with a balance wheel has had its escapement restored. Many early lantern clocks were converted to short pendulum verge escapements later in the 17th century and were often further converted to long pendulum anchor escapements at a later date. Redundant holes in the top plate are the usual evidence of such conversions.

Lantern clocks originally ran on woven ropes, which were threaded over spikes on the ratchet wheels. They were often converted to run on chains; if so, the ratchet wheels will have had their points filed down.

Pierced frets at the top of lantern clocks have sometimes been damaged and required replacement. These frets are cast in one piece with their feet: if a replacement has been fitted its feet may not match the original holes, which will be detectable. Any signature that appears at the base of the front fret should be checked for authenticity.

In recent years the increasing value of lantern clocks has led to the production of many counterfeits, some using movements taken out of simple 30-hour country longcase clocks. Others, such as the large number of examples signed "Thomas Moore, Ipswich", are brand new, though given the appearance of age by being chemically treated or buried in earth for a while.

▲ **A 17th-century lantern clock with its original verge escapement**
The dial centre is signed "Davis, London". The heavy, arrow-shaped steel hand is an attractive feature. The frets to the front and sides are particularly unusual and these are often damaged. This clock is exactly as you would hope for, but any evidence of winding holes in the front dial of clocks of this type would indicate a fusee movement has been fitted.

▶ **A fine quarter chiming bracket clock, Langley & Benjamin Bradley, c.1730**
These views show a substantial and beautifully executed three train, seven-pillar fusee movement with verge escapement. The plates are beautifully decorated with winged cherubs, birds, insects, two cavaliers, a female mask head, a basket of flowers and foliate engraving.

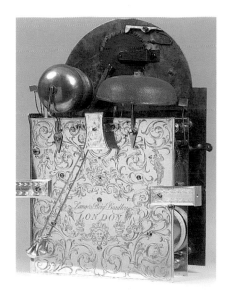

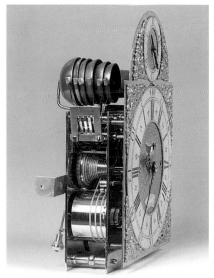

There is some shrinkage of the timber which is always a good sign of age and indication that it has not been restored.

The spade hands are unusual in that they are made of gilded steel.

The chapter ring, which was originally white, is now dull brown from the smoke of ages.

▲ An untouched black lacquer tavern or Act of Parliament clock, William Chalken, c.1750–75
Only minimal restoration has been carried out to this case as well as slight retouching of the lacquerwork, and the piece bears all the marks of its 230-odd years.

Act of Parliament Clocks

These large wall clocks take their name from the Act of 1797 which put a sales tax on clocks, though similar items had been made since the early 18th century. They were made for public places, such as inns, and were often lacquered. Recently a number of copies have been made that are very convincing at first sight, though a close inspection will often reveal inappropriate and inferior materials, such as plywood.

Dial Clocks

Dial clocks were introduced into Britain in the mid-18th century and were popular until the early part of this century. Although they are not much faked yet, early examples are now sufficiently valuable to merit careful scrutiny.

The first examples had painted wood or engraved and silvered dials similar to those of longcase and bracket clocks. They were usually signed by a London maker. The movements had short pendulum verge escapements with a fusee in the train. The cases were generally a rich, dark mahogany with a broad turned bezel and a substantial wood or brass ring securing the glass. The hands were of pierced blued steel or, very occasionally, brass, and were similar in design to those of contemporary bracket and longcase clocks.

During the early part of the 19th century the number of examples increased dramatically and the silvered dial passed out of fashion, being supplanted by painted metal – usually tin. Examples do exist in which original painted dials have been exchanged for engraved, signed, silvered or brass dials to give the impression of an earlier date.

Later in the 19th century these clocks changed very little in detail, but just enough to make them less valuable. The dials and glass became flat and the brass bezel less substantial. Hands became plainer, sometimes with simple spade ends; minute hands might have no decorative shaping at all.

Check that the clock belongs in the case by examining the retaining screws in the edge of the dial. All three or four of them should align with holes in the frame and there should be no redundant holes.

Skeleton Clocks

There is no simple guide to establishing whether a skeleton clock is genuine, made up from old parts or an outright fake. Many examples were produced during the 19th century as it was common practice for provincial clockmakers to contrive a skeletonized clock as a window display. These clocks were readily made up by taking the wheels from an old dial or bracket clock and replanting them within a set of pierced, skeletonized plates. Such clocks often had painted metal dials, whereas their more sophisticated contemporaries were likely to have their dials engraved and silvered.

Skeleton clocks are as easy to make up now as they were then, and their increase in value has made it a commercially viable proposition to produce them. Timepiece clocks are the most often faked.

All the wheels of superior skeleton clocks are finely pierced, normally with five or six crossings. Bracket clocks rarely had more than four crossings as the wheel work was not on display. The under-dial wheels driving the

Carriage clocks commonly have a lever escapement mounted on a platform on the top of the movement rather than the backplate. This type of escapement does not have a pendulum and so is especially suitable for travelling clocks.

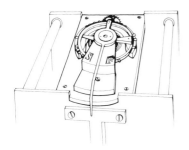

▼ **The top section of a carriage repeat-strike clock**

The replacement platform has been silvered in an attempt to disguise its lack of age.

The handle has been removed and the mounting holes plugged.

hands of a cased clock are almost never pierced, though the copier with an eye for detail will rectify this when using them to make up a skeleton clock.

The base can sometimes reveal more than the wheel work. A new wooden base should always be regarded with suspicion. Odd-looking feet supporting the clock frame should be examined, as should the studding that holds the clock to the base: a common sign of replacement or alteration is the fitting of over-large feet to add height to a clock that has been placed under a non-original dome.

Skeleton clocks are not usually signed on the movement because of lack of space. When a signature appears engraved on a plaque fitted to the base it is very important to establish that the entire assembly belongs together.

Carriage Clocks

Carriage clocks were introduced early in the 19th century and are traditionally held to be modelled on the *pendules d'officiers* used by Napoleon's commanders. It was the perfection of the lever escapement and the low cost of manufacture, combined with their exceptional accuracy, that led to the mass production of these clocks.

English examples are rare by comparison with their French counterparts, of which hundreds and thousands were made between 1850 and 1920. More recently several French and Swiss companies have recreated them, not as forgeries but simply as copies of a continuously popular style. They are obviously new, although a small number are around that have been "aged" by dirtying the case and the movement.

The clock is very likely to be modern if the dial, which should be enamel and very smooth, is thin and slightly corrugated, with the white very white and the black very black. Some clocks are stamped with serial numbers on the back plate, and if these are composed of more than five digits the clock is unlikely to be old.

Beware of alterations to carriage clocks. A recent modification has been the replacement of the side glasses with modern electrotyped metal or porcelain panels. They are inferior in quality, being decorated in acrylic or cellulose paints which have a soft and greasy appearance, and sit ill with an original plain white dial.

Although mass-produced, carriage clocks were finely if not heavily gilded and some signs of wear should be expected if the gilding is claimed as original. The best-quality examples were fire gilded and can occasionally be found still in perfect condition. Original gilding should be preserved if possible.

One particular "enhancement" to be aware of is the alteration of a quarter-striking (*petite sonnerie*) clock to a full *grande sonnerie*. It is not technically difficult to lengthen the slide on a quarter-striking clock or to fit the complete mechanism and to turn such a clock into a *grande sonnerie*. However, the modification means that the clock will not strike in the *grande sonnerie* mode throughout a full seven-day period – the barrel on a *grande sonnerie* clock is larger than its quarter-striking contemporary. The ideal way to buy a *grande sonnerie* carriage clock of doubtful history is therefore on eight days' approval.

Glass

Coloured glass

In the late 18th and early 19th centuries, English and American coloured glass became more popular and was produced cheaply and with basic attention to detail. This milk jug may be genuine but it is known that small American factories made similar wares at the end of the 20th century. The lack of wear on the foot suggests this piece is modern.

Comparing two glasses of similar style

The amethyst wine glass (left) made c.1910–1920 was copying the type of early 19th-century glasses typical of this genuine green glass (right) with a capstan stem. Closer examination of the underside of the feet of both glasses reveals that the later copy has the pontil mark indented in relation to the foot, which has no visible marks of the tools. On the genuine glass the foot is much flatter, the pontil mark is more pronounced and there are irregularities left by the glassmaker's tools.

Despite the fact that it is only a relatively small amount of glass that fetches high prices – prices comparable with works of art in other fields – there is quite a substantial amount of glass on the market that could deceive collectors. Some of it is undoubtedly made or altered to deceive buyers and enhance prices; much more is the result of honest reproduction. While it is only sensible to assess all antique glassware with careful knowledge, a blanket of suspicion should not be cast over old glass in general.

Whether a piece of glassware could be deceptive depends to a considerable extent on the seller. The maker of an entirely legitimate reproduction cannot be accused of deception, but the subsequent seller, by ignorance or design, may mis-describe a piece and so render it spurious. It would be unjust to refer to the factories making reproductions of 18th-century English glass in the 1930s as fakers, but it would be kind indeed to describe as anything less than fraudulent people who know their provenance yet try to sell them as authentic articles.

Knowledge is the key, and the purpose of this chapter is to record the kinds of glassware that have been reproduced or faked and to give some indications of how to identify them. Reading will provide the collector with the history of glass production, a knowledge of factories and individual makers, and descriptions of glassmaking processes. But book-learning can never be the sole guide. Because relatively little glass is marked in comparison to ceramics or silver, handling as much glass as possible and identifying the different types of glass body, is an essential way for collectors to gain expertise and confidence. Opportunities for handling glass are available from a number of sources.

Acquiring Knowledge

Collectors' societies often provide members' days when glass is brought for discussion and identification. The Glass Association, the Glass Circle and the Carnival Glass Society cater for most tastes and can put collectors in touch with each other. Each society publishes newsletters and journals for the spread of information. Museums provide many examples to look at and learn from, both in their permanent galleries and in the many temporary exhibitions. At Broadfield House Glass Museum at Kingswinford in the West Midlands, the collections include a "Black Museum" containing fakes, forgeries

and reproductions designed to assist collectors to distinguish between the genuine and the copy. The major salerooms provide excellent opportunities to view and handle important glasses not readily available elsewhere. A great deal can also be learned from good dealers, who, incidentally, by supplying a proper descriptive receipt bind themselves to their honest opinion and will make amends if they should be proved wrong. A handful of specialist glass dealers make a point of collecting fakes and reproductions and make them available to collectors in their shops and by organizing joint exhibitions. Specialist fairs are another good way to see large amounts of glass and exchange views with dealers and other collectors. The biannual Glass Fair held at the Motorcycle Museum, near the National Exhibition Centre at Birmingham, is the best known and longest running of these fairs. Regular visits to glass and china shops will also keep one up to date with new developments in revival reproductions. It is worth collecting any promotional material for future reference.

Modern Factory and Museum Reproductions

In recent years the business of creating reproductions of antique objects has become widespread and glass is no exception. For the novice collector the spread of reproductions among genuine items in antique fairs and shops can be a minefield. Fortunately, some of the larger antiques fairs now have special areas devoted to reproductions, allowing a close examination of the copies.

Codd's Patent Bottle

Glass collectors will recognise the ubiquitous Codd bottle containing a glass marble in the neck to act as a seal. The idea was patented by Hiram Codd in 1874. In 1996 Codd bottles were being made in Taiwan for export to Japan and other Far and Middle Eastern markets. J. H. Edgington, a British glass collector, reported seeing them in production at the rate of 30 per minute, complete with pinched neck. His report featured in *The Glass Cone*, the newsletter of the Glass Association, no.46, Summer 1998 issue. Reproduction bottles can be confused for older specimens when they have genuine old labels applied to them.

Satin Air Trap

This 19th-century technique, popular with American and British factories, involved trapping air bubbles in a variety of patterns between two layers of glass. When the glass was cold it was given a satin finish by dipping in acid or subjecting the glass to acid fumes. Amongst genuine examples some satin air-trap pieces were lighter in weight than known 19th-century items and were also in different profile shapes. A chance visit to a Murano glassmaker's house by a British glass collector and historian has identified these items as Venetian from the 1950s. Catalogues and other printed information provided by the glassmaker gives conclusive proof.

Fenton Art Glass

The Fenton Art Glass Company in West Virginia in the United States has been in operation since 1905 when it was responsible for some of the finest Carnival glass of that period. The history of the firm is one of continuous quality development and production. Often using traditional processes and techniques,

▲ **A modern reproduction of a Codd's Patent bottle made in Taiwan**
This was made for the Japanese drinks market and even has Japanese marks on the base.

▲ **A 1950s Venetian vase copying the late 19th-century satin air-trap technique**
New evidence has recently come to light from Murano that, during the 1950s, one factory was producing many pieces such as this. The vases are usually larger and more ornate than the original American and English versions.

CARNIVAL GLASS

This brightly coloured, pressed, iridescent glass was introduced in North America in 1908 and continued to be made by American, British and European factories throughout the 20th century. The name implies that the glass was given away as prizes at fairs and carnivals but this only applied to the later, very cheap, amber-coloured glass. The classic Carnival glass, known as "the poor man's Tiffany", was too good to be disposed of in this way.

▼ **Reproduction Art Nouveau glass**
Reproductions of pieces by Emile Gallé and Daum have flooded the antiques market in recent years. Produced in Romania, they are easily purchased over the Internet and in the wrong hands could easily deceive the beginner and expert alike. This forgery was made in the last few years. Only the sharpness of cutting is unlike the original.

▶ **Identifying later Fenton copies**
The two-handled vase is a genuine example of Burmese glass made by Thomas Webb and Sons in Stourbridge about 1886. The small posy bowl, made by the Fenton Art Glass Company in America, is close to the colour match of the Webb vase but the tell-tale sign of its origin is that the decoration is transfer-printed and shows the dots of the printing process. No genuine Burmese ware was ever transfer-printed. The posy bowl also bears a lozenge mark and the name "Fenton" but this could easily be ground out by a forger.

some of their ranges have a Victorian look to them and are close to English and especially Stourbridge 19th-century originals (see below), including Vaseline glass, Burmese glass, crimped rims, and twisted handles on mottled, coloured baskets. Carnival glass is also made occasionally especially for the many Carnival Glass Societies in America. There is no doubt about the integrity of this excellent company but, because the majority of the items are little known in Britain, British collectors should be aware of the pitfalls that may face them. Instances have been reported where modern Fenton pieces have been sold under Victorian descriptions with prices to match. In the more flagrant abuses, the offending dealers have apparently been warned off. Collectors can obtain catalogues of the latest products direct from the company or can access their web site (**www.fentonartglass.com**).

Modern Gallé Copies

Emile Gallé (1846–1904) created some of the finest Art Nouveau cameo glass from his workshops in Nancy in France. As prices for genuine pieces reached into six figures, they became a target for reproductions. The large number of these reproductions, which are readily found, are made in Romania and sold over the Internet. One of the web sites refers to a maker called Montessy, a devoted disciple of Gallé, who married a Romanian girl after the Gallé factory closed in 1931. They lived in Azuga, in the Valley of Praque, in Romania. With the help of Bohemian glassmakers, close copies of Gallé were created. Production seems to have been disrupted under the communist regime but when that regime ended production started up again.

The lamps, vases and bowls are created in the same way as the originals with a number of different layers of coloured glass which are then acid etched to create cameo landscape and floral scenes. All of them bear the "Gallé" signature in cameo relief and have an additional mark of "TIP" which is thought to denote "Gallé type". The initials "TIP" are separate from the "Gallé" name and can be easily ground off by the initial buyer. The web sites (**www.tip-galle.com** and **www.giaion.tripod.com**) show what is available.

► **Three modern Czech reproductions acquired in Novy Bor in 2001**
They are (left to right): copies of a German *roemer*, popular from the 15th to the 17th centuries, a cone-shaped beaker found across Europe during the 5th century AD and a *daumenglas*, literally a thumb glass, made in Germany or Holland in the 16th and 17th centuries.

▲ **A modern Czech reproduction of 18th-century Bohemian and German flasks**
Bought at the Glass Museum in Kamenicky Senov; there is no intention to deceive but on the secondary market it could fool the unwary.

Reproductions from the Czech Republic

The Czech Republic has a large number of glass factories ranging from vast enterprises to independent one-man studios. The range of items from these glassworks is staggering. Crystalex, one of the largest companies, makes thousands of items for export to Russia, the Middle East and Japan. At the other end of the scale, Pavel Rybacek, at his studio in Novy Bor, makes very plausible reproductions of Roman, medieval, and 17th- and 18th-century glass. Another independent maker in Novy Bor, Vaclav Stepanek, blows imitations of iridized Tiffany and Loetz vases. Vaclav Stepanek is one of the greatest glassblowers in the Czech Republic and has created pieces for notable artists such as Stanislav Libensky and Dale Chihuly, and has worked at the International Glass Symposia at Novy Bor and at Frauenau in Germany. His promotional literature refers to the "replicas of Gothic, Baroque and Art Nouveau glass produced in the style of the famous glassworks in Klastersky Mlyn in the Sumava (Czech Republic). All the works produced are signed and marked with the year of origin. Special attention should be paid to the 'Collector series' of reproductions of Gothic glass, which are produced from originals in the depository of the West Bohemian Museum in Plzen."

The rim has been ground flat.

The glass is much whiter than its 18th century counterpart.

EUROPA.

▲ **A modern Czech "Europa" beaker imitating mid-18th-century German and Bohemian enamelled glass**

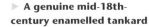
► **A genuine mid-18th-century enamelled tankard**

This piece has been finished by hand and shows a rounded edge.

▲ **A modern reproduction imitating early 19th-century Biedermeier *Transparentenamel* tumblers**
This high-quality piece was bought in Novy Bor in the Czech Republic in 2001 for a few pounds. Out of context at an antiques fair, it could easily pass as the genuine article.

▲ **Antique Moser glassware of the kind that is still being produced today**
This late 19th-century bowl is in dark blue glass with an etched and gilt border of female figures.

At the end of the 19th century glass factories in the former Czechoslovakia were responsible for exporting vast numbers of so-called "Mary Gregory" glasses (see page 99). The glasses were named by collectors after an enamel decorator who is known to have worked at the Boston and Sandwich Glass Works in the United States. Research has identified that Mary Gregory only enamelled snow scenes onto glass. The glasses with scenes of boys and girls flanked by foliage originated in Czechoslovakia. For a number of years, copies, mainly in ruby glass, have been exported from that country. Removed from a trade stand display, with the original label removed and seen amongst other antiques, these vases can be deceptive.

In the 1930s the London firm of John Jenkins introduced a range of pressed "Barolac" glass, made for them in Czechoslovakia. The firm reintroduced the series in the early 1980s in these patterns: Palm Trees, Cherries, Aquarium, Sea Horse, Pansy, Poppies and Trees. Vases and bowls were not marked but are very close to the frosted milky appearance of the originals.

The great Czech firm of Moser base some of their current lines on their 19th-century designs. After studying antique examples in books and museums it should be easy enough to spot the new versions. One range to be wary of, however, is that of the ruby and brown vases and bowls with a continuous band of etched and gilt classical figures.

Bohemian and German glass factories have been responsible for producing accurate copies of Biedermeier shapes, especially the tumblers which were popular in the early 19th century and are now highly collectable. In the 1980s the German firm of J. Oertel sold a good-quality range of *Transparentenamel* beakers. Other 18th- and early 19th-century techniques which were, and are still copied, are *Schwarzlot* (black-painted decoration) and *Zwischengoldglas* (two close-fitting cylinders of glass with gilded decoration trapped between them).

In Vienna, the famous glass firm of J. & L. Lobmeyr offer reproductions of goblets based on the Vienna Secessionist-inspired designs of Otto Pruscher from the 1900 period. It is important to state that there is no intention to

▲ **A "Burmese" vase**
Often thought to be by Webbs of Stourbridge, and although it dates from the correct period, i.e. 1880–90, this vase has a propeller mark which has been proven to originate from a Bohemian factory.

▶ **An English cased-glass punchbowl**
Cased glass has been exported from Czechoslovakia for over 150 years following its introduction in Bohemia. The technique spread quickly throughout Europe and North America in the 19th century and is still popular with glassmakers and collectors. Such a vast output creates enormous difficulties in attribution and dating.

This English punchbowl and stand is relatively easy to date because the bowl was a popular Edwardian shape continuing in production in the 1920s. The idea of bowls on separate stands first appears in the late 19th century but some cased and cut glass, which can be proven to be from the 1840s, could be mistaken for modern glass because of its clean and bright appearance. Perhaps the most difficult items to date precisely are the ubiquitous hock glasses with coloured bowls on tall, clear stems.

▲ Lalique marks

The vast majority of Lalique articles, but not all, bear a mark, some examples of which are shown here. The style of the mark varied with time, though facsimiles of René Lalique's signature appear in all periods. The marks were variously moulded, sandblasted and wheel cut; if moulded marks appeared indistinct, an etched mark was often added for clarity.

The full mark, "R. Lalique France" dates from before 1945, though the "France" was not always added. "Lalique France" dates from 1945 or after. The size and shape of all the marks can vary according to the size and form of the object being marked.

with this range or with any of the other reproductions referred to in this section. It is the description and handling of these honest reproductions by later unscrupulous owners which can lead to problems for collectors.

Problems with Continuous Reproduction

The one area of reproduction which can create difficulties in accurate dating is the continuous production of a design over many years. In Finland the Iittala glassworks have made the famous Alvar Aalto vases since they were designed by the architect in 1936. The 1967 Orchidea and Alpina designs of Tapio Wirkkala are similar examples.

In France, the glass of René Lalique has maintained its high reputation for sophisticated design since the 1920s. However, many of those shapes are still continued and dating them means relying on 1930s publicity and pattern books, details of signatures and reference to the most recent company catalogues.

The difference in price between coloured Lalique pieces of the Art Deco period and clear or frosted, which can be up to seven times greater, has meant that fakers have been tempted to change the colour of the clear glass using modern technology. In the late 1980s and early 1990s, collectors of Lalique scent bottle became aware of an increase in the number of amethyst coloured bottles appearing on the market. This sought-after colour always fetched high prices and suspicions were aroused. Eventually the news transpired that the faker or fakers would take original 1930s clear glass scent bottles or even later more recent examples in the same style, and subject

▼ Pre-1945 Lalique vase

The crisp modelling was achieved by using compressed air to blow the glass into the mould.

▼ Factory mistake

This Lalique vase is signed "R. Lalique France" but the lettering is back to front – this is almost certainly an innocent mistake at the factory, as no faker could afford to be so negligent.

The signature includes the pattern number which can be checked with original catalogues.

The inclusion of the initial "R" proves it was made before 1945, the year of Lalique's death.

▼ Modern copies

This piece may be of American or Taiwan origin and is of modern manufacture but is based on examples which date from the mid-19th century. These pieces turn up regularly at antiques fairs.

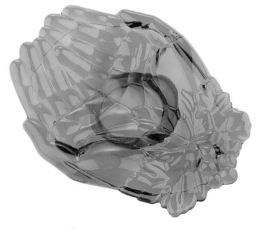

▶ A selection from the display by Hoffman of Vienna and Prague shown at the 1862 London Exhibition

These styles continued in Northern Bohemia into the 1880s but are often dated 40 or 50 years earlier, especially the decanter with the applied snake, the central vase and the handled jug on the right. It would come as no surprise to find these pieces described as either French or English *c*.1840–50, but the decoration is generally too ornate and fussy for that period. The *Humpen* is much too slick and brash to be mistaken for a 17th- or 18th-century original. Some early 19th-century fake *Humpen* were made by Johann Georg Buhler who worked in Munich.

The ruby-cased vase engraved with figures may have been made by F. Zach, who worked during the third quarter of the 19th century, possibly for a time in England. A covered cup by Zach, now in the Metropolitan Museum of Art in New York, was featured in the 1910 catalogue of the J. Pierpoint Morgan collection where the author tried to prove it was made by a 17th-century engraver, even suggesting that he had been a wood carver who worked sporadically on glass. It was not until the 1964 article in *Apollo* entitled "The Glass Engraver F. Zach: 17th or 19th Century" by Robert Charleston appeared that the oft-repeated 17th-century attribution was finally disproved.

them to intense ultra-violet radiation in professional equipment. The radiation acted on the chemical make-up of the glass, transforming it from clear to amethyst. In one reported case in Australia, the culprit is said to have placed the parcel containing the scent bottle directly into the equipment, subjecting it to radiation and then shipping it back immediately to the owner. A similar effect of colour change from clear to amethyst can take place when glass has been left in the open air and where there are intense levels of light, but this change will require years rather than the few minutes with modern equipment.

Museum-inspired Reproductions

The development of retail shops within museums has led many museums to look at items in their collections as source material for reproductions offered for sale as souvenirs of a visit. The Metropolitan Museum of Art in New York for example, sold replicas of an early American mould-blown tumbler in its collections. When the clear glass tumblers passed into second-hand ownership, some collectors were taken in by the copies until they spotted the initials "MMA" which had been placed within the overall design to differentiate the replicas from the original. At the reconstructed 1608 Jamestown Glasshouse in Virginia, the visitor can buy copies of bottles, drinking vessels and candlesticks "of authentic 17th-century English design".

Roman glass in museum collections has been the inspirational starting point for Mark Taylor and David Hill in England. Mark and David are, respectively, a glassblower and an artist who work together producing a wide range of high-quality reproductions of ancient Roman glass vessels entirely by hand. Research and experimentation feature strongly in an effort to gain insights into the techniques of glass production during the Roman period. Starting with blown vessels, they went on to introduce mould-blown beakers with charioteer scenes, and engraved and cut pieces. In 2001 they introduced reproductions of Roman mosaic glass vessels. Each example is signed, dated and numbered, with a record kept at the studio to prevent future confusion. Roman glass is also the inspiration for a commercial range planned by Peter Rath in his design atelier at Kamenicky Senov in Northern Bohemia. The efforts of Taylor, Hill and Rath are based on solid research and are genuine attempts to identify alternate methods of glass production especially as the larger glass companies lose traditional methods or close their operations completely.

▲ Reproduction Egyptian sand-core vessels

These two vessels, copying Egyptian sand-core vessels, were made in Murano about 1900. The originals were made on a core of sand; these copies were blown.

▼ Reproduction jug

This jug is probably 1920s or '30s Venetian and is a very good copy that is almost successfully "genuine".

Ancient Glass

Forgeries of Egyptian glass sculptures began to appear early in the 20th century. In 1912 the British Museum purchased four glass canopic jars now shown to be fakes, probably made in Egypt; other items include Shawabti figures, statuettes and small animal sculptures. Common features were the purple-blue colour, the occasional remains of mould marks, and hollow moulding – originals were always cast in the solid. The maker cast the forgeries from moulds taken from ancient pieces; detection therefore relies on technical examination and methods of construction. Almost all of the forgeries have been deliberately broken and repaired, with some portions missing to add the appearance of age.

The most notable glass products of the Roman Empire were the cameo glass vases of the 1st century AD. In 1878 the Venice & Murano Co. showed imitations at the Paris Exhibition; Pauly et Cie, another Venetian firm, made similar versions. The glass used for Venetian cameo was a soda lime glass which resulted in softly modelled outlines giving an impression of age. A pitted surface, common to all Venetian cameos, helps the illusion. Two vases which have deceived until recently are a 1st century AD Roman vase in the Toledo Museum in Ohio, which was published in the first guidebook to the glass collections, and a tall vase in the Moore Collection at Yale University Art Gallery, described in 1927 as "Hellenistic first century BC".

The Mainz firm of Ludwig Fellmer was a major producer of Roman shapes. A page from their pattern book, published by Spiegl in *Glas Des Historismus*, shows simple flasks and bottles and more complex jugs and vases with trailed and pincered decoration, as well as mould-blown vases in barrel shape reminiscent of the genuine "Frontinus" marked pieces of the 1st century AD.

Modern sources for ancient glass forgeries are the Israeli, Turkish and Egyptian glassmakers; they work in primitive conditions, using clay moulds taken from original glasses. The wares they make are determined, as always, by market prices: the most popular fakes are small mould-blown bottles or altar cruets decorated with Christian symbols. Artificial ageing can include acid etching, putting a covering of sand onto the surface of the hot glass, and the application of chemicals while the glass is hot. Occasionally the forger will glue genuine flakes of iridescence onto the surface of the copy.

▶ Made to deceive

This small vase is a deliberate forgery from a workshop in Damascus which specialized in glasses with Christian and Jewish symbols.

The vase has been dipped in acid to give a false patination.

A flange of glass remains on the neck where the mould was badly fitted.

The white stain is too obvious an attempt at weathering. It was produced at the same Damascus workshop as the vase bottom right on page 85.

▲ **Amber flask**
This amber flask with interlocking circles is based on a 3rd century AD original. It was bought in Damascus in 1979.

▲ **Hexagonal flask**
This hexagonal flask has very faint images of the Menorah and other figures. It is another deliberate attempt to deceive.

▲ **Designs drawn from the 1886 pattern book of the *Rheinische Glashutten***

Modern chemicals sprayed onto glass can induce a deceptive flaking effect. Weathering is an important part of ancient faked glass as it very conveniently disguises joins, as well as possible discrepancies in colour matching.

The Corning Museum of Glass in upstate New York has identified some ancient glasses as "marriages" of genuine broken fragments. The identified conglomerate vessels show ingenuity in combining quite disparate elements, such as sticking together two genuine and complete objects to form a hitherto unrecorded shape.

German Historical Reproductions

In the last half of the 19th century, archaeological excavations, the development of museums, exhibitions of famous glass collections, publications such as Ruskin's *Stones of Venice* and pattern books crammed with eclectic designs created a fashion for historical reproductions which swept Europe.

In Germany, the style known as "Historismus" covers all copies from Frankish claw beakers to 18th-century enamelled *Humpen*. The *Rheinische Glashütten-Aktien-Gesellschaft* – the glassworks of the Joint-Stock Company in Koln-Ehrenfeld in the Rhineland – was the most important factory for this work. Founded in 1864, it made table glass and bottles but from 1879–90, under the directorship of Oskar Rauter, it concentrated on revivals of Roman, Venetian and old German styles. Designs used blown-glass techniques with a little cutting and engraving but no painting or gilding. Subdued colours included the characteristic "antique-green". The flawless quality of Köln-Ehrenfeld glass means that it is impossible to mistake it for anything else.

In 1865 Carl Heinrich Müller moved from Thuringia to Hamburg where he established a glassblowing workshop. His copies of 16th- or 17th-century Venetian goblets were made by lampwork and sold as authentic pieces by dealers in the Netherlands. From 1876–7 Muller combined his stylistic and technical innovations to create many dragon-stem goblets and covers which, almost without exception, were classified as 16th- or 17th century. Increased awareness and research into 19th-century glass records has helped to identify these fakes.

▲ **Reproduction "Historismus" vases**
On the left, clear glass with applied prunts painted green and with engraved scrollwork. Possibly from the Koln-Ehrenfeld factory in the 1880s (height 16cm/6⅜in). On the right, a four-handled green vase with slight irridescence. It bears a very faint circular mark "SAALBURG", and was made by Loetz Witwe, Austria, for Tschernich & Co., Haifa, about 1890–1900 (height 18½cm/7⅛in).

▶ Fritz Heckert beaker
A beaker of soda glass with air bubbles, figures on either side of the coat-of-arms, the name "IONES TAMATZ" and the date 1624. Another "Tamatz" beaker in the Corning Museum is dated 1610. Both were made by Fritz Heckert, who based them on examples in the Kunstgewerbemuseum, Berlin (height 12cm/4¾in).

▲ A Venetian cameo glass vase, dating probably from the 1870s
Venetian cameo glass of this period can be deceptive. The metal used was a soft soda lime glass, which was inclined to pitting. This, combined with the softness of the relief cutting, can give a misleading impression of great age. English cameo glass of the same period shows much crisper, sharper carving in the harder metal.

At Petersdorf in Bohemia, Fritz Heckert operated a glass-decorating works from 1866 and added glassmaking facilities in 1889. His pattern books illustrate an astonishing variety of deliberate imitations of *Humpen*, decanters and beakers enamelled with figures, coats-of-arms, inscriptions and dates. Genuine glasses in museum collections would provide inspiration but Heckert's enamelling is flat and without modelling.

The Venetian Revival

The fashion for historicism coincided with the revival of the Venetian glass industry in the 1860s. In 1861 the Museum of Murano was opened with the express intention of stimulating this revival by offering antiquarian models, including Roman glass and Venetian glasses from the classic periods of the 16th and 17th centuries. This achieved the desired result and for the next 40 years Venetian glassmakers dealt almost exclusively with copies and variations based on their glorious past.

The most famous company was that set up by Antonio Salviati in 1859 with English patronage, but there were numerous others, often specializing in certain aspects of antique reproductions. One example was Francesco Borella, who made objects with gold leaf decoration based on Roman examples discovered in the catacombs. Rosa Barovier Mentasti provides a detailed account of the entire period in her book *Il Vetro Veneziano*.

▶ 19th-century Venetian reproductions
This bowl demonstrates the extreme accuracy of Venetian reproduction. It is one of a group of *millefiori* and mosaic bowls made by the Venice and Murano Glass and Mosaic Co., founded in 1859 by Salviati (diam 16½cm/ 6½in). It is a good example of the historicizing attitude inspired by the museum in Murano. In 1878 the Paris Exhibition catalogue referred to "Reproduction of Roman *Murrhine*, including Roman *Paterae* or bowls of various colours." Some bowls have a cane with the letters "VM" – possibly for the maker Vincenzo Moretti, but more likely to be the trademark of the company. Like the originals, the bowl is fused in a two-part mould and ground on both sides. They were made in small numbers due to cost – a 30½cm/12in bowl cost 5,000 francs.

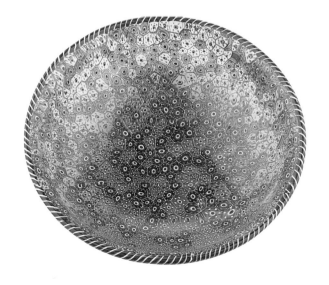

▲ Early 20th-century copies
Two Venetian glasses made about 1900 in imitation of earlier styles. The wine glass could be sold as 18th century but the enamelling on the bowl is not known in early Roman or Venetian glass and should not deceive.

▲ Venetian copies
The revival of the Venetian glass industry from 1860 onwards led to many reproductions influenced by earlier periods, especially the 16th and 17th centuries. This small beaker with the inscription "Caro Bevi" (good drink) is a good example.

The obsession with the past has never totally left Venice. The houses of Scalabrin and Daltin and Valle Valerio make enamelled and gilt versions of 16th-century marriage goblets and processional bowls; Antico Forno, Paolo Rossi and Piero Ragazzi specialize in reproductions of archaeological finds and mosaic glass, while Vetraria Alt make imitations of 19th-century paperweights and ornaments.

Following the exhibitions of Venetian glass in Paris and London in the 1860s and '70s, European and American glassmakers joined the rush to create exact 16th-century copies. English glassmakers were able to examine the originals in the collection formed by Felix Slade which was displayed as early as 1850; it was donated to the British Museum in 1868 and published in 1871. Jenkinson in Glasgow, Northwood in Stourbridge and Lutz in America created serpent-stem goblets and *latticino* vases and bowls with a high precision worthy of the originals.

18th-century English Glass

Collectors of 18th-century English glass have a number of pitfalls to contend with. They are in three categories. First, there are the deliberate fakes, of good quality and proportions with all the right combinations of feet, bowl and stems, but the quality of the metal is suspect. Next are the glasses in designs that never existed in the original repertoire and where the material is quite obviously wrong. The third category – and the most difficult to spot for the beginner – are the glasses of 18th-century date produced in Europe and Scandinavia in imitation of "verre d'Angleterre", the fashion for which swept Europe after the discovery of lead glass by Ravenscroft in the 1670s and the subsequent development of an English national style.

Continental glassmakers undertook visits to English glasshouses in an effort to discover their secrets while English glassmakers were enticed abroad to work in developing glass industries. A notable example was James Keith, a master glassblower from Newcastle who emigrated to the Nostetangen factory in Norway in 1755. The impact of the English style on Norwegian glass is evident until 1830 and is echoed in Finnish, Swedish and Dutch glass. The Peter F. Heering collection of Danish glass contains many examples

◄ Copies of 18th-century glasses
Two English reproduction goblets made in the middle of the 20th century and based on mid-18th-century examples. The engraving and the air-twist stems are of good quality but the glass itself is far too perfect and lacks any signs of the glassmaker's tools.

◀ **A modern copy of an 18th-century decanter and glass**
This decanter and wine glass, engraved with an English privateer and the inscription "Success to the British Fleet", were copied from 18th-century examples. Made in 1939 by Stevens and Williams in Brierley Hill, they may have been made in support of the war effort.

▼ **Modern colour twists**
Colour twists inside the stems of wine glasses became popular in England from the 1760s. The example immediately below dates from the middle of the 19th century; the lower glass probably dates from 1920–30.

often thought of as English. The whole question of Scandinavian imitations needs to be more widely publicized. Even now it is possible to come across glass described in saleroom catalogues as English and dated to the early 18th century, when in fact it is Scandinavian and 50 years later.

Much 18th-century glass began to be reproduced during the 19th century by glassmakers eager to compare their own skills with those of their predecessors. The appearance of deliberate fakes in the early 20th century coincided with early research into the history of English glass and an increase in auction sales. In 1897 Albert Hartshorne published *Old English Glasses*, the first complete survey of the subject; the next 30 years saw publication of the classic works by Francis Buckley, Grant Francis, H. J. Powell, W. A. Thorpe and Dudley Westropp, among many others.

With the revival of the Adam style in the Edwardian period, the glass firms churned out imitations of 18th-century glasses to match the reproductions of period furniture. A glance through company pattern books, especially in the Stourbridge area, for the appropriate dates reveals page upon page of lookalikes. Silesian and baluster stems do not occur very often; the outright favourites were air and opaque twists with some facet-cut stems and the occasional drawn-trumpet stem. The large firms of Stevens and Williams, Thos. Webb & Sons, H. G. Richardson and Walsh of Birmingham were the chief producers and may have supplied the Birmingham retailers Hill-Ouston. The catalogue issued by that company in 1934 offered a bewildering assortment of cut, blown and engraved glass with some emphasis on reproduction and "antique" services and individual items. Special attention was given to wine glasses, which are the most accurate of the antique copies and the most frightening for collectors.

Pattern books, catalogues and photographs of fake glasses are obviously of great help when it comes to identifying forgeries, but there is no substitute for constant handling. Only in this way can both knowledge and a sixth sense be acquired. Each period of glassmaking used certain techniques peculiar to its own time which, when recognized, can give clues to date and place. An awareness of these methods will allow the collector to spot the types of fake that appear in the Hill-Ouston catalogue. Out of all the techniques the most contentious and misunderstood feature is the pontil mark.

▶ **Part of a page from the pattern book of H.G. Richardson and Sons, Wordsley, 1910–16**

Many of the glasses were bought in from other makers, including F. & C. Osler of Birmingham, to be cut and engraved, often by freelance decorators. The facet-cut stem wine glass at the top could be bought with matching tumbler, jug, finger bowl and monteith (although the last two items both meant a double-lipped wine cooler). Matching services often consisted of glass bought from different firms. In 1918 Richardsons made red and white twist glasses mentioned in the pattern book as "foreign reproductions made on gadget" (see page 92).

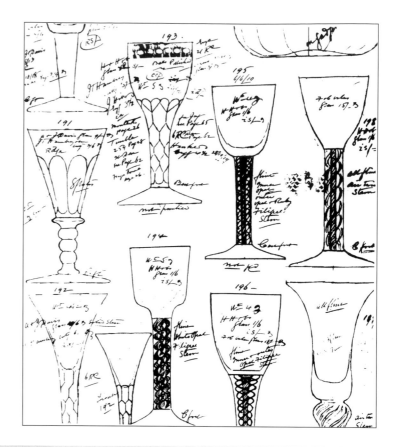

▶ **A selection of reproduction 18th- and 19th-century drinking glasses from the 1934 Hill-Ouston catalogue**

The Hill-Ouston Company was based at the Alexandra Works, Macdonald Street, London W1. This catalogue was the ninth issued by the firm. The goblets are often seen at antiques fairs masquerading as genuine 19th-century examples.

SLAG GLASS

A generic name given to pressed glass of the late 19th century with marbled colouring of purples, greens, blacks, blues and whites. It was said to derive from the addition of the waste by-product from steel furnaces. Some technologists doubt whether that material would constitute a compatible mixture with glass. Modern copies from original moulds have been made at the Davidson factory.

E 7069   E 7173   E 8548   E 7068

E 8166
ARCH RIB GOBLET   E 7066
JACOBEAN RUMMER   E 8795
ARCH RIB GOBLET   E 8509

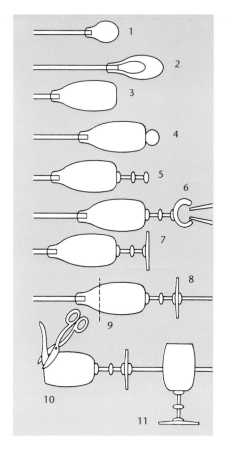

◀ **Making a three-part glass**

A three-part glass is made by a chair – a team of four glassmakers, each one assisting with part of the process.

(1) The blowing iron is dipped into the pot of molten glass for the gather.

(2) It is rolled on the marver and blown out.

(3) Gradually the bowl is shaped either by hand or by blowing into a mould.

(4) A small gather of glass is applied to the base of the bowl.

(5) It is formed into the stem.

(6) The foot is then added either as a blown foot, consisting of another bubble attached to the stem and opened out.

(7) Alternatively another gather, fixed to the stem, is squeezed into shape by the footboard. Once the foot is made the glass is ready to be transferred from the blowing iron onto the pontil rod for any final shaping.

(8) A small bit of hot glass is gathered on the tip of the pontil rod and stuck on the exact centre of the underneath of the foot. The blowing iron is cracked off (9).

(10) The glass is reheated, the bowl is opened out and the rim is sheared. Excess glass on the rim was always sheared off on 18th-century glasses, leaving a nick or bump in the rim.

(11) Finally, the glass is broken off the pontil rod and taken to the annealing lehr.

The Pontil Mark

The pontil mark is simply the scar left when the finished glass is broken off from the pontil iron. During the 18th and 19th centuries most tablewares were transferred to the pontil rod in order to allow excess glass to be sheared away, to shape the pouring lip and to add the handles on jugs. The practice continues to this day for certain items such as jugs and large bowls. Virtually all handmade glass, whether it is contemporary or antique, will carry signs of a pontil mark. It is not a guarantee of age.

The appearance of the pontil ("punty" or "puntee") on 18th-century glassware was a feature that was not lost on the makers of reproduction glasses. One Stourbridge firm that specialized in this trade was H. G. Richardson and Sons. From c.1840s–'80s the company pioneered many new techniques, but by the early 20th century they were concentrating a large part of their output on reproductions. The drawings of "old glass" in their pattern books often bear the additional note "pontil not ground" or the equivalent: "not punticd".

There are genuine 18th-century glasses that do have ground pontils. Facet-cut wine glasses are one example where it was simple enough to grind the pontil as part of the cutting process. The cutting wheel leaves a more or less circular area of polished glass in various diameters, some as small as the original pontil, others going across the entire foot. More expensive pieces would also have the scar removed, including cruet bottles and containers fitted into silver or plated stands. The flat base helped the glass to stand firmly and avoided damage to the stand or to table tops.

▲ **A wine glass, *c.*1910, held in the gadget as it would have appeared during manufacture**

During the 19th century in England the gadget was introduced as a speedier alternative to the pontil rod. It consists of a hollow steel tube about 135cm/54in long, containing a spring-loaded rod. The working end of the gadget consists of two jaws which open when the plunger is operated. The foot of the hot wine glass is slid into the jaws, which are clamped back to hold it while the bowl is opened out and the rim is sheared. The action and the pressure of the jaws leave a ghost image on the top surface of the foot. The mark left on the underside is a characteristic "T" or "Y". When the glass has been completed the plunger is pushed to open the jaws again and release the glass.

The period for the introduction of the gadget has been given as *c.*1760–1800. This seems too early, however, as no glasses of that date carry the ghost image of the jaws. The majority of glasses with the mark date from the 1860s onwards and it is likely that the gadget did not come into use until about this time.

A variation on the classic pontil mark is a type sometimes called a waffle. It worked on the same principle, but the molten glass on the end of the pontil iron was impressed with a criss-cross pattern, using the glassmaker's pincers. The result was that only four small points were stuck onto the glass, making it easier to remove the iron. It is seen most often on European glass, including Venetian. In the 20th century some of the "Monart" vases made by John Moncrieff of Perth have a raised circular pontil, usually matt, which may occasionally still bear the factory paper label. Studio glassmakers sometimes use an oxyacetylene torch to reheat the pontil, thereby softening the sharp edges and eliminating the need to grind it away. Other studio glass firms will impress their trademark into the pontil while it is still hot.

The collector will come across glass without any visible sign of a pontil. The classic example is the majority of Roman blown glass, although there are odd exceptions to this rule. Some glass which is handmade is stuck onto a large flat disc of glass on the end of the pontil and any unsightly marks on the edges of feet or bases may be ground away. In such instances other factors need to be looked at to give a clue to age. Glass that has been pressed in metal moulds will not have the pontil mark; examples include 19th-century items and mass-produced moulded 20th-century glass such as Crystal d'Arques.

Other 18th-century Fakes

Engraved Jacobite and Williamite glasses have been produced continuously since the originals were made and therefore accurate dating becomes a priority. In the case of Williamite glass, one needs to look at shape, style and colour as the engraving tends to follow an established tradition of William III on horseback surrounded by various mottoes and inscriptions, including many references to the Battle of the Boyne on 1st July 1690. With Jacobite glass suspicion is usually aroused if the glass carries too many explicit references to the Young Pretender such as roses, oak leaves, stars and Latin phrases and dates – the originals supported the Stuart cause with more subtle allusions. Some "Jacobite" engraving – including the diamond-point "Amen" subject matter – has been added onto genuine period wine glasses.

▶ **A reproduction and a genuine Jacobite wine glass showing how close modern copper wheel engraving is to its 18th-century counterpart**

A genuine and rare Jacobite glass (left) with an engraved portrait of Bonnie Prince Charlie, dating from the middle years of the 18th century. The identity of the engraver is not known. On the right is a "controlled" fake, blown by a student in the glass studio at Broadfield House Glass Museum about 1995, and engraved by Kevin Andrews, one of the best engravers in the Stourbridge district.

The portrait of the Prince was copied from a genuine glass but the portrait on the reverse, of Charles disguised as a servant girl, is not known on any genuine Jacobite glass.

◀ Two Jacobite goblets highlighting the difficulty in identifying an original
The tall goblet has the typical rose and buds engraving with the motto "Fiat" (Let it be) but the glass is known to date from about 1930 in Stourbridge. The goblet on the right is one of the rarest known Jacobite glasses from the mid-18th century.

▼ Reproduction commemorative glassware
Commemoratives celebrating the victory by William III at the Battle of the Boyne in 1690 proliferated in the 18th and 19th centuries. This glass probably dates from the early part of the 20th century and is a deliberate forgery.

There is a very real difficulty in judging whether any engraving is contemporary with the glass; 18th-century engraving was of medium quality and is easily imitated. Some historians have attempted to decipher certain hands by looking closely at the details of Jacobite glass but there is still no hard and fast rule that can be applied.

It may be of some consolation to collectors to know that certain glasses have not been faked. Among these are "Lynn" glasses with horizontal ribs which have only risen in price in the last few years, and ratafia glasses which for some reason have also escaped the attentions of the forger.

The foot shows deliberate faking of wear with crude file marks.

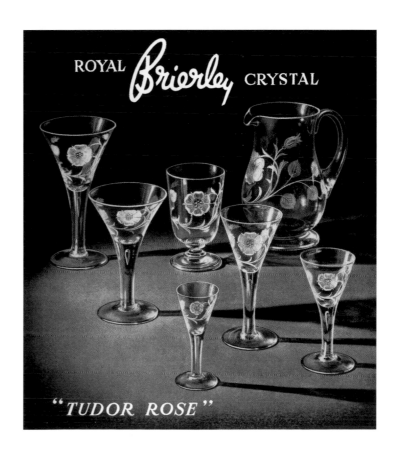

ROYAL *Brierley* CRYSTAL

"TUDOR ROSE"

▶ An advertisement from *Pottery Gazette*, July 1951, for Royal Brierley's "Traditional Jacobite Drinking Glasses Recreated"
The blurring of accurate periods between Tudor and Stuart was obviously of little concern.

Decanters

Decanters from the late 18th century have been much copied, whereas the earlier cruciform shapes have been left alone. Replicas of club-shaped decanters in blue and green with gilded imitation wine labels were imported from Czechoslovakia in the 1930s but are too shiny and glossy and their gilding is of poor quality. More recent fakes which have appeared are white opaline mallet-shaped decanters with painted medallions; Portugal may have been the source for these. They are good copies but their extra thickness and the fact that too many appeared at once gave them away.

Irish decanters impressed with the names of the glasshouses such as Waterloo, County Cork; B. Edwards, Belfast; and Waterford Penrose and Cork Glass Co. have been favourite targets. The Cork fakes appear most often. Look for the bright quality of the metal, clearly readable lettering (sometimes with only the word "Cork") and a noticeable degree of overblow over the edge of the base mould. Fake stoppers were blown into a badly fitting mould and one half was slightly staggered, resulting in a bad fit.

A Typical Selection of 18th-century Coloured Decanters on the Market

▲ The grain of the stone- or iron-cutting wheel has left striations which are a feature of 18th- and 19th-century cut glass. The hollow facets on the body are typical of the 18th century. The stopper, which seems original on first inspection, shows a different composition to the body under ultraviolet light suggesting either that it is a contemporary stopper, but from a different factory, or that it is a good later copy. Stoppers can easily be ground to fit decanters which have lost their originals. Sometimes both stopper and decanter will carry matching marks scratched on at the factory to ensure that they were not split up.

▲ The shape of this decanter is exactly right for the period 1770–80. However, the cut decoration of large stars on the shoulder and the leaf pattern around the base are unusual. It may be that it is a rare pattern and is an original, or alternatively the decoration may have been added later. On balance, and until some other proof comes to light, one would accept that it is genuine.

▲ Everything is right about this decanter which has a scene of a Bristol glasshouse gilded on one side. The profile of the decanter, the three neck rings and the bull's-eye stopper are exactly the right proportions for a piece dating from about 1800. The wear on the gilding over 200 years cannot be faked.

Cut Glass

The correct identification of cut glass must be one of the most difficult areas of all glass authentication. In England the same methods of roughing the initial design followed by smoothing remained unchanged from the early 19th century until the 1950s. By 1900 the technique of acid polishing was gradually being introduced, which gives some help to collectors. Polishing on a brush wheel with putty powder retained the crispness and grain marks of the stone wheels but acid polishing removes all these signs and tends to round off the edges of the cuts. However, by the early 20th century some accurate reproductions were still finished by brush polishing to achieve the authentic texture of much older examples.

By the late 19th century the quality of the glass had improved considerably, tending towards "whiter" clarity without the slight greyish tinge of old glass. This comparison becomes obvious if the collector can place a modern cut glass next to a known 18th-century glass. A recognition of this brightness combined with a knowledge of the preferred 19th-century shapes of jugs and other items gives at least two clues to help unravel this puzzle.

Irish Cut Glass

Many of the firms who specialized in reproduction 18th-century wines also turned out some very good copies of "old Waterford glass". After 1918, old glass, especially Irish, began to make high premiums and it began to be faked. Further confusion was added by Hartshorne and in 1916 by J. H. Yoxall, who perpetrated the myth of the blue tint in Waterford glass. As early as 1920 Dudley Westropp, the first sensible authority on Irish glass, discounted the theory quite adamantly: "I would wish now, once for all, to state that the glass made in Waterford has not the decided blue or dark tint always ascribed to it." Even after such a categorical statement the legend continues.

▲ **1916 dated pattern of H. G. Richardson & Sons showing a replica of a 1790 decanter, together with a pattern for decoration**
The notes mention "rough stoppered", "fine rib moulded", and "pushed up to stand not puntied".

▶ **Irish cut glass turnover rim, _c._1930s**
Turnover rims, as seen in this large cut-glass vase, are generally attributed to Irish glass factories at the beginning of the 19th century. This example was made a hundred years later, about 1930, in England

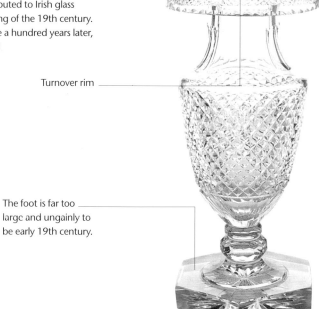

Turnover rim

The foot is far too large and ungainly to be early 19th century.

▲ **H. G. Richardson reproductions of "George III" cut-glass designs, early 20th century**

▲ **"Demi-crystal Reproduction Antique Designs" of early 19th-century glass from the Hill-Ouston catalogue, 1934**

The misleading comments made by Yoxall were reiterated by Mrs. Graydon-Stannus who apparently inherited a glass factory in Ireland and became fascinated with Irish glass. From 1926 to 1936 she operated the "Gray-Stan" factory in London which introduced mottled and bubbled glass in the current art glass fashions. It is generally accepted throughout the antiques trade and by glass historians that she was responsible for confusing the history of Anglo-Irish glass and originating Irish reproductions to substantiate her theories. Some genuine glasses, including drawn trumpet wines, were "enhanced" with new areas of flat cutting. In 1920 she published a small book, *Old Irish Glass*, and followed it a year later with a larger revised edition. The text of the book is full of inaccuracies and many glasses are misrepresented – including the candelabra, candlesticks and chandeliers which often feature 20th-century drops and arms, marble "Bossi" pedestals and metal fittings.

Chandeliers and Candelabra

The difficulties in identifying genuine cut-glass objects are multiplied when it comes to chandeliers and candelabra. An invaluable source of information can be the 18th-century trade cards of London glass dealers, but at the end of the 18th century it was already customary for chandeliers to be dismantled and re-formed into the latest fashion. That tradition means that one can never be absolutely certain how much alteration has taken place. The huge market for lighting fixtures in the 19th century has furnished the restoration trade with a readily available supply of components which can be reassembled at will.

Drops for chandeliers were pressed in a mould before being given a final cut to sharpen the edges; a similar idea appeared in 19th-century hollow ware when cutting shops used pressed blanks. The benefits included a saving on the expense of the rougher plus the cut designs being already impressed into the article. It is almost impossible to recognize this type of cutting, especially if it is well done. Some Continental glass, currently sold at markets and discount warehouses, is advertised as hand-cut, but a close examination of the surface will reveal the flow marks of pressed glass.

Identification by Technique

A bewildering variety of techniques and machinery to improve glass production and give novel methods of decoration were patented in the 19th century. The dates of their introduction can be an invaluable help for identification.

Venetian Diamond Pattern

Apsley Pellatt and Benjamin Richardson introduced the Venetian Diamond pattern during the late 1840s, using compressed air to blow glass into metal moulds. The finished effect was of a close diamond quilting with the criss-cross ribs in fairly high relief. Other firms, such as Powells, later took up this form of decoration. But because the idea of moulded glass is normally thought to be a process of the later 19th or 20th century confusion arises the pieces are often wrongly dated.

Acid Etching

The use of hydrofluoric acid as a decorating medium was first realized in Sweden in the 1770s, but it was only in the mid-19th century that its full commerical potential was exploited with the opening of acid-decorating workshops. The process was two-part: first, the outline was etched and then a second dip in the acid gave the shading effects. Because the acid acts in a uniform way the shading has a matt, satin-like frosted finish with no appreciable grain or pitting.

A variation of the technique became popular from the 1890s and is seen often on glassware made for hotels and shipping lines. Instead of the two-stage process a copper plate was carved with the required design. A fluoride-etching paste was filled into the design and transferred onto the glass using tissue paper. The paste etched the glass very lightly, giving a clear if somewhat faint design without the deep linear outline of the first process. Top-quality 19th-century acid etching has not been faked as it is almost impossible to achieve the same quality of result – plus the fact that any modern attempt would cost far more than the genuine article.

In the 1870s engineering firms began to market geometric etching machines which led to the mass production of glasses decorated with linear patterns, including circles and the Greek key. Since then many countries have capitalized on this quick form of decoration; much of it has come from Belgium. It can be difficult to date these glasses because there is little difference in quality in the actual etching. In the 1970s a great deal of Portuguese acid-etched ware of very good quality appeared. The Stourbridge glass firms abandoned etching in the 1970s, preferring sandblasting as a decorative technique.

Sandblasting

In 1870 the American Benjamin C. Tilghman patented a sandblast machine which was exhibited three years later in the Vienna Exhibition. The patent specified "a stream of sand or other abrasive powder, usually dry, but sometimes mixed with water, projected with more or less force and velocity to strike and pulverize the surfaces of glass, stone, metal and other materials upon which it is directed".

First use of the sandblast was on window and plate glass, then it was employed to mark glasses with the government weights and measures mark. From the 1880s it was used on cheap pressed tumblers with commemorative inscriptions. Even at low pressure the sandblast gives a very granular texture to the designs that is quite different in appearance and touch from wheel engraving or acid etching. Letter and numbers will show gaps where the ties in the paper stencil held the central portions of the characters. It is advisable to distinguish this technique as it is commonly referred to as "engraved" in an attempt to give it an upmarket image.

Intaglio

Intaglio is another term that causes confusion. In general use it means any decoration that is incised into the surface of the object, but in 1891 John Northwood I at the Stevens and Williams factory developed a new form of engraving which he also christened intaglio. The new process was a halfway stage between copper wheel engraving and cutting – it did not have the

---

FLINT GLASS

Lead glass is given a variety of terms which can confuse the collector. The oldest, "flint glass", goes back to George Ravenscroft, the discoverer of lead glass in 1674, who followed Italian practice and believed he had to use flints or pebbles for the basic raw ingredient. Flints were calcined and ground to give the silica that is now much more easily provided in the form of sand. Until the 1970s glassmakers still used the term to mean clear, transparent glass. In its molten state glass is known as "metal".

Another confusing term is "crystal glass" which should refer to cut glass, which imitates the form and sparkle of a cut gem or crystal. Glass itself does not have a crystalline structure as minerals do; in scientific terms it is a super-cooled liquid.

▲ **This Czech car mascot is based on Longchamps of Lalique and illustrates the sandblasting technique**
Although it lacks the convincing artistry of the original mouldwork it is still rare and attractive and has a value to collectors.

"APPRENTICE'S PIECES"

This misleading term is sometimes used for any glass that appears a little more ornate or unusual. It is often conjured up by dealers when they have run out of any other information and has even been used to describe an 18th-century Liége openwork basket and stand. Only pieces with a definite provenance should be accepted as the apprentice's final show of skill.

Handle Design

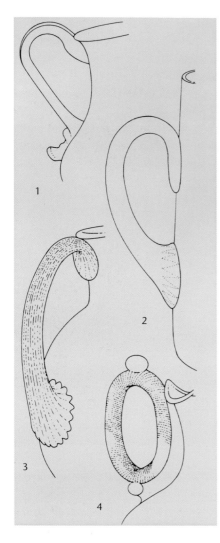

(1) The "pump" handle was used throughout the 18th century. It continued in use sporadically even after 1860.

(2) The "dab" handle was pulled up from the base to give a thinner join at the top.

(3) The "shell" handle was introduced in the late 1860s. It was moulded and then applied onto the glass. The shell was also used for feet and as a purely decorative feature.

(4) The "rope twist" is seen in a number of variations, often wrapped around the neck of a jug. The technique is similar to that used to make the incised twist stems of 18th-century wines.

finesse and drawing-like qualities of wheel engraving nor was it restricted to the geometric patterns of cutting. Decoration was still by means of revolving wheels but of small diameter, from 2.54cm/1in to 10.16cm/4in, and made of stone. Since it was introduced it has gradually overtaken other forms of decoration so that it now forms the main decorative process in most large glass factories.

The characteristic patterns consist of flowers and leaves, the curving C-shape scroll possible with the intaglio or "tag" wheel being especially useful for the latter. The profile of an intaglio cut reveals one very sharp edge that dips in at right angles into the glass while the other edge is much broader and flatter and shades away back to the surface of the glass.

The Design of Handles

During the 1860s various methods of applying handles to jugs and vases superseded the traditional method in which a hot strip of glass was attached at the top of a jug, near the lip, pulled downward and attached at a point lower on the body. About the mid-1860s the method was reversed, providing a stronger join at the base of the handle. Handles were now given more attention, resulting in many adaptations – see the examples left.

Glass in the United States

Glass is collected in the United States with an enthusiasm and vitality reflected in the large number of clubs and societies covering every specialized topic. These organizations have done much to keep track of forgeries and reproductions. For example, in 1985 the Heisey Glass Club purchased all the Heisey moulds on the closure of the Imperial factory to prevent them from being used to make forgeries.

Pressed glass has been the mainstay of the American glass industry since its introduction in the 1820s. In widespread use today, it has created problems for collectors. In writing his book on milk glass, E. McCamly Belknap felt the chapter on fakes was the most important to help differentiate between antique and reproduction. For example, the Westmoreland Glass Co. in Pennsylvania continued to make clear pressed and milk glass reproductions of early American originals alongside their own creations from 1889 onwards. The later addition of the initials "W" or "WG" helps to trace their products. A similar situation arose with the works of John E. Kemple in Ohio.

◄ **A Murano jug imitating 19th-century Mount Washington Burmese glass, 1970s**
Although the shape is right, the poor colour and texture are not.

MARY GREGORY GLASSWARE

"Mary Gregory" is the name given by collectors to glassware from around 1900 decorated with white enamelled figures of boys and girls because it was thought a known American decorator of this name was the artist. Fresh evidence now disproves this theory. The original glasses were made in glassworks in Bohemia in the former Czechoslovakia but modern copies abound from the same source.

An original Bohemian jug painted in the Mary Gregory style, c.1890–1900

Modern pressed glass

These three pressed glass pieces were bought from the same stand at an antiques fair which immediately gave cause for concern. Rather than being from the 1880s and 1930s they are modern American reproductions. The Clown saucer and the Dog Kennel are popular subjects and extremely marketable while the Art Deco "Bottoms Up" cup is known to be faked due to the originals now fetching very high prices.

▲ A Shirley Temple jug

Collectors should be aware that Shirley Temple commemoratives have been in virtually continuous production ever since her rise to fame in the 1930s. This milk jug is difficult to date accurately and needs further research and advice from American glass experts.

In 1949 Kemple had acquired 150 old moulds and very quickly unsigned milk glass appeared from the factory and was sold through two large outlets.

Fortunately moulds do eventually wear out, so production is limited to some extent. But old pressed glass can still be difficult to attribute because the companies who supplied the moulds often sold copies of the same mould to factories in America and England. In view of the major complexities, the best advice to the aspiring collector is to join one of the many glass societies and get to know the subject by talking to fellow collectors.

In the area of blown glass the classic American style is the blown 3-mould. In 1941 the McKearins bought a group of glasses supposed to come from the Mutzer family early in the 19th century. After some initial doubts the group was proved to be fake, possibly made in Pennsylvania between 1920 and 1929. About 50 pieces have been located since. In New Jersey the Clevenger Brothers Glassworks made reproductions which could be ordered by mail as late as the 1970s. Other typical American patterns like the Lily Pad or the Hobnail are prime targets.

Copies of art glass include the expensive Peachblow and Burmese. Imitations of "Wild Rose" Peachblow from New England were made in 1950 but not in original patterns and with poor chalky colours of white shading up to red. Burmese imitations, shading from a weak pink to yellow, suddenly appeared in antiques shops in England in the 1970s. Of a grainy, sugary texture, they probably came from Murano (see opposite page).

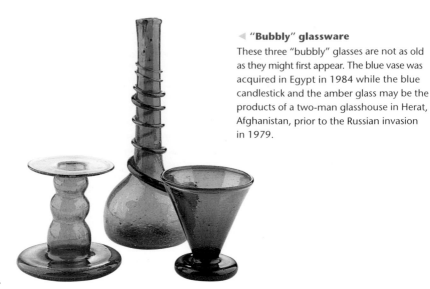

▲ **"Bubbly" glassware**
These three "bubbly" glasses are not as old as they might first appear. The blue vase was acquired in Egypt in 1984 while the blue candlestick and the amber glass may be the products of a two-man glasshouse in Herat, Afghanistan, prior to the Russian invasion in 1979.

▼ **An example of "bubbly" glassware from the 1934 Hill Ouston catalogue**
This range had enough of an air of "old country glass" to be passed off as early 19th-century Nailsea or Wrockwardine. The supplier is unknown.

E 5431
Height 13½"
Dia. 12"
AMBER

Bubble Glass

Most of the glass vessels with masses of bubbles within the body that can be found today should be considered as 20th century until it can be proved otherwise. It was only at the end of the 19th century that the idea of using bubbles as decoration resulted in the conscious imitation of ancient Roman glass. In the 1880s Christopher Dresser designed the "Clutha" range for Couper and Sons of Glasgow which featured deliberate imperfections, bubbles and irregular handles and rims. Following the success of Clutha, Stevens and Williams used "Caerleon", the name of the Roman site in South Wales, for a range of bubbled and iridized vases.

By the 20th century bubble glass offered a profitable market, especially as it could be melted easily and quickly and did not require highly technical finishing skills or machinery. The cruder and simpler it looked, the easier it was to sell. Green is the predominant colour achieved naturally by using low-quality sand with a high iron ore content.

In 1927 in America, the Consolidated Lamp and Glass Co. patented "Catalonian Old Spanish Glassware" in a range of about 40 different pieces, mainly vases, plates, salad bowls, iced tea and water sets, and sugars and creams. The range was offered in "brilliant" colours of Emerald Green, Spanish, Rose and Crystal or in "soft" colours of Honey, Amethyst and Jade. Characteristic features are swirling ridges and small bubbles, with larger distinct bubbles scattered at random through the glass. By 1928 the Diamond Glass Ware Co. of Indiana, Pennsylvania, advertised "Barcelona Glass – A Reproduction of Early Spain" which imitated the wrinkled look of "Catalonia". In September 1932 Henry Beach, a direct importer in El Paso, Texas, advertised Mexican Bubble Glassware, noting that it had "all the charm of true craftsmanship, made in Mexico by the peons of the age-old manner of their ancestors – but produced under the supervision of our own agent". Another "El Mexicano" range from the Morgantown firm was advertised in a Marshall Field catalogue of 1933 in green or frosted glass. At the same time, Bryce Bros of Mt Pleasant, Pennsylvania, introduced "El Rancho" pitchers, vases, salts and peppers in reddish-orange or greenish-blue milk glass.

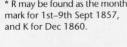
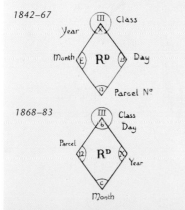
Maker's Marks

Glass is marked less frequently than pottery and porcelain simply because any lettering would detract from the appearance, especially on clear glass. The most famous glass mark is the applied raven's head seal of George Ravenscroft, which was used literally as a seal of approval for his new lead glass. In the 18th century factory marks are non-existent but engravers' and enamellers' signatures do appear – usually of well-known and "expensive" names such as William Beilby and Isaac Jacobs.

During the 19th and 20th centuries, trademarks on glass became more common. The most often seen 19th-century mark is the diamond-shaped registry mark of the Patent Office (see left). After 1883 it became a Registered Number. The letters and numbers in each corner of the diamond mark provide a key to the date of registration and the name of the manufacturer. On pressed glass the diamond mark is not always an infallible guide because there are known discrepancies between marked pieces and the records kept at the Patent Office. Although the diamond mark is seen mostly on pressed glass, where it features as a raised design, it can also be found as a transfer-printed mark on glass of the 1840s, or as an engraved mark on coloured or engraved glass of the late 19th century.

The obvious place to look for marks is on the underside of the foot, but it is worth examining every inch of the glass in case they have been placed in some hidden corner. On cut glass the foot may be so ornate that the mark may be placed at the top of the stem of a wine glass or at the base of a jug's handle. American "Brilliant" cut glass of the late 19th and early 20th century was so heavily cut that the trademark was often placed inside the piece, usually in the bottom centre. Badged marks applied with acid or sandblast are often so faint as to make them almost invisible. Wear and tear on the foot can erase all or part of a mark whether it is painted, engraved or etched.

Any signed or marked glass is worth collecting even if initially there is no information about the maker. That information probably does exist somewhere and by locating it a glass that seemed of no consequence may acquire added significance both in historical and financial terms.

Some glass authors have listed the trademarks on glass found in their collections, or marks which they have found in the course of their research. Some of the best early work was done by Cyril Manley, who listed his finds in his book *Decorative Victorian Glass*. Dr. Helga Hilschenz in *Das Glas des Jugendstil* provided similar lists of Continental marks and signatures. But the most complete listing of glass marks was published by Carolus Hartmann in 1997 with his *Glasmarken Lexikon 1600–1945*. This impressive work took 10 years to research, contains 11,000 marks, and is split into three sections for ease of reference. Section 1 gives dates when marks were used, section 2 lists artist's biographies and histories of the firms, and section 3 gives indexes of the list of abbreviations, terminology, glossary of specialist terms, index of place names, index of glass museums throughout the world and a bibliography. Written in German, the book is an invaluable source for glass collectors, even those without German as a language.

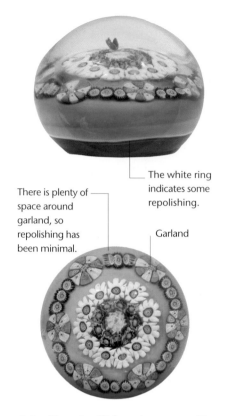

The white ring indicates some repolishing.

There is plenty of space around garland, so repolishing has been minimal.

Garland

▲ **Looking at a Clichy colour ground in profile and from above**

▲ **A genuine Paul Ysart signature**

PAPERWEIGHTS

Although some paperweights have been faked, it is more likely that collectors will be faced with a lack of originality due to damage – scratches or chips. Almost all French antique paperweights have been repolished, as even light scratching detracts from their beauty. An equal amount should be shaved off the whole area of the paperweight and its correct profile will be retained – but what is a correct profile? Even within the same factory there were different profiles – Clichy, for instance, have several different shapes. Antique miniatures, however, have a very similar shape.

Some judgment can be made about the amount of glass on the top and sometimes below, but this takes experience. In the case of Baccarat, they set up their canes at quite different levels. So a close-pack with the canes quite near the surface could be absolutely right. If the general shape of an antique weight is rather flat, be suspicious. Clichy colour grounds show a white ring if they have been polished on the sides – sometimes it may be next to nothing, other times it might be unacceptable. Look at the pattern on the top – if an outer garland is falling over the edge it has certainly been repolished.

The valuable antique weights have never been faked, so one is unlikely to be fooled into spending five-figure sums on a worthless object! The faking centres around date canes and signature canes made in the 20th century – naturally those worth more money. The fakes are well documented and fall into the following categories; (1) Paul Ysart weights (2) The English weights with "1848" canes (3) Baccarat "Dupont" weights and (4) Murano weights.

Paul Ysart Weights

Few Paul Ysart weights are signed on their base (see detail left); those that are always have a provenance as they were sold direct to collectors or given as gifts. Ysart's weights have two types of signature canes: "H" canes and "PY" canes. Those weights with "H" canes are definitely by Ysart; however, those with "PY" canes can be a problem. Between 1987 and 1989 supposed Paul Ysart weights were offered to dealers in large quantities and suspicion was aroused. On comparison with authenticated Ysart weights they were found to be fakes. The weights all had a "PY" cane to identify them; however, they differ in several notable ways from the originals as seen below.

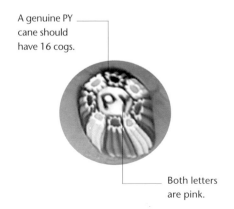

A genuine PY cane should have 16 cogs.

Both letters are pink.

▲ **Genuine Ysart signature cane**

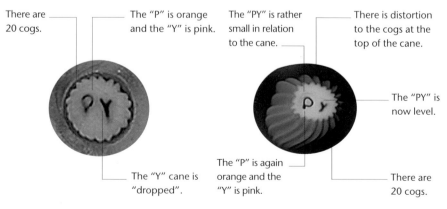

There are 20 cogs.

The "P" is orange and the "Y" is pink.

The "Y" cane is "dropped".

▲ **Series 1 fake Ysart signature cane**

The "PY" is rather small in relation to the cane.

There is distortion to the cogs at the top of the cane.

The "PY" is now level.

The "P" is again orange and the "Y" is pink.

There are 20 cogs.

▲ **Series 2 fake Ysart signature cane**

▲ A good-quality Paul Ysart fake

The clearly "dropped" "Y" cane (Series One fake, see detail page 102) is really the only clue.

▲ An English paperweight by Arculus, dated 1848, *c*.1920

There is little difference in value between undated weights and those with the falsely dated cane.

▲ A Murano weight with fake central date, *c*.1930s

This fake date cane should not fool any collector apart from the novice.

English Weights

For a long time it has been known that the "1848" cane in "old Whitefriars" weights was a fake if the canes were bright blue. The pastel-coloured canes were then presumed to be the original, although the weights or bottles in which the canes occurred looked remarkably similar (as one would expect of a faked object, anyway). In the 1990s new research revealed that the firm of Arculus, which became Walsh-Walsh, had made fake weights in the 1920s and '30s and doubt was thrown on the supposition that any 19th-century Whitefriars weights existed or indeed that there was an original English dated "1848" weight. The consensus is now that the "1848" cane was invented in the 1920s and not copied from an original.

There remain a lot of unanswered questions about English weights. From the point of view of a collector the crucial point is that the 1848 date cane is considered to have been made in the 1930s. This presupposes that the collector is able to recognize the weight as English because, of course, the date cane 1848 occurs quite genuinely in antique French weights.

Baccarat "Dupont"

The French firm of Baccarat made magnificent weights in the Classic Period (1845–60), but by the 1920s and '30s, paperweight-making was only being carried on in a small way.

Baccarat Dupont weights are worth considerably less than the equivalent Baccarat Classics so it is very important to be able to distinguish between them. None would market for more than £1,000/$1,450 and the least desirable Dupont – the Scrambled, about £100/$145. Key distinguishing characteristics are: (1) They have smaller canes than the classic; (2) different combination of colours, mostly rather pale; (3) some fake date canes – 1815 is an impossible date since paperweights were first made in 1845, but also possible dates such as 1847;(4) the date cane is sometimes placed centrally which would not occur in a genuine weight; (5) pansy weights are sometimes dated in contrast to antique treefloral weights, which were never dated; (6) patterns known include interlaced foils, cinquefoil, rondello, concentric and pansy; (7) they are usually polished flat.

Murano

Murano is the "glass" island off Venice. Their paperweights are, generally speaking, rather poor quality. At some point during the 20th century, possibly the 1930s, they made *millefiori* weights with fake date canes. Like Dupont, they liked to put the date cane in the middle. That should be enough to set alarm bells ringing – if one sees a date cane in the middle it is not a genuine French antique.

The most serious fake paperweights are the Ysarts, because they are often good quality and very similar to the originals, and the difference in value is considerable. Similarly, you would not want to mistake a Dupont for a Classic Baccarat. The English 1848 date canes are not a great problem. It is unlikely that the Murano with its fake date in the middle would fool anyone, but if anyone unscrupulous got hold of one it might cost a novice collector a lot more than he would be happy to pay! The best protection is to acquire knowledge and experience by handling items as much as possible.

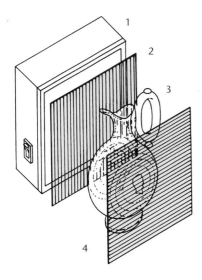

◄ **A Polariscope**
This is used to reveal the flow lines of glass and therefore is able to show interruptions to those lines where a break has been mended or where parts have been added. The box (1) holds a light source behind a diffusing service. The light then shines through a polarizing screen. (2) The sample (3) is set between this sheet and the analyzer (4), a second polarizing screen with its axis set at 90 degrees to the first.

THE ULTRAVIOLET LAMP
An ultraviolet lamp will help to identify the composition of glass. The complex nature of glass chemistry can create difficulties and therefore the readings are not completely infallible, but as a general rule it will help to distinguish between soda and lead glass. A lead content will give a light blue tinged with purple, whereas soda shows a distinctive green-yellow.

The Repair of Glass

The question of repairs is a subjective matter and everyone must decide their own priorities about alterations. Collectors tend to prefer not to have any visible signs of damage, whereas museum curators would rather show the object in its original condition. Repairs can be acceptable provided the proportions are not destroyed: for example, on 18th-century glass the foot will always be larger in diameter than the bowl; anything less should cause suspicion.

Over the years the techniques of repairs have changed – the old way of trimming a foot went vertically through the rim, giving a flat edge. When the underneath of a foot is chipped or flaked, instead of trimming the edge the underside is skimmed out. This results in a thinner foot with some loss of the original striations and loss of wear marks. Any artificial wear produced by rubbing on emery paper will show random scratches often going inwards from lines of natural wear. One Midlands factory is said to have employed a retired glassmaker to grind the feet of 18th-century reproductions on the back doorstep. As with any antique object when trying to ascertain if wear is genuine, consider which part of the glass could have been in contact with the surface. If the scratches are generally deep, look unnatural and go too far inwards, then the glass has been altered.

"Marriages" of two separate glasses, such as the bowl of a wine glass joined to another stem, can be passed off as a genuine glass. The stuck join has to be at a definite joint – probably where the stem joins the bowl or the foot – which helps to disguise the deception. Removal instead of addition also takes place: a rummer with a broken foot can be transformed into an acceptable tumbler by cutting away the unwanted glass stem and leaving a ground-out pontil.

The introduction of modern glues and resins specifically for glass has been of immense benefit both to the bona-fide restorer and the forger. "Superglues" set hard on exposure to the ultraviolet rays in ordinary daylight, but on coloured glass the colour filters out the ultraviolet and the adhesive does not form a strong join. It may be that these glues are not as long-lasting as epoxy resin glues.

Wax and silicone rubber moulds used with polyester resins have revolutionized the restoration of ancient glass where a considerable amount may be missing and requires an infill. Certain resins have an inherent abraded look that suits ancient items; others may discolour. More importantly, they allow the work to be reversible.

Base Metals

This chapter is concerned with several metals – pewter, copper, brass and bronze – but the general approach to authenticating objects made in any of them is similar. It can be divided into five areas, as follows:

Methods of Manufacture

Over the centuries the techniques of making all forms of metalware have varied, some methods declining while others rose in importance. A sound knowledge of how objects were made at various times in history is a great asset when seeking to date metalware. For example, the types of seam used in copper and brass work are good guides to dating.

Makers' and Other Marks

This is perhaps the easiest check where reference works illustrating makers' marks exist. Only a small proportion of objects do have makers' marks, however. But there are other marks which can be useful: housemarks, ownership marks and initials, full coats-of-arms or crests engraved on items can all help with dating. To give but one example, coats-of-arms have been rendered in different styles according to their period; establish the style and you can begin to date when the work was done.

Style

This is a dangerous area if knowledge is used inflexibly. Similar objects were made over several decades and it is often not possible to establish a neat, chronological order. Patterns do emerge, however, and identifying the style of a piece suggests a broad period during which it might have been made.

Observation

You can learn a lot by feeling an item as well as by looking at it. Handle it, run your fingers over its edges, turnings and hinges. Try and identify where the wear is. It is extremely unlikely that you will come across a 17th-century object in pristine condition; no wear usually means little age.

▲ **A pewter candlestick composed of genuine tankard lids soldered onto a candlestick stem**
This was probably put together in the 1930s.

▲ **Dating by the style of armorials**
The same coat-of-arms in the 19th-century style (top) and as represented in the 17th century (below).

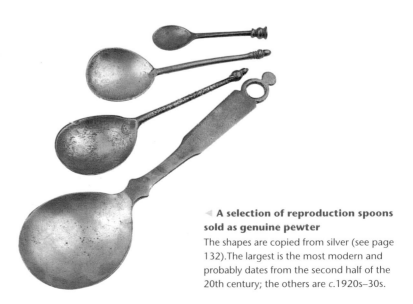

◄ **A selection of reproduction spoons sold as genuine pewter**
The shapes are copied from silver (see page 132). The largest is the most modern and probably dates from the second half of the 20th century; the others are c.1920s–30s.

▶ **A page from the Pearson-Page catalogue published in the 1920s**
This illustrates examples of reproduction pewter available at that time. Many of these items, now over 60 years old, have acquired some of the appearance of age and can be deceptive when they turn up at antiques fairs and shops.

Alloys

For economic and technical reasons the alloys used by coppersmiths, brassfounders, braziers, blacksmiths and pewterers have varied over time and a knowledge of the alloys can provide definitive answers. To carry out this check requires access to analytical equipment.

There is a sixth aspect of authentication which no book can teach: experience. No amount of advice, no list of facts, no practical guidance can give you the experience that is needed to make sound judgements. The more metalware you handle the more you will see and understand, for it is never enough just to apply a set of rules and come out with a dogmatic judgment. Assessing an item is a matter of balancing the probabilities. If all the indicators point one way then you can be reasonably sure of your attribution, but where the evidence conflicts, you need to be more tentative.

There are two sources of potential difficulty: genuine fakes, which were carefully made to deceive; and reproductions, which at their first sale are offered for what they are but at subsequent sales may well be sold, sometimes artificially aged, and claim to be the item of which they were originally a copy. This gives rise to the largest group of fakes on the market.

▶ **A modern fake Billy & Charley (recto and verso)**
Made of different alloys from the 1850s onwards. The makers used whatever cheap material they could find. Note that the date of 1002 is shown in Arabic numerals rather than the Roman numerals you would expect if this date were genuine.

Billys and Charleys

One of the more infamous events in forgeries using metals was that due to William Smith and Charles Eaton who, working on the construction of the London Docks near Wapping in the 1850s, found a few pilgrims' badges made of pewter. They discovered that there was a market for these amongst antiquarian collectors, so they set up a workshop counterfeiting these items, henceforth known as Billys and Charleys, in lead or copper alloys. Many dealers and collectors believed the fake articles to be genuine and it took a court case and a raid on their workshop to expose the fraudulence. It is now difficult to see how this did not happen earlier – from the errors in dress styles depicted on the badges, the fabricated Latin inscriptions and, perhaps most of all, from the dates on the pieces that were in Arabic numerals instead of Roman.

Despite all the revelations there are people who still collect Billys and Charleys, the original forgeries, and in more recent times there are forgeries of these forgeries appearing on the market!

▲ **A mid-19th-century fake Billy & Charley figure and ampoule**
These are made of cheap alloys and cast in a mould. The top one is dated 1330.

PEWTER

Pewter is an alloy of tin. For 450 years or more it was one of the most important metals found in the home. People of all classes used it for eating and drinking, and about the house. The rich man might have had many dozens of plates and dishes but even the pauper owned at least one battered pewter plate.

Being a soft alloy, pewter had a comparatively short working life; as soon as they needed replacing, damaged objects were usually traded in for newly worked pewter. Hence there are few survivors of the tens of thousands of items that were in daily use, so 17th-century pieces are the earliest that can normally be found. This was the period of maximum production in Britain and Europe, but the manufacture of pewter continued at a high level in the 18th century and in the United States it reached a peak in the 40 years after the War of Independence. Pewter continued to be made in the United States into the 19th century, at a time when the craft was in great financial difficulties elsewhere. During the 19th century, a variation of

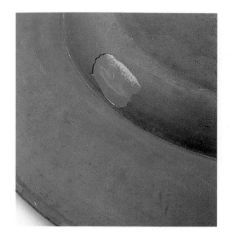

▲ **This large 17th-century charger shows evidence of flaking from oxidization**
Despite its appearance, this type of oxidization is perfectly normal and only a cause for concern in that it is unstable.

pewter – a hard alloy of tin made in sheet form with the help of steam-driven machines and known as Britannia Metal – became widely used.

Most commonly found now are 18th-century pewter plates and dishes, 19th-century drinking mugs and Britannia Metal tea and coffee pots, but almost anything one can think of which was used in the home has been, at some time or another, made in pewter.

Pewter was first collected in Britain in the late 19th century. Most British fakes were made in the 1920s. They are well made, often "repaired" to set the collector's mind at rest. Unless it is polished almost daily, pewter soon develops a patina or film of thin oxide which is difficult to replicate and this type of oxidization is one of the things collectors look for to confirm age. Unfortunately, it is possible to fake oxidization and all good fakes have this simulation of age carefully applied to their surfaces. Collectors should familiarize themselves with the appearance and colour of authentic patina.

Because the early fakers wanted to make money they nearly always copied the more valuable objects, such as 17th-century candlesticks and flat-lidded Stuart tankards. In contrast, reproductions of quite ordinary items were widely made from the 1920s onwards. These were perfectly fairly offered for sale for what they were, but time has aged them and the unwary can be deceived. Unscrupulous people have also set out to age reproductions. For example, in recent years a flood of acid-stained black pewter of little age has been offered for sale in auction rooms and has often been wrongly identified as old. Reproduction pewter is widely stored in France among grass cuttings to give it a kind of patina, and other chemical methods of dulling surfaces and making them look old have been tried.

Another category of fake with which great care has to be taken is the genuine item which has been "improved" to increase its value. Genuine late 17th-century plates can have their value increased threefold by adding a wriggle-work decoration; plates from the workshop of Alderson, George IV's pewterer, can be made into "Coronation" plates by the addition of the scroll: "GR IV". In the United States, genuine antique plates have had copies of American marks added, thus greatly increasing the value.

Methods of Manufacture

Most pewter is cast in moulds. These were often made of bronze but moulds were also made of iron, wood, clay and stone. Simple shapes such as plates and spoons could be cast in a two-part mould, but complex forms, such as tankards or flagons, needed multi-part moulds. The various parts of a casting had then to be soldered together. When a casting came out of the mould it had a rough, unfinished appearance. Surplus metal had to be trimmed off and the rough surface polished down on a wheel, using a hard tool or abrasive.

Pewterers tended to complete the undersides of their pieces carefully, using a wheel and turning off the metal in a widening concentric ring (see opposite page). So look for evidence that the object has been cast in a mould, not raised over a form or stamped out from sheet metal; look for quality craftsmanship on the seams and turning; be sceptical about anything that has not been turned off on the bottom or under the base.

One way of bringing together small parts for fastening was to cast a part of an object directly onto the rest of it – for example, a porringer ear onto the

▲ **A wriggle-work plate, 1670**
The narrow reeded rimmed plate is engraved with a crowned portrait bust of William III flanked by the Royal Cypher "WR" within a band of wriggle-work foliage. It is marked with ownership initials "IT", and an unrecorded touchmark: "CR" or "CB", and dated 1670 with a floral device. This piece is perfectly genuine but look out for 17th-century plates or pieces that have been "improved" with the addition of later decoration or dates.

side of a porringer or a lid onto the thumbpiece of a flagon or tankard. To do this the mould was clamped into place on the partly completed object with a pair of pincers protected by a piece of linen. The joint was then poured and the impression of the linen remains (see below).

Flatware – that is plates, dishes and chargers – needed to resist heavy use and it was found that by hammering them round the booge (the area between the rim and the bottom of the plate) a stronger structure could be obtained. In Britain most plates were hammered, but American flatware is less frequently hammered. Few reproductions are hammered.

Rarely did the reproduction maker follow the old skills; they needed modern machines for quick production. Virtually all reproduction pewter falls at this hurdle.

▲ Dents caused by hammering
Hammering around the booge is a technique used to strengthen pieces, but it is not seen on reproduction items, and rarely on American pieces.

▽ ▶ A genuine Stuart tankard, *c*.1720
Genuine tankards should show natural bumps and bruises from use – pewter is very soft and the natural way to set a tankard down is front edge first; consequently this area is often slightly dented.

Comparing Two Tankards of a Similar Style

The linen mark where the handle was cast directly onto the body.

A typical ram's horn thumbpiece you would expect on a tankard of this date.

These concentric rings on the base are evidence of the metal being finished by turning.

▽ ▶ A tankard copying the 18th-century Stuart style, *c*.1910

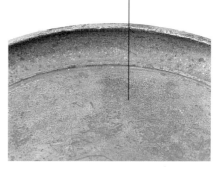

There is no sign of a linen mark suggesting the piece was raised over a form.

There is no evidence of turning on a wheel to finish off the piece.

▲ **An example of a fake mark**
This fake mark on a late 20th-century plate is composed of different elements copied from genuine marks. Many provincial pewterers used "London" in the mark as this was considered a selling point, so this is something copied by the fakers too.

▲ **A fake touchmark on a fake plate**

▲ **An example of fake housemarks**
Housemarks were generally tavern marks. This example is shown on a very late 19th-to early 20th-century baluster jug with a ball-and-wedge thumbpiece.

The Styles of Pewter

To be able to date pewter you have got to be able to put a provisional period to an object from its appearance. This will not be an exact date, for stylistic changes did not occur in a smooth, even way, but its shape and appearance ought to suggest to you a likely period in which an object would have been made. Reference books (Cotterell and Hornsby, for example – see the Bibliography) are invaluable in this regard, to professionals as well as to amateurs, and the more illustrations they have, the better; but they need to be complemented by experience in handling objects.

Makers' and Other Marks

Fakers and reproduction makers have used "genuine" marks on their work, so a mark by itself is no safeguard. Likewise, genuine pewter was often not fully marked, so fine things may lack the proof of who made them.

The nature and size of marks usually struck has also changed. Early marks are very simple, basic shapes with two initials, usually small; they were struck on handles, the front rims of plates and so on. By the late 18th century large, complex marks with full names and even addresses were being used and these appear, because of their size, underneath plates. Stuart tankards normally have marks struck either on the lid, if it is flat, or inside the base, but during the early 18th century a tendency developed for marks to be struck on one side of the neck, close to the handle. In the mid-17th century a secondary system of marking became popular – pseudo-hallmarks. These were normally struck four times and they are useful both to help identify a maker and offer confirmation of the period. It is not possible to establish a set of rules – makers tended to put their marks where they wanted – but by handling pewter, examining where marks are struck and looking at illustrations of pieces a working idea of styles of mark and where they normally appear will emerge.

Other marks seen are those placed there by early owners. Ownership marks take three common forms: a small group of housemarks, often

▼ **Genuine marks on a plate by John Duncombe of Birmingham, *c*.1745**
Duncombe was refused admission to the Guild in 1707, illustrating that not all pewter makers were registered at the Guild.

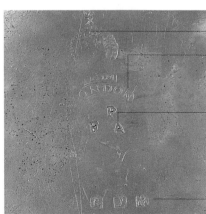

Touchmark, ie. the maker's mark.

London cartouche (not a guarantee that the piece was made in London).

The Triad mark (often a sign that the piece was a marriage gift), is made up of the initial of the surname, the initial of the Christian name of the male (bottom left) and the initial of the Christian name of the female (bottom right).

Pseudo-hallmark: The pewterers introduced these in response to the hallmarks used by silversmiths but pewter marks cannot be read in terms of year or place of manufacture in the same way as silver.

▲ 19th-century verification marks
These marks were required by law to be stamped on measures used in the sale of ale or dry goods, and are valuable pointers to age.

▲ An 18th-century plate
This piece shows the typical signs of knife cuts and natural wear from use. It is very difficult for the faker to simulate the naturalness of genuine wear.

▲ A modern Irish half gill measure
Although it has a touchmark of 94 Main Street, Cork, it was probably made in Birmingham, England. Note how sharp the edges are – pewter is too soft an alloy to retain sharp edges so if this piece were old the edges would be worn and smooth.

obscure in meaning, struck on early pewter – generally before 1600; a triad of owner's initials widely punched on pewter from the early 17th century into the 19th but less common after 1750; and crests and coats-of-arms.

With some experience you can usually identify the period in which initials were struck. Just as with handwriting, so punches followed the letter forms of the day. The way in which coats-of-arms were ornamented followed the broader style of the period. Not only can the style of an armorial help to date an object, but if the arms can be identified important provenance is added to the piece.

When an object was made for use in a tavern or market its capacity had to be confirmed by the authorities. Pewter and brass mugs and measures are often found with these verification marks stamped on the rim and they too help to confirm the period in which an item was used.

The Condition of Old Pewter

Look at every surface of a piece of pewter. How did it get its bumps and bruises? Are they consistent with real wear? Fakers tend to bang away, adding marks of wear without regard to the way an object is naturally used. A pattern of even wear over the entire surface is unnatural. If it is a plate, is there an irregular pattern of knife cuts, or are there just a few, evenly marked across the surface? Are the edges, bottom, hinges and neck of a flagon or tankard worn soft with use or are they sharp and even?

Most alloys of tin will oxidize over time but it takes at least 50 years for genuine oxide to develop. Is the oxide where you would expect? In damp parts of an object or where it got less use? Real oxide can erupt into unpleasant bubbles and these are hard to fake. Likewise, genuine light oxide cannot be copied properly. Most attempts to create oxide are poor although the true faker of the 1930s did obtain some skill. Fake oxide is always found with small holes in it rather than rounded eruptions. This is because it was put there with a drill and acids, rather than occurring naturally from within.

The Alloys

The traditional alloy of pewter common into the 17th century consisted of tin and copper with small amounts of other elements such as lead. In Britain and Europe all objects, such as flatware, which needed to stand up to hard use, contained above 90 per cent tin with perhaps 2–6 per cent copper. Measures, flagons, balusters etc, with their more complex shapes needing careful casting, were made of a softer alloy with less tin and more lead. Apart from Roman pewter few items contained more than 20 per cent lead. Later in the 17th century the proportion of copper gradually decreased, and a popular "hardmetal" appeared with a high tin content. In the United States, most new pewter was made from old metal and a slightly lower-quality alloy was common for flatware.

Changing Styles

▲ **An English "ball knop" brass candlestick, 17th century**

▲ **A George III brass candlestick, late 18th century**

▲ **A 19th-century brass candlestick**

▶ **A typical collection of brass, steel, pewter and copper items dating post c.1850 that can be found at auction**

COPPER, BRASS & BRONZE

Copper by itself, although suitable for some tasks, is too soft for many purposes; it is also difficult to cast. Alloys were therefore adopted, each based on a different hardening agent. The most common alloys were bronze and brass.

Bronze is made with tin added to copper, and brass has zinc in the alloy. In practice, other elements are also found, and "pure" brass or bronze was seldom used in the past. The lines of division between alloys are not as easy to establish as was at one time thought.

An enormous range of objects used in the home or workshop was made in brass, bronze or copper from the Middle Ages into the 20th century. Most commonly found these days are 18th- and 19th-century brass candlesticks, 19th-century copper and brass kettles, and 19th- and early 20th-century copper saucepans, jardinières and boxes. In addition, there is a mass of reproduction brass and copper of the 1920s and '30s; some of the pieces are copies of earlier designs, others are more loosely based on earlier styles.

In the Middle Ages Britain had sufficient tin but was obliged to import both copper and zinc. The first British copper appeared on the market in late Elizabethan times but it was not until after the restoration of Charles II in 1660 that the British copper mining industry expanded. It did so very speedily and by the early 19th century Britain was supplying nearly all the world's copper ore and British centres such as Birmingham were making millions of brass and copper objects for export. Brass, bronze and copper manufacture started out in this way but by the late 18th century was becoming increasingly mechanized and factory based. In the United States copper and brass were imported from Britain in substantial quantities, both as raw materials and as completed goods. As a result, it took some time for local manufacture to become established, but by the 19th century large quantities of brass and copper were being made in the United States.

Until after the Second World War there were few fakes of British or

American copper, brass or bronze pieces as the originals had little value. Plenty of popular reproductions were made in the years between the wars, however, and many of these have now acquired genuine age and wear.

In Europe metalware was popular well before the 1914–18 war so European fakes a hundred years old do exist. In addition, several museums offered for sale first-class unsigned replicas, copies of important objects, in the late 19th century. Fakes are currently thought to be being made in Spain and Italy and include copies of wall sconces, alms dishes, ladles, candle moulds and other popular and valuable forms. These are well made and are excellent facsimiles.

▲ **A 16th-century woodcut published by Hartman Schopper, showing a coppersmith at work**

Methods of Manufacture

Copper and its alloys, bronze and brass, each have specific properties and qualities which determine their usage. Copper is malleable and resistant to corrosion, with a high melting point. Therefore, although it was suitable for use in a variety of cooking implements, these had to be tinned, as vinegars, fats and fatty oils become cupreous on contact with copper. Because of its malleability, copper lends itself to being gilded and also chased in the same way as silver. Therefore it was also used for decorative objects, from the ecclesiastical to the domestic. A major drawback of copper, however, is that it is not suitable for casting and has very rarely been used in this way.

Brass is hard and durable, it can be exposed to both air and water, and its surface can also be treated in various ways. Therefore, many brass and all copper objects were made from raised sheet metal. Once the metal had cooled it was hammered by hand to make thick, uneven sheets. By the 19th century, these sheets were being produced more economically by steam power and rolling mills, resulting in thinner and more even sheets.

Thus the method of manufacture is a good guide to dating and authenticity. On early pieces, uneven hammer marks are often still visible. The method of joining objects in sheet metal is also an indication of its date. Up until the early 19th century, dovetailing was the traditional way to form joins. Precise dovetails were cut on the opposing sides of the metal and then hammered together to form a waterproof join. Although most modern reproduction pieces employ this method the dovetails are more imprecise.

In the 19th century, the overlap seam began to be used and ran concurrently with the dovetail. This method required the two opposite

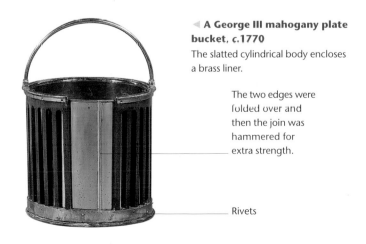

◀ **A George III mahogany plate bucket, c.1770**
The slatted cylindrical body encloses a brass liner.

The two edges were folded over and then the join was hammered for extra strength.

Rivets

▲ Until around 1790, candlesticks were made in two parts and joined with a vertical seam as shown here
Breathe heavily on the candlestick and the solder line should become visible. Alternatively turn it over and the seam should be clearly visible on the underside.

edges to be bent over each other to form a narrow flange which was then hammered flat.

Casting was also used to make brass and bronze items. Bronze is not malleable and is unsuitable for hammering. It can, however, withstand high temperatures and was used for cooking utensils such as three-legged downhearth cauldrons. Objects that were cast, whether by the *cire-perdue* or "lost wax" process, – a costly method as it could only be used once – or in "sand moulds", would need finishing to smooth rough edges, using chisels and by lathe-turning, the latter leaving irregular marks quite distinct from those left by machine lathes.

Cast brass candlesticks are common. The stem was solid-cast until about 1690, when hollow-casting began to be used. The stem was then cast in two, with a separate foot, within a "sand mould". After cleaning, the two halves were brazed together and the foot was similarly attached. 18th-century candlesticks are always well-finished under the foot, with chisel and irregular lathe marks clearly visible, in contrast to the many reproduction candlesticks now available on the market. By about 1790, solid-stem candlesticks were again the norm, though the foot was still cast separately. Complicated single-piece casting in brass would date the object post-1860.

Where handles had to be attached to the body of an object, such as a copper saucepan or a coffee pot (see below), rivets were normally used. Early ones are thick and hammered on both sides to complete the joint. Thin rivets, often only on one side, are a sign of late 19th-century production. The use of solder for attachments is an indication of a similar date.

Items were also produced in copper and brass by stamping. As thinner sheets of metal could be produced by the last quarter of the 18th century, this accelerated the press-and-die method of production. Sheets of metal were laid over a raised model of the pattern to be used, and then stamped out mechanically. Thus a wide variety of objects, ranging from buttons to furniture mounts, could be produced quickly and economically.

▼ An illustration of traditional manufacturing techniques

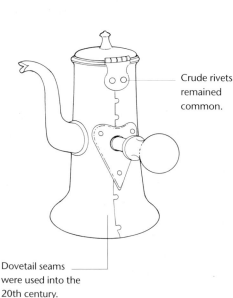

Crude rivets remained common.

Dovetail seams were used into the 20th century.

▼ A pair of candlesticks by R. L. Llewellyn Rathbone, beaten copper, 1902

Hammering and rivet joints were old techniques used by the Arts and Crafts artists.

The Alloys

While the alloy from which an object is made can seldom confirm by itself whether the article is old or not, knowing what an object is made of is a very useful dating tool. We can confirm whether it has the same kind of composition as is found in other genuine examples. The alloy used can also help to identify the national origins of some obscure objects, as different countries appear to have used different alloys according to local costs and the availability of raw materials.

In the case of brass, however, analysis can take us a stage further. Before 1770 mineral zinc was not available – only calamine, an oxide of zinc. Combining calamine with copper was difficult, as the zinc tended to evaporate when added to the crucible. Until the discovery of mineral zinc it was not possible to make a brass alloy with more than 30 per cent zinc and to get the level above 20 per cent was very difficult. A simple test for the proportions of zinc may, therefore, tell us at once whether an object was made before or after 1770. Most 18th-century brass has several trace elements in addition to copper and zinc; "pure" brass is likely to be modern.

Makers' and Other Marks

Few copper, brass or bronze objects, other than the mass-produced items of the 19th and 20th centuries, are marked by their makers. Little help is offered therefore by makers' marks alone, although naturally the makers of some objects have been identified and recorded. Some 18th-century brass-workers and a number of 17th- and 18th-century skillet and mortar makers are known.

As with pewter, some help may be offered by inscriptions, owners' initials and housemarks. Care must be taken, however, with inscriptions found on copper and brass. Reproduction makers made their products more interesting by adding inscriptions and false owners' names to many objects. For example, there are dozens of tobacco and snuff boxes with dated inscriptions to be found, all modern. Look at the nature of the lettering and try and compare it with genuine inscriptions on objects in museums. Modern letters appear rather thin and scratchy and often far too sharp.

▼ **A 17th-century brass candlestick**
Of typical shape, this candlestick shows all the signs of wear you would expect from a piece of this age which has seen everyday use – such as bumps and bruises to the base.

The Condition of Old Metalware

Take an object and run your fingers over all its surfaces. Is it smooth where it would naturally have worn? Are there rough corners and edges? Are there clear signs of wear and are they where they ought logically to be? Your fingers can often tell you more than your eyes. Where there are repairs, try and work out how the damage took place. Is it plausible?

By and large people prefer their copper and brass polished, so some of the evidence of age, offered by the patina and so helpful in pewter, is not always available for copper and brass.

Some late 17th- and early 18th-century brass and copper objects of high quality were originally silvered. It is wise to check all the crannies of a piece for evidence of this as it confirms an early manufacture, even if it means that the object is now not as it was originally made. Later brass and copper pieces were sometimes silver plated and still later they were electroplated – again it is worth looking for evidence of this type of treatment.

Sheffield Plate

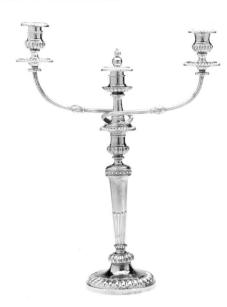

▲ **A Matthew Boulton candelabrum**
A candelabrum of the type for which Matthew Boulton was justly famous, with applied silver and lead-filled borders. It dates from the early 19th century.

Note the colour difference at the edge of the "let-in" silver piece.

▲ **A wine cooler engraved with a coat-of-arms, made by J. Watson, *c.*1810**
In the late 18th century a pure silver disc or heavily plated shield would be inserted into the piece to allow a crest or coat-of-arms to be engraved safely. In the early 19th century a patch of pure silver was burnished onto Sheffield Plate objects to provide a base for engraving.

Sheffield Plate properly describes a process of fusing silver and copper that was accidentally discovered by Thomas Boulsover in 1742. It was applied to the manufacture of domestic articles from the 1750s to the 1850s, and no article may legally be sold as Sheffield Plate unless it is made both by the precise process and within the period.

Not all Sheffield Plate was made in Sheffield, however. Large quantities were made in other manufacturing towns in England and the process was copied abroad. Russia, Poland and France all produced fused silver items, though their quality and style were generally sufficiently inferior to make them easily recognizable. To date, there is no evidence of any large-scale production in Ireland or North America.

Boulsover enjoyed some success with his discovery, but not enough. By 1769 he had given up making fused plate, but Joseph Hancock, now known as "The Father of Sheffield Plate", had taken up the process for the manufacture of domestic items. Matthew Boulton established his Birmingham factory in 1762, and with his partner John Fotherfill produced high-quality work. Boulton was among the first platers to adopt the sterling silver thread process, invented by Roberts and Cadman, by which a silver wire was soldered to edges to hide the raw copper that would otherwise show through. Boulton stamped such pieces with the words "SILVER BORDERS" and his marks, the double- or single-rayed sun.

The Process

The first form of Sheffield Plate was arrived at by binding, with a brass wire, an ingot of sterling silver to an ingot of copper that was hardened with about 25 per cent brass alloy. The bound ingots were then heated in a furnace until they fused; when cool, they were rolled into thin sheets. This was single plating. After 1770, however, double plating came in. The method was similar, but now the copper ingot was sandwiched between two ingots of silver. The resulting sheets accordingly showed silver on both sides and could be used for making articles such as sauce boats and entrée dishes which required silver to show inside as well as out. Where a surface was unlikely to be seen, but nonetheless required a finish, it was tinned. Original tinning is steely grey in colour and, if it is in good condition, counts as a plus point.

Fused plate articles were made in much the same way as their solid counterparts. This created a problem, the solution to which gives us a guide to authenticity. The hammering and annealing required to raise a seamless vessel contributed to the edges of the work fraying. Makers masked this by cutting the sheet at an angle, allowing the upper or outer edge to be drawn over and under ("lapped") to keep the edge tidy and conceal the raw copper. It is thus only on the very earliest examples of Sussex Plate that a raw copper edge can be seen. This problem also existed on items produced by seaming and die-stamping. The application of a hollow silver wire or thread (after 1785) proved an effective alternative. Wire was applied until the mid-1820s, the technique having run concurrently with applied decorative borders – first the bead, then the gadroon and finally the foliate and shell motifs – since the 1790s. These borders were made of stamped silver filled with lead.

▼ An electroplated wine cooler, 20th century

The rim is dented – a typical sign of wear.

Linear decoration, such as coats-of-arms, are usually flat-chased rather than engraved to avoid the copper showing through.

Worn plate may appear pinkish where the copper is showing through.

No seams or joins are visible as these are hidden by the layer of deposited silver.

A major innovation in 1768 was the production of plated wire, which enabled the construction of delicate wirework baskets and other decorative containers. The refined effect of wirework was a natural partner to the elegant designs of the Adam period; work of this period was enhanced by piercing, bright-cut engraving and the application of either stamped-out or applied reeded wire or bead borders.

Electroplating

The technical innovation that hastened the decline of the Sheffield process was the introduction of German silver, in which a mixture of nickel and brass was applied between the copper and the silver. By 1836 a refined nickel called Argentine was used as a total replacement for the copper. Then, in 1840, a patent was registered for an electroplating process which was to prove the end of Sheffield Plate.

However, by the end of the 19th century there was a considerable demand for the Old Sheffield look and electroplating onto copper as well as Argentine became popular. This is where mistakes can occur. When silver has worn through to expose the copper underneath (called "bleeding"), it has been assumed that the article must be Old Sheffield. But this can only be so if the silver is of sterling standard – electroplating is done with pure silver. Initially the sharpness of colour and the feel may be a guide, but the forger can now create an old "skin" or patina. In the last resort a solution of nitric acid dropped on the surface will decide – it will turn sterling silver blue but has no effect on pure (electroplated) silver. A replated Old Sheffield item can be told by its slightly greasy feel.

Most of the Sheffield Plate that appears on the market is in relatively good condition, whereas much 19th-century electroplate is very much the worse for wear. This is in part because the method of making Old Sheffield articles – annealing and raising – actually strengthens the metal. If an article can be easily impressed or dented it is unlikely to be Old Sheffield.

Style and Decoration

Gradually, Sheffield Plate became as popular as silver – and not just because it was cheaper. In some homes, plated articles were used in preference to their equivalents in sterling silver. For Sheffield Plate to be this popular it had to be as fashionable as silver: shapes and forms of ornament had to be fully up to date and every bit as stylish as their sterling counterparts. An item that is offered as early Old Sheffield that is not stylistically true to its period is unlikely to be authentic. This rule of thumb does not, however, apply throughout the whole period of Sheffield Plate: in the last two decades of the process, fused platers kept their expensive Regency steel dies in use.

◄ A candlestick, c.1825
This piece has been over-polished so the decoration is losing its detail and the copper is showing through the plate.

English Silver

The silver hallmarking system, introduced in the late 15th century in the form which has lasted to the present day, is one of the earliest types of consumer protection. The 21st-century dealer and collector is extremely fortunate to have this system to back up his knowledge of style and form. The hallmark will indicate to the purchaser that a piece is of sterling or Britannia standard, in addition to revealing its age. This provides a system for double-checking the instinctive judgment of a piece against the marks of one of the official Assay Offices. The faker of silver articles has to be that much more inventive than fakers in other areas of antiques, as he has to produce not only the piece but also the hallmark.

The ultimate guardian of honest trade practice is the Assay Master at Goldsmiths Hall. In addition to being responsible for the assaying and marking of all new wares, the Assay Master chairs the Antique Plate Committee which sits regularly to examine suspect pieces submitted for scrutiny. The Committee is made up of experts in the trade. As well as attending meetings their duties include informing the Assay Office of any suspect piece they may come across. The Assay Master will then require other members to examine the item and either confirm or contradict the original suspicion.

The focus of this attention naturally falls on the auction market, as that is where the majority of traders purchase pieces. Occasionally a piece will be withdrawn from sale because it is suspect. This makes London unique in that an amateur collector has unparalleled protection against being duped at auction. If a piece were to escape the eye of one of the Antique Plate Committee members, which is unlikely, the major auction houses have a reputation to maintain, and some of them give a five-year guarantee which offers additional protection. The British Antique Dealers' Association requires its members to reimburse the full monies invoiced should any piece be discovered to be fake or intentionally mis-described. This Association also offers an arbitration and disputes procedure which can be used by members of the public and of the trade and this can frequently be of help to effect a mutually satisfactory conclusion to a previously difficult difference of opinion. The Trade Descriptions Act can also be employed in extreme cases.

▶ **Unauthorized additions and alterations**

This silver coffee pot has genuine hallmarks for 1566 and a maker's mark, an incuse fleur-de-lys. These marks were struck when the silver was originally worked as an Elizabethan communion cup similar to this typical, unaltered genuine silver communion cup from a similar period (far right). Later, when the base, handle, spout and lid were added, the object was not resubmitted to the Assay Office; therefore the new additions have not been marked, and the piece contravenes the Hallmarking Act of 1973, even though these alterations were never intended to deceive.

Duty Dodgers

A few early 18th-century silversmiths dodged duty by making an item and incorporating marks from an older piece. These were produced mainly c.1719–58, when the duty was sixpence per ounce. Typical candidates were coffee pots, teapots, two-handled cups, casters and sauce boats on spreading feet. These are normally marked on the base and therefore a disc of silver with an earlier mark could be inserted in the base. Always check both that marks coincide with dating by style, and that the marks appear in the correct places. Coffee pots, teapots, cups and casters are usually marked in a cluster on the base. If three or more base marks are in a straight line it is likely that a disc has been inserted. Coffee pots with straight tapering sides are ideal for this, as the base is made as a separate piece and soldered in. The other categories require the soldering in of a disc within the depth of the applied foot. This would otherwise be visible from the interior, where the solder line would show. Check for a double base by giving it a sharp tap with a pointed object; if a pimple appears on the inside there is no double skin.

▲ **Silver wine fountain weighing 575 oz**
This very large piece was made for George Booth, 2nd Early of Warrington in 1728 by Peter Archambo I, a Huguenot goldsmith. In order to avoid paying the excise duty (6d per oz), Archambo submitted a small silver object to the Assay Office for testing and marking instead. Having paid only a small amount of duty, the marked area of the small object was then inserted into the foot of the huge wine fountain. Therefore the wine fountain itself was never submitted to the Assay Office and the correct duty never paid.

◀ **Teapot base**
This detail of the base of an unassayed teapot shows where the silversmith has "let-in", or inserted, a hallmarked silver disc cut from a piece of redundant 18th-century silver, thereby avoiding paying duty on the total weight.

Fakes

The most common method of faking silver involves removing the marks from an older or a more valuable item, or one by a celebrated maker that is in poor condition, and then soldering them into a less valuable piece. Most types of object have characteristic configurations of hallmarks. For example, mustard pots are usually marked in a group on the base, while salvers are nearly always marked in a straight line. Marks that have been "let-in" are often positioned incorrectly, distorted, or missing altogether.

▲ ▶ **Rose bowl**
The uncharacteristic slanted line of the George III hallmarks on this Victorian rose bowl suggests they are a spurious addition. If you breathe heavily on any suspicious areas you should be able to see a faint solder line if, indeed, it has been altered.

▶ Modern fakes

This fork and spoon bear counterfeit marks purporting to have been made in London, 1689, by the goldsmith William Mathew. Both items are engraved and marked on the reverse. These pieces were auctioned by a London craftsman in 1985 and sold for £48,000 ($70,000) although the money was never paid. Suspicion had been aroused after some spoons, supposedly marked "1621" and "1683", which had been auctioned in 1985, were submitted to the Antique Plate Committee and found to be clever forgeries. In May 1986, the maker of all these pieces pleaded guilty to various charges, including forging hallmarks, and was sent to prison. The fact that these pieces were successfully auctioned for such a high price illustrates how difficult it can sometimes be to determine whether an item is genuine or not.

The Categories of Fake Silver

There are two distinct categories of fake silver: articles with forged hallmarks and hallmarked pieces which have been altered or incorporated into others. The former, until recent years, were fairly easy to spot by comparing the marks presented with marks which were known to be genuine; the evidence now points to greater sophistication being employed by forgers to reproduce facsimiles of marks, and microscopic examination is sometimes necessary. The latter is usually detectable by diagnostic examination.

The Analytical Method

Every piece tells a story if you know what to look for. First, look closely at the style and decoration of the piece and ask yourself some key questions.
- Are the different decorative techniques used contemporary with each other and to the purported date?
- Are there co-ordinating stylistic factors between the decoration?
- Does the quality of workmanship reflect the date?

◀ An altered silver goblet

This hot-water jug has been fashioned from a Neo-classical silver goblet of 1788, by the addition of an insulated handle, an upper body, cover, and lip decorated with a gadrooned rim. The awkward proportions and placement of the marks provide valuable clues as to how this piece has been reconstructed. Hot-water jugs are normally marked on the base or near to the rim, and on this example the marks suspiciously appear beneath the rim – where they would be found on a goblet.

The questions to ask, after forming an initial impression based on style, are then these:

- Do the hallmarks agree with your initial impression of date?
- Are all the marks there?
- Are they distorted or in an unusual position?
- Are any subsidiary pieces lacking the correct marks?
- Are there any signs of repair, such as patches or rough soldering where separately made pieces have been attached?

Tankards

Perhaps one of the most common fakes is the conversion of an 18th-century tankard or mug to a more useful jug. This was done extensively during the 19th century and these pages show some typical examples.

The covered tankard became unfashionable in the 19th century and provided the innovative silversmith with an object that could be converted into a variety of items. The most common alteration was to make it into a jug for hot or cold liquids. The illustration below shows a perfectly legal alteration of a tankard to a different use. Tankards do have very recognizable forms – the outline form of the handle; the lid with thumbpiece. Another common clue is the fact that there are four hallmarks on the base and inside the domed lid. Tankards are the only pieces that have this combination of four marks on the base and lid as a matter of course.

Genuine coffee pots can be subjected to the addition of decoration alone. This is not illegal and while in Victorian times it would have enhanced the appeal and value of a piece, today it will probably diminish it by a factor of five.

Comparing an Original with an Altered Piece

▼ **A genuine tankard of baluster form with a moulded girdle and dome cover**
It is engraved with a contemporary crest and is by Isaac Cookson, Newcastle, 1747.

▼ **A hot-water jug adapted from a similar tankard to the one left**
Probably by John Kidder, 1771. This authorized alteration is marked and was made by Henry Holland in 1876.

The spout has been added.

The ivory fillets have been inserted at the time of alteration to stop the heat passing through the handle.

▼ **Converted punch ladles**
18th-century punch ladles are ripe for conversion. Feet and a handle can be added to make a cream boat, as shown in the illustration below. The double-lipped variety is found with two handles and four feet added. Pap boats are also subjected to this type of alteration.

◄ **Later decoration**
This tankard from the 1690s has been decorated in the 19th century, which will lower the value of the piece, although it is not an illegal alteration.

The stepped lid, scroll handle and thumb-piece are all characteristics of 17th-century tankards.

Classical ornament of putti, fruiting vines, masks, shells, are all typical 19th-century decoration.

Later Decoration

The alteration to, or imitation of, older styles was not just a phenomenon of the late 19th century. As early as 1810 the large manufacturing silversmiths of Garrards and Rundell, Bridge and Rundell were reproducing late 17th-century Baroque style and mid-18th-century Rococo style pieces (see page 126). Many pieces were altered to the "antique style" so sought after by dilettanti in the early 19th century. The end result would be an eclectic mix of styles and periods, such as bodies made from Queen Anne ale jugs, chased with mythological battle scenes. The spouts might have been cast from a mid-18th-century piece and the handles modelled on the 17th-century caryatid type.

Cream Jugs

In the past, cream jugs or boats were created by converting a number of obsolete objects. The most common are caster to pitcher cream jugs (as below), punch ladle bowls to small cream boats (left), and pap boats to similar but larger vessels by the addition of feet and handles.

▶ **The conversion of casters**
Small baluster casters have been converted to more useful pitcher cream jugs by the addition of handles and spouts. Occasionally they are difficult to spot, but usually poor craftsmanship, discolouration of the skin, or heat marks where the additions have been soldered, should point to a conversion.

Teapots, Stands and Kettles

Teapots were rarely converted to other objects but were often modernized by adding decoration, a new spout, finials and handle. These can usually be spotted by following the analytical method outlined on page 120.

Teapot stands, which were common in the late 18th and early 19th centuries, have been used to manufacture "antique" teapots. Nearly all the stands are hallmarked in a straight line and not at the points of the compass as on the base of a teapot. Teapot lids should be hallmarked, and if these marks are missing or differ from the base mark then warning bells should sound. Small bullet teapots of the first half of the 18th century also need careful examination, as it is now known that some were made up by unscrupulous use of the silver and marks from a mug or tankard.

Tea kettles, like teapots, were often updated, but are not commonly faked. Always make sure that all separate parts are correctly marked and there should be little chance of being fooled. On one type of fake, however, the marks from an 18th-century tankard base have been let in to the base of the kettle while the tankard lid is used to make a burner, which is fixed to the tripod stand. The test here is to look carefully for any distortion of the hallmarks, to make sure the lid has a good mark, and, if the burner is removable, to check for a hallmark on the stand. The burner, which is small compared with a tankard lid, is the place where the marks will be most obviously distorted if it is a fake.

Tea/coffee or hot-water urns are sometimes found made from a cup and cover by adding a tap; alternatively, urns are occasionally found converted to cups by the removal of taps.

The wine funnel has been subjected to various adaptations. The most common is calling the bowl of the funnel a tea strainer. By blocking the perforations in the bowl it can become a small sugar basin or salt cellar. The replacement of the spout by a pedestal foot can make a goblet. If the foot is not made so tall, and a spout and handle are added, a milk jug can be made. It is highly unlikely that these adaptations would be made now that wine funnels are fairly rare and valuable.

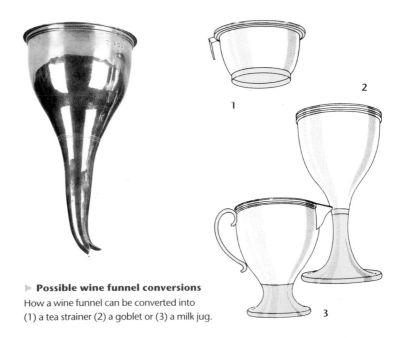

▶ **Possible wine funnel conversions**
How a wine funnel can be converted into
(1) a tea strainer (2) a goblet or (3) a milk jug.

Brandy Saucepan Conversions

▶ A genuine early 18th-century brandy saucepan with a turned wood handle

(1) Remove the handle, add a wire scroll handle to an example with a spout to create a cream jug.

(2) A Plymouth or Exeter-type cream jug. These have been suspect in the past because they are so like conversions from brandy saucepans.

1

2

1

2

▲ Sugar basins have been turned into teapots (1) by removing one handle, replacing it with a spout, and adding a lid. A simpler conversion (2) is to make a sugar bowl into a tea caddy simply by adding a lid.

Sugar Basins, Argyles and Brandy Saucepans

Large sugar basins were needed for unrefined sugar and the size of these is such that with the addition of a handle, lid and spout a small teapot can be created. The argyle (gravy pot) with internal insulator removed is occasionally found passed off as a rare bachelor's teapot.

Brandy saucepans are sometimes found with their handles removed to be sold as sugar basins. Spouts can be added to early 18th-century examples or replaced on later examples. There has also been controversy in the past about a type of cream jug that looks like a 1730s brandy saucepan with its turned wood handle removed and a simple wire scroll handle added (see above). These have now been accepted as genuine, but only if they are made by Exeter or Plymouth silversmiths who used this style.

Candlesticks

Until the third quarter of the 18th century the majority of table candlesticks were cast. It is possible to make a mould from a candlestick that has been hallmarked and thus achieve a very accurate replica, including marks. The innovation of electrotypes in the mid-19th century added yet another dimension to the art of copying.

Candlesticks cast from one another, including marks, can be spotted by careful comparison of the placing of the hallmarks and any obvious flaws. With loaded candlesticks there is a possibility that marks have been "let in" to the edge of the base. The "let in" mark is most likely to have come from table silver, and if a maker's mark is visible it will probably be identifiable as a "spoonmaker's". Seams where the piece has been soldered in are also likely to be visible. On loaded candlesticks, the detachable drip-pan or nozzle is almost invariably marked with the maker's mark and the lion passant on London examples, whilst fully marked on Birmingham or Sheffield models. There can be exceptions to this rule, particularly on London-made examples but it is best to be wary of unmarked nozzles after about 1775. Before that time, however, the marking of nozzles, though required, seems to be a little more erratic. Experience, "eye" and careful analytical judgment will hopefully aid the collector to reach the right conclusion. If uncertainty persists it is best, perhaps, to exercise caution and leave them alone.

Later silver is marked on the outside.

Early candlesticks are marked underneath, high up on the ogee line.

The baluster stem is typical of most late 19th- and 20th-century examples but are fairly plain, with bands of die-stamped decoration.

◀ Modern candlesticks

Modern reproduction candlesticks such as these are readily available on the market.

▲ Marks and their position

Candlesticks made in the first half of the 18th century are cast, and are invariably marked underneath the base with the marks spread out. The exception to this rule is Irish-made candlesticks, which are quite often marked on the outside surface of the base. From the middle of the 18th century, the majority of candlesticks (although not all) were filled with pitch ("loaded"), and it became the normal practice to mark them on the outside of the base, on the rim of the foot, so that the marks could be seen.

Always examine candelabra carefully, as an old trick is to solder the nozzle sleeve to a branch so that it bears the same mark as the candlestick. Candelabra branches should be marked with date letter, standard, duty, town and maker's mark, depending on their period. All detachable parts should also bear corresponding marks.

Chamber candlesticks are now popular again as they are ideal for small dining tables. Again, check the detachable pieces. Hallmarks will not appear on them if the chamber stick has been constructed from an epergne dish (especially the period 1720–60), a wine funnel stand, salt cellar stand or counter tray. Wax jacks are also known to have been made up from these same items.

Snuffers and their accompanying trays have been comparatively free from interference, but are occasionally subjected to the addition of handles and feet. They are also a convenient style for converting into inkstands by the addition of simple rings to hold the glass inkwells. The absence of or difference in hallmark on the inkwell covers will reveal the truth.

Trays and Salvers

It is not often that one comes across tea trays that are wrong, but when viewing a potential purchase check the mark to see if it is distorted at all or struck too close to the border. Either of these factors could reveal reshaping

▲ This 1875 urn is a late Victorian copy of a 1780s example

It reflects the classical styles popular in the late 18th century and is decorated with a beaded border typical of the period, but the proportions and the slightly clinical look identify it as a Victorian copy. The marks will tell you exactly what it is so there is no question of any attempt to deceive.

▶ Honest replicas

Making honest replicas had a brief period of popularity in the 19th century. This large Victorian ewer by James Garrard, London, 1893, is typical of Garrard & Rundell's work. It is almost an exact replica of an earlier piece with baroque-style strapwork and classical decoration but it lacks the flow of the original. Candlesticks made at this time in the 17th-century style are easily identifiable by their over-large size compared to the originals, but they are honest pastiches of the period.

▶ **Identifying and dating a piece**
Using the analytical method described on page 120, always ask yourself key questions when looking at a piece. What is the style? In this instance, is it Rococo or Rococo revival? What style is the armorial? What do the marks tell you? If the marks are 1860, as here, it clearly confirms that the style has to be Rococo revival and the piece is therefore exactly as it purports to be. If the style and the marks don't match up, alarm bells should ring and further checks should be made.

or additions to the borders. Tea trays are sometimes made up from oval salvers or meat dishes by the addition of handles and feet. In these cases the handles will often not match the design of the border, which they will normally do on a "right" example.

The most commonly found alteration of a salver is from a plain Georgian example to a decorative Victorian presentation piece. If an inscription does not coincide with the mark, or if the style is not quite what one would expect, then check carefully to see if there are any odd creases or seams which might denote an added border and/or feet. Occasionally one will find that the border has been hallmarked at the time of the addition. The marks are usually tiny and difficult to spot, but must be there if an altered salver is to be sold legally.

In the second half of the 17th century and the first quarter of the 18th there was a vogue for the salver on foot, or tazza. When the fashion for tazzas waned many had their central "trumpet" foot removed and three or four small feet added at the borders. These are usually discernible by an examination of the centre of the underside where some sign of the position of the central foot will remain. I have also seen these conversions reversed. It is therefore important when examining a salver on foot to see that it is struck with the obligatory lion passant or leopard's head erased mark. This should always be the case except on some provincial or late examples of the second quarter of the 18th century onwards.

THE FAKER

Many fakers are superb craftsmen, but they often are caught out by their own hubris. If the maker of the fork and spoon on page 120 had resisted crafting pieces of such unusual quality that inevitably would cause a stir in the market, he would have been more likely to have completed the fraud successfully. Pieces of exceptional quality always have a provenance – they will have been sold at auction or been recorded in a collection at some time; it is extremely unlikely that pieces of this calibre would ever just materialize with no market background and be "right".

Plates and Dishes

Dinner plates, soup plates and meat dishes, which were produced in their thousands for affluent 18th-century families, were usually of plain circular design until 1740. After this date the vogue was for shaped circular plates with gadroon borders, and many plain services were returned by patrons to their silversmith for updating. If they were not re-marked, the original marks will have been distorted and partly lost during the refashioning.

Another inventive use for the dinner plate during the last hundred years has been rehammering them into more saleable and appealing rose bowls and strawberry dishes. Again, stretched marks will give this away. More difficult to detect is the conversion of soup plates into dinner plates by removing the centre of the plate, cutting it down, rehammering and soldering back into the border. An original scratchweight is always a useful check, as soup plates tend to be between 7½ and 15 per cent heavier than dinner plates. Entrée dishes have been remarkably free from tampering, but the addition of decoration and the replacement of detachable handles should be watched out for.

Soup tureens and sauce tureens are in the same category, with the following additional points: look out for let-in marks on pedestal feet, and make sure a full set of marks appears – otherwise the piece may be a converted liner. Soup tureens made in the period 1805–40 often had detachable liners. These liners will have the same set of marks as the tureen except that the town mark (leopard's head or mask in the case of London) will have been omitted.

The faker has in the past found a variety of uses for both the tureen liner and the wine cooler liner. Whilst the former can be turned into baskets, bowls or tureens, the latter can, by the addition of lids, become biscuit barrels or ice buckets. Cake/dessert or sweetmeat baskets are extremely popular and apart from converted liners mentioned above, dismantled epergnes and converted goblets are the two most common deceptions.

▶ **Scratchweights**

Often the number and weight of each item in a set was inscribed on its base. This may show how many items were in a set and, by a change in weight, if a piece has been altered. The weights are made up of ounces (oz), penny-weights (dwt), grains (gr). There are 20 penny-weights in an ounce. One ounce equals one troy ounce.

This would be the number of the piece within a set, for example of 12 plates. If the number is so high as to make it improbable that it could relate to pieces in a set, it could be an inventory mark. These were made so the butler could easily check pieces in the plate room and would either be scratched on by the butler himself or by the silversmith when the piece was made.

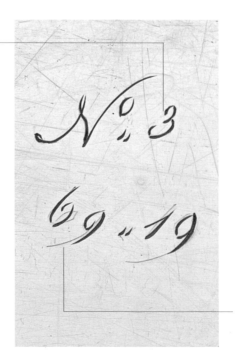

This piece weighed 69oz = 19dwt when it was first sold. It probably weighs slightly less now due to cleaning and wear but this should be a variance of no more than 3oz or so. Any more should beg the question of what has been removed from the original piece. If the piece weighed more than the 69oz = 19 dwt you should be looking to see what could have been added at a later date.

A George III Cow Creamer by John Schuppe, 1763

A Dutch Cow Creamer, late 19th century

▲ **Comparing cow creamers**

18th-century English silver cow creamers are very rare and if you come across a silver cow creamer it is much more likely to be a 19th-century Dutch one, although it could have English marks. It was not illegal for the Dutch silversmiths to copy the English marks. Once brought into Britain, the pieces were then sometimes marked at the Assay Office with a foreign import mark, i.e. the date followed by an "F". The Dutch cow creamer above has London import marks for 1889.

Cow Creamers and Porringers

Popular interest in collecting silver was immortalized by Bertie Wooster's antics with cow creamers and porringers. The cow creamer in its original form was almost exclusively made by John Schuppe in London between 1750 and 1775, while the "modern Dutch" replicas were made from the 1880s onwards. The 18th-century examples are clearly identifiable from the hallmarks: claims for those without should be given a wide berth. However, the modern Dutch cow creamer is worth one-tenth of the value of an 18th-century English one.

Porringers, on the other hand, need careful examination if one is to avoid buying a fake. Many William III/Queen Anne-style examples, decorated with curved lobes and fluting below a corded girdle, have been created from Georgian mugs and tankard lids. Careful examination of the hallmarks for distortion and signs of a seam where hallmarks may have been let in will reveal the truth in most cases.

Beakers are not very common in English silver and caution should be

► **A George II boat-shaped sauce boat, c.1730**

The "halo" around the crest shows a difference in surface patina and suggests that an earlier crest has been removed. This makes the silver thin and vulnerable and affects the value. Pushing gently on a suspicious patch will reveal if any original engraving has been removed. Breathing heavily on suspicious areas should reveal solder lines of any "let in" areas.

▼ **Possible conversions of a goblet**
A goblet can be converted into (1) a sweetmeat basket, and a goblet bowl into (2) a wine funnel.

1

2

taken over 17th-century examples that bear the hallmark on the base. There is a chance that these may have been rebodied. Be careful to compare the wear and colour of both body and base.

Other conversions and fakes to be looked out for that are not quite so common are:

- tankard lids converted into bleeding bowls;
- dish rings with marks from a spoon let into the rim;
- wine coasters converted to soy frames by the addition of a handle and feet;
- cruet frames converted into wine coasters by the removal of handles and feet;
- wine coasters converted into decanter wagons by soldering two together and adding carriage wheels;
- punch ladle bowls converted into salt cellars;
- salt cellars converted into mustard pots by the addition of lids and handles;
- snuff boxes turned into vinaigrettes by adding grilles;
- vinaigrettes converted into pill or cachou boxes by the removal of grilles;
- teapot stands converted into toast racks by soldering on bars.

▼ **An altered christening jug**
This small christening jug, 1840, has been converted into a cream jug with the addition of a spout. This type of alteration is illegal unless the spout is hallmarked.

This alteration has been marked on the spout and is, therefore, perfectly legal.

The proportion of the piece is unbalanced with the addition of the spout.

Rough patches can be seen around the soldered edges of the new spout.

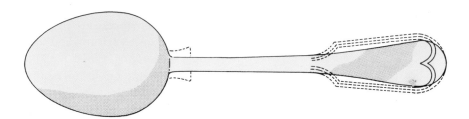

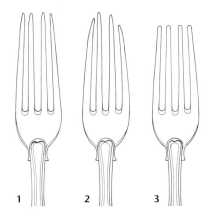

▲ **Alterations due to wear**
Worn flatware is one of the only types of silver
not to be worth much more than melt value
of the metal, as satisfactory repair is almost
impossible. Flatware can be found in varying
conditions.
(1) A fork in fairly good condition.
(2) A fork damaged by years of scraping
across plates leading to wear and bending
of the tines.
(3) Worn forks that have been subsequently
trimmed level to disguise the wear. This
becomes apparent when compared with
an unaltered example, but otherwise can
be difficult to spot.

Flatware

The first purchase that is likely to be made in silver, not unnaturally, is that
of a service of flatware, a generic term for spoons and forks. This should not
be confused with the term "cutlery" which is specifically to do with knives:
sadly it has become so confused that people, when referring to a "cutlery
service", believe that they are referring to a service of knives, spoons and
forks. Common usage, however, does not make it correct.

Flatware will produce few fakes but some tampering. The fakes, or,
perhaps, subtle alterations is a more apt description, can be seen in early
flatware (c.1700 to c.1750), which is now becoming increasingly rare and
consists of forks made out of spoons. Forks, most particularly dessert forks,
are always much more difficult to find than spoons. Therefore, it makes sense
that the conversion of spoons into forks is a more viable and commercial
proposition.

The tines, or prongs, of a three-prong fork are quite strong and a weak
tine would most likely indicate that a transformation from a spoon to a fork
has been effected. To turn a spoon into a fork is not a difficult problem; the
problem lies in making the tine into a good solid feature, and even this is
not impossible. A single example thus transformed may be difficult to
recognize in isolation but the collector, when offered a dozen three-pronged
forks, should beware if the "set" are of all, or many, different dates and yet
have all equal tines. (Try bending the tine and it should, as said above, be
strong, not weak and thin.)

These conversions of table silver are all illegal, but one which is not is
the alteration and matching up of patterns – as long as no extra metal is added
and as long as the form is not changed substantially. Fiddle pattern is not
as popular as Old English, so it is not unknown for the former to have the
shoulders at the top and base of the stem trimmed away to form the latter,
as shown above. Old English pattern, in turn, is not as sought-after as the
more decorative forms of the same design. It is, for example, not impossible
to "manufacture" Old English Thread, Featheredge, Beaded and Bright-Cut
engraved patterns from the plain form.

Spoons

In the Victorian era there was a vogue for presenting "Berry Spoons" as
gifts. The majority of these are plain spoons which have been embossed with
foliage, fruit or flowers in the second half of the 19th century, as seen in the
example overleaf. Their value is, strangely, usually double that of the plain
spoon, reversing the price trend that is followed by later-chased hollow ware
(mugs, tankards, coffee pots, etc.). The "modern" strawberry was

▲ **A typical George III berry spoon,
1780, decorated in the 1870s**

not cultivated and popularized until the early 19th century, but a lot of these spoons are marked pre-1800. Sauce ladles have occasionally been treated in a similar fashion and sometimes pierced to form sugar sifters.

Broadly speaking, however, the ordinary spoon and fork is not a natural focus of the forger's attention and it is possible to collect flatware with a fair degree of equanimity. Rather, it is the more specialized form of flatware that can demand the attention of the faker or "improver".

Specimen Spoons

For many years there has been a strong interest in collecting early English spoons, the general definition of which is spoons (and the occasional fork) made before 1700.

Until about 1660, these spoons bear no relation to the spoon with which we associate the word today. The bowl is of a generally fig-shaped outline with a narrow hexagonal stem which is usually topped with a finial of some sort. Possibly the best known of these finials is the Apostle. These spoons have a figure on the top depicting one of the Apostles, each of whom is differentiated by the emblem which he carries. For instance, St. Peter is depicted with a key; St. Andrew with a saltire cross; St. Bartholomew with a flaying knife and so forth. Obviously, the one Apostle who is left out is Judas Iscariot and he is generally replaced by St. Paul who was the Patron Saint of London. Our Lord is shown with his right hand raised in blessing and an orb and cross in his left.

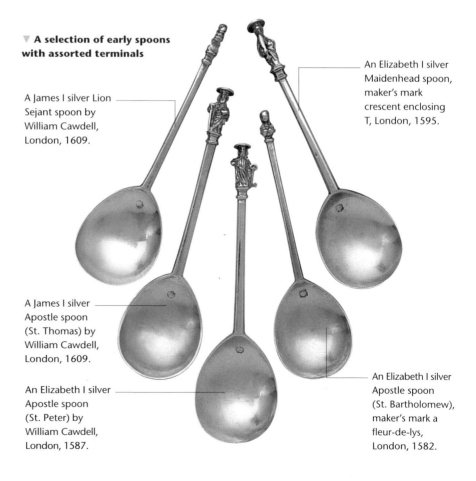

▼ **A selection of early spoons
with assorted terminals**

A James I silver Lion Sejant spoon by William Cawdell, London, 1609.

An Elizabeth I silver Maidenhead spoon, maker's mark crescent enclosing T, London, 1595.

A James I silver Apostle spoon (St. Thomas) by William Cawdell, London, 1609.

An Elizabeth I silver Apostle spoon (St. Peter) by William Cawdell, London, 1587.

An Elizabeth I silver Apostle spoon (St. Bartholomew), maker's mark a fleur-de-lys, London, 1582.

▼ **Identifying the Apostles**

It is possible to recognize the individual Apostles by the emblems they hold in their right hand, although sometimes these are difficult to discern easily.

Left to right, top to bottom

St. Matthias, St. James the Greater, St. Jude
St. Matthew, St. Andrew, St. Simon
St. Thomas, St. John, St. Peter
St. James the Less, St. Philip, St. Bartholomew

Apart from Apostle spoons there were a host of other finials such as diamond points, acorn knops, lion sejants, maidenheads, seal-tops and all of these, as well as the trefid spoon, which is the obvious precursor to our more standard modern spoon, are amply written about in a number of specialist books.

However, unlike the bulk of later flatware, these have been the subject of substantial faking or improving with varying degrees of sophistication and success.

The simplest, most artless, form of faking was done in the late 19th and early 20th centuries and this took the form of cutting off the slightly spreading top of a Hanoverian pattern dessert-spoon and soldering an Apostle on the top as well as slightly reshaping the bowl. These are pathetically easy to spot and do beg the question as to whether they were ever really intended to deceive.

Casting a spoon from a genuine original is a less simple way of faking and, at first glance, can well imitate the genuine article, but on closer examination it should fail the text. The marks are likely to be a little "fuzzy" or granular and, by putting careful pressure on the stem, it will bend relatively easily – a sure sign of a cast spoon.

More sophisticated still is the replacement of the finial of a seal-top with an Apostle. The spoon, in this case, will probably look slightly out of proportion but considerable experience is needed to see the slight difference. As in all things the greater knowledge a person develops of the genuine the more the person will balk at something that does not seem right. Sometimes this is obvious, more often it is a slight wariness, a feeling of unease. This knowledge and a sixth sense is the best bulwark against deception for both the professional and the amateur.

▶ **A fake silver Apostle spoon, Glasgow**

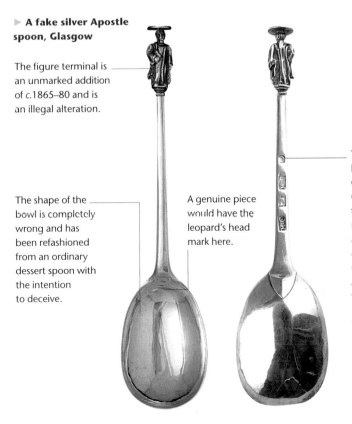

The figure terminal is an unmarked addition of c.1865–80 and is an illegal alteration.

The shape of the bowl is completely wrong and has been refashioned from an ordinary dessert spoon with the intention to deceive.

A genuine piece would have the leopard's head mark here.

The stem bears the hallmark of Milne & Campbell and the Glasgow hallmarks for c.1757–80. The marks are spread out as you would expect on a dessert spoon. On an original Apostle spoon you would find them bunched closer together near to the bowl with the leopard's head mark on the reverse positioned at the front of the bowl.

American Silver

The makers' marks of the 17th-century firm of Hull and Sanderson, Boston. With reasonable technical ability for die-sinking such punches can be simulated. The more one can examine authentic punched marks, therefore, the more likely it is that a wrong one will be spotted.

Marks used by John Coney, Boston.

Marks used by Peter van Dyck or Dyke. Their relative simplicity and minor variation indicate how easy it would be for a skilled forger to simulate them.

Maker's marks used by Jacob Hurd of Boston, recorded from 1723. Some makers used their initials only, others their surname, yet others marked their work with initials and surname.

Marks used by Philip Syng Jr, of the famous Philadelphia family.

Two versions of Paul Revere II's mark.

Two of the several marks used by Samuel Kirk of Baltimore between 1830 and 1846. The figures refer to the weight of the piece. If Kirk's work were not so well known, the wide variety in his marks could be taken as an invitation to add to his catalogue.

American silver of the Colonial period – with the temporary exception of that made in New York until the mid-18th century – relied very heavily for its designs on English models (in New York, the Dutch influence was stronger). The possibility instantly arises of wrong attribution in some cases if one is judging by style alone. A substantial number of pieces could have been made in either country.

The fact that the United States did not adopt the hallmarking system could lead one to suspect all sorts of misconduct. If, under the strict supervision of the Goldsmiths Company, English silversmiths could perpetrate deceptions such as those described on pages 118–133, what could American silversmiths not have got up to without any form of regulation?

The Marking System

To forge an English hallmark requires the making of four, five or even six punches. However, American silver of the 18th century normally bore only a maker's mark. This might be the maker's full name stamped in a rectangular punch or it might be just his initials, but either way, it is a great deal less trouble to forge these marks than those of an English Assay Office.

There is no simple way to gauge whether a marked piece is genuine. Comparison with the mark on an article known to be genuine by reason of its provenance can help to confirm the authenticity of a mark or to raise doubts about it. It is in the end largely a matter of experience, however; of establishing whether the marks look right – whether they have been punched where one would expect, whether the silver looks new or has the patina and wear appropriate to a piece that is 200 years old.

There are three main ways to fake silver with American marks. The first is to make a copy of something that one would expect to find made in the Colonial or Federal periods and stamp it with a fake punch, thus making an out-and-out fake. The second is to take a piece of English silver of the period, erase the hallmarks and add an American maker's mark with a forged punch. This is rather more difficult to detect than the first deception as the piece will be authentic in every detail of style, wear and patina. The third is to find a beaten-up but perfectly genuine American spoon, cut out its mark and solder it into a larger piece; a thin line of solder can, however, usually be seen when this has been done. (See page 119 for an example of a "let-in" mark.)

Wrong attribution of marks is another possibility. There is a not inconsiderable amount of antique English silver stamped with a maker's mark only. Such items, judged by their style alone, could often have been produced in either the United States or Britain. If found in the United States, it is a natural assumption that they are American until proved otherwise – an assumption that may be made innocently or by turning a blind eye.

The Safeguard

Whereas in theory American silver was wide open to abuse, in practice there is a powerful safeguard. It is that comparatively little silver was produced in the United States during the Colonial period. Most of it is now in major

◄ **George II bullet teapot**
Bullet-shaped teapots are rare
and fairly important objects
and at one time this teapot,
bearing only the maker's mark
"S.B." was optimistically
believed to have been made
by Stephen Burdett in
New York about 1730.

Apart from the fact that
it could be shown quite
unequivocally that the mark
was in fact that of Samson
Bennett, and therefore the
teapot was made in Falmouth,
Devon, the bellflower motif
from which the spout springs
is entirely typical of Exeter/
Plymouth/Falmouth.

collections and has been carefully scrutinized and recorded. An unrecorded
piece coming on the market would be noticed immediately and would
need, if it was not authentic, to be a very good fraud indeed if it was to get
past the expert assessment it would undoubtedly receive. Despite the close
regulation of silver in Britain it would probably be easier to get rid of a
dubious piece of 18th-century English silver than of its exact counterpart
from, say, Boston, simply because it could be buried in yet another routine
sale of antique silver.

Proper Attribution

Silver should not be assessed from its mark alone – nor should the mark or
marks be the first thing you look at, for they can prejudice a more balanced
judgment. The overall design should be the first aspect to consider, followed
by condition and then the details of decoration.

In the matter of design, the student of American silver has some interesting
and subtle problems to contend with. New England silver of the 17th century –
to all intents and purposes Boston silver – is instantly recognizable to someone
who is familiar with English silver of the period. Many of the 24 goldsmiths
working in Boston in 1680 had served their apprenticeship in London and
they brought on their apprentices in the same tradition. Not only were they
London trained, but as well as making silver themselves, they regularly
imported pieces from London, as many extant bills and letters prove.

◄ **A coffee pot by Joseph and Nathaniel
Richardson, Philadelphia, c.1790**
Whereas it is true that American silversmiths
were following English patterns closely, there
were on occasion time lags, of which this is one.
The Rococo outline and very Rococo spout of
this example would have been considered
dreadfully outmoded in London at this date.

Note that with the exception of the
contemporary initials the pot is left entirely
plain and unchased, as one would expect.

▲ **A three-piece tea service by Asa Blansett of Dumfries, Virginia, c.1800**
Though there would have been differences with a London-made tea service, this does show an American goldsmith working in a pretty much up-to-the-minute design as opposed to the coffee pot by the Richardsons on page 135. American examples such as this can be either plain or bright-cut.

The prosperity of the Colonies meant more work for silversmiths, and they established themselves in many New England towns, such as Newport and Providence, Rhode Island; New Haven and Hartford, Connecticut; Ipswich, Massachusetts; and many others. From the end of the 17th century the great city of Philadelphia was supporting a large number of goldsmiths, pre-eminent among them the first members of the Richardson dynasty. Outside New York, all these smiths were working in current English styles.

New York was a law unto itself. The names of smiths alone give one a good idea of what to expect: Cornelius van der Burch, Jacobus van der Spiegel, Cornelius Kierstede and Peter van Dyck were making items as closely patterned on Dutch models as the Richardsons' work resembled that of London goldsmiths. The descendants of these same smiths, however, were within a couple of generations succumbing to the fashion for English silver that dominated New England, but at the end of the 17th century and during the early years of the 18th, two styles were in production contemporaneously and were sold alongside virtually identical imported wares.

As the 18th century progressed links with London remained strong, but certain features became characteristic of American silver and helped to differentiate it from English wares. The lions rampant and angel-head terminals applied to New York tankards and to the pierced galleries of the

▶ **A tankard by John Coney, Boston, c.1690.**
A fine example of Coney's work. Note especially the cherub's head on the handle terminal: this feature is particularly American and very rare on English-made tankards. The position of the mark is also informative. American-made tankards, mugs and cream jugs are usually marked on the left of the handle, while English-made pieces are almost invariably marked on the right. If an example turns up bearing a maker's mark only and punched to the right of the handle, make doubly sure that it is not English of provincial make.

The cherub's head terminal is typically American.

The maker's mark of John Coney appears on the left of the handle – an American characteristic.

vase-shaped sugar bowls of the Neo-classical period are just two examples. Forms changed too – witness the unusually large (not to say enormous) Philadelphia coffee pots of the late 18th and early 19th centuries.

Porringers

For some reason, there is one object made in Colonial and indeed in Federal America that steadfastly maintained its popularity despite its demise in England early in the 18th century – the single-handled porringer. Quite what these porringers were for is a matter for heated debate and various convictions; what is certain is that they were not bleeding bowls as they are frequently called in England.

Large numbers of American-made porringers are marked only on the handle. This raises the possibility of removing a handle, taking several casts from it, making several more bowls and multiplying at a stroke the number of early porringers without undue difficulty. Marks that have been cast rather than punched tend to show a certain roughness, however; a slight pitting to the background can be seen with a glass, whereas a punch leaves a cleaner impression.

The 19th Century

The tendency to establish an indigenous style that was asserting itself in the latter part of the 18th century was disrupted in the first few decades of the 19th. After the split with Britain it was natural that there should be some dissociation from English models, and this was accompanied by a leaning towards France in its Empire and post-Empire periods. This quasi-French style was not altogether successful, however, and rarely poses possibilities of confusion between French models and American adaptations of them. The style shows at its best in New York, but even there it was relatively heavy, lumpish and derivative.

From this period on, errors of attribution (and the possibilities of

▲ **A single-handled porringer by Samuel Casey, Kingstown, Rhode Island, c.1760**
The late date clearly demonstrates the extraordinarily long survival of these objects in America, long after they had ceased to be made in England. Like so many American porringers, it is marked on the handle only.

▲ ▶ **A silver soup tureen on stand by Samuel Kirk and Son, Baltimore, c.1880**
These are excellent examples of the high quality of the chasers' art in the United States in the mid- and late 19th century. Samuel Kirk's output from the second decade of the 19th century showed the greatest strength, originality of design and superb quality of chasing.

deception) arising from confusion between Dutch, English and French originals and their American counterparts become less likely. In mid-century a great surge of both design and technical ability, particularly in New York and Baltimore, led to the creation of an emphatically American style. Led by Joseph Kirk of Baltimore, it reflected the European Rococo Revival and exhibited a marked penchant for robustly chased and cast work decorated with complex Classical architectural scenes. The enormous American water jug probably came into style at this time. The lavishness of their decoration, together with the size of many of the more distinguished examples of this period, mean that these pieces are unlikely to be fraudulently reproduced or made up.

Later in the 19th century both Tiffany and Gorham were responsible for a great deal of silver and base metal work made in the Aesthetic taste; their forays into Art Nouveau were equally successful. This period of silversmithing in America has been ignored by collectors until relatively recently, when there was a dramatic surge of interest, with price increases to match. American silver of this period is arguably better made and more innovative than at any other, the technical skill displayed being some protection against faking.

Alterations

A besetting problem in English silver, alterations can be made for reasons of innocent expediency or to enhance prices. The kinds of alteration to be found on American silver are, necessarily, similar to those effected on English silver: tankards to jugs, for example (see page 121).

While pieces of American silver that have been altered at some time in the past exist, it becomes progressively less likely that alterations will be made now or in the future. Authentic items from the 18th century now fetch such high prices that they will be preserved as they are, which incidentally means that the would-be "improver" has to pay a fortune for his raw material and is therefore most unlikely to be able to make a profit from his work.

▶ **Later decoration**
This relatively modest cream pitcher (near right) by John Bayley of Philadelphia, c.1770, is a perfect candidate for enhancement by later (19th- or even early 20th-century) decoration. Most American cream pitchers of this period are plain but a number of them have been chased to bring them "up to date" in the 19th century. That is not to say, however, that one does not occasionally find a genuinely chased example as can be seen on the pot (far right), made by Joseph Richardson, Sr., of Philadelphia, c.1760.

AMERICAN MARKS

In the USA there are no mandatory marks, unlike England. However, makers customarily stamped wares with their own marks, and the shapes of the enclosures around these marks can help with dating:

- End 17thC – shield/quatrefoil/ trefoil/heart
- Early 18thC – oval/circle
- Mid-18thC – cartouches
- By 1800 – rectangles
- Early 19thC – banners/lunettes/ simple intaglios

In parallel with alterations to the form of pieces, a great deal of relatively plain American silver was chased up in the mid-19th century with fruit and flowers. This was done merely to update pieces and with no intent to deceive, but the embellishment can be so obtrusive as to render the qualities of the original invisible.

Training the Eye

Because of the way that American silver developed – at first in close imitation of two European styles, then developing a domestic identity but remaining open to foreign influence – authentication by style alone can be quite difficult. The marking system is of value, but it leaves much unsaid. There is, accordingly, no substitute for looking at lots of silver and developing a feel for what is authentically American.

A knowledgeable dealer is the best assistant and protection a collector can have, for he or she will assist with their knowledge and protect with their reputation. Excellent collections, such as those at Boston, Yale, the Metropolitan Museum and Winterthur, to mention but a few, were formed to inform and should be used accordingly. The third and indispensable source of experience is books, both the catalogues of major collections and more discursive works, a few of which are mentioned in the Bibliography.

Pottery & Porcelain

Today no-one would regard a Bow blue-and-white copy of a Chinese or Japanese exportware plate as "fake"; nor would they regard a Qianlong crackle-glazed Guan dish copying a Song Imperial original as a "forgery". We use these words "fake" and "forgery" when discussing deceptive 19th- and 20th-century copies of earlier pieces, yet there was almost certainly less interest in the differences between Chinese and Japanese or Chelsea and Bow in the 17th and 18th centuries. Such niceties were the province of an extremely small group of cognoscenti, a circle including such celebrated collectors as the Duchess of Portland and Lord Holland.

Manufacturers recognized that their customers were for the most part concerned with what was fashionable, whether in the Chinese or the Meissen style, and that utilitarian qualities were of secondary importance. As long as the "china" looked right and up-to-the-minute, that was sufficient. Although a few manufacturers, such as Derby, chose Meissen as their criterion, most chose Chinese porcelain, as can be seen from the patent applied for in 1744 by Thomas Frye and Edward Heylyn. These gentlemen wished to make "a certain material whereby a ware might be made of the same nature or kind, and equal to, if not exceeding in goodness and beauty, China or Porcelain ware imported from abroad". In this enterprise they eventually succeeded, but in some cases they also attempted to copy a Chinese reign mark as additional evidence of authenticity.

The First Fakes

Faking porcelain – as opposed to merely copying or working in a particular style – probably began in the late 18th century, when Paris enamellers purchased large quantities of Sèvres porcelain, painted them in the factory style and added the conventional interlaced "L" marks. Such specimens are everywhere and this has led to some erratic attribution, since the bodies are perfectly "right" and the enamels and gilding can be very good. Some of the

▼ **An authentic late 16th-century Isnik tankard**

Decorated in a typically bold palette under a brilliant transparent glaze. Both Cantagalli in Florence and Samson in Paris produced copies of this kind of ware.

◄ **A copy of a late 16th-century Isnik tankard**

It probably came from the Cantagalli workshop but the mark (normally a singing cockerel) has been deliberately gouged out of the base (see page 158). It should probably be designated a fake rather than a mere copy as it has been altered to enhance its desirability.

The painting is weak and lacks detail when compared with the original.

A typical European tin-glaze unlike the brilliant glaze of its model.

The palette is less bold – the green is too grey and the blue is a rather sticky-looking ultramarine.

A fake Toby jug, late 19th century
A lead-glazed copy of an 18th-century "The Squire" Toby Jug. The turquoise jacket is a colour that was never used. The translucent off-white crackled glaze is not blue enough compared to the original.

Sèvres blanks were bought by Thomas Martin Randall of London and Madeley, who also decorated them in the factory style. A few examples of Randall's work have in the past proved good enough to be displayed in a major museum as factory-decorated Sèvres.

The advent of the Industrial Revolution and the consequent redistribution of wealth among the expanding middle classes created a demand for both antique and fashionable china such as Sèvres. Since supplies of old porcelain and pottery were limited, factories such as Merkelbach and Schiffer in Germany, Samson in France and Cantagalli and Doccia in Italy catered for the demand by producing very deceptive copies. Some of these pieces appear not to have been marked, or if they were marked, the marks have since been removed in order to deceive (see page 158).

With continuing demand for rare items in the late 19th and early 20th centuries, forgers had a field day. In porcelain and pottery, connoisseurshop was in its infancy, as can be seen by contemporary publications such as W. W. R. Spelman's *Lowestoft China*, in which the author illustrates at least 60 items which are not from the Lowestoft factory. This does not mean that collectors were ignorant of the faker's art. There are also many references to dubious pieces. Captain Price, for example, in his *Astbury, Whieldon, and Ralph Wood Figures and Toby Jugs*, published in 1922, refers to the many fakes of the "Squire" toby jug.

In the field of English pottery, the 1920s were arguably the most active years for the forger. One of the most celebrated cases is that of the Astbury or Astbury-Whieldon figures and groups, which began to appear towards the end of the decade. Such figures were then, as now, very expensive collectors' pieces and would naturally merit the attention of the forger. In 1929 Herbert Read wrote, "I am not acquainted with any forgeries of the Asbury-Whieldon type. The delicately coloured glaze would not be easy to imitate." But they were imitated. As Ross Taggart observed in his article in *The Arts Quarterly*, "It would seem that it was at virtually this precise moment

A pair of fake Astbury-Whieldon figures
As prices for this type of piece rocketed, they have come to the attention of the fraudster. The originals are modelled with more detail and character than these forgeries. Here the bases have been simplified too much. On the right-hand figure the glaze is too glassy, resembling melted chocolate!

► **A forged horse and rider, "Tang dynasty"**

This was a forgery made c.1900 in China. As the railways were driven across China numerous tombs were discovered. The excavated figures and pottery became popular in the West and consequently an industry grew up in China to satisfy this demand. The forgers had the benefit of original moulds and local clays were readily available. New figures were created from broken fragments (which can cause false readings in thermoluminescence tests unless several samples are taken), and the "new" composite figures now have a century of wear on them. The main clue to this example's lineage is the over-emphasized facial features. Quality of the forgeries does vary and the modelling can be very stiff compared to the originals.

▲ **An authentic Tang dynasty horse and rider**

The modelling is much more expressive and lively compared to the fake.

▲ **A pair of early 20th-century copies of Wei dynasty tomb figures**

Soon after tomb figures first reached the West at the beginning of the 20th century, forgers both in China and Europe took the opportunity to replicate the simpler unglazed types such as these. At first these forgeries fooled many collectors who had little experience with early pottery, but eventually they were detected by comparison with genuine excavated pieces. The copies are generally stiffly modelled and heavier in construction, although some are good enough to require a thermoluminescence test to confirm a late date. Tang pottery is made of a pinkish buff clay but Wei is almost black. These figures are made of a coarse red brick-like material cunningly covered in black slip.

that the forgeries began to appear."

In a saleroom on 4 June 1931, three Astbury figures and a pew group marked "Wedgwood" were entered as lots 66 to 69, "The property of a Collector". All sold well and no-one was suspicious, that is until the following year. Ross Taggart writes, "When these were first known, they were in no way suspected by the leading auctioneers, reputable dealers, and discriminating collectors. It was Mr Kiddell (of Sotheby's) who first began to doubt them in the light of another pew group that was shown to him and was undoubtedly wrong. When this was brought to the attentions of Messrs Rackham, Honey and Elliot, the "Wedgwood" pew group was still passed as genuine. It was only with the appearance of the "Wood" piece that the true character of both became apparent."

It was also around this time that the first pieces of Tang tomb pottery arrived in Europe, and within less than five years the forgers were busy not only replicating this period but Sui and Wei pottery as well. Without the benefit of thermoluminescence testing, attribution, especially of the unglazed figures, must have been extremely difficult. It was A. J. B. Kiddell again who managed to ferret out the duds from the genuine. For his pains he was presented in 1923 with a specially commissioned fake of a Wei pottery equestrian figure which is currently stabled in Sotheby's celebrated "Black Museum".

Spurious Marks

The use of spurious marks was widespread. In England the Meissen crossed swords mark was copied or parodied by Worcester, Bow, Longton Hall, Lowestoft and Champion's Bristol in the 18th century, and by Derby and Minton in the early 19th century. In France the interlaced "L"s of Sèvres and the "VP" monogram of the Marseilles factory were universally abused, doubtless for commercial gain. The Meissen crossed swords were copied by a large number of minor Thuringian factories in the late 18th century and 19th century.

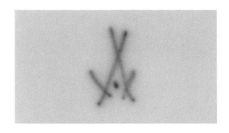

▲ **A genuine Meissen mark**
This example is slightly unusual as the dot was only included 1764–73.

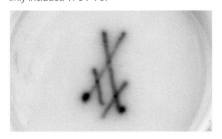

▲ **A Chinese copy of a Meissen mark**
This mark of underglaze-blue crossed swords appears on a Chinese copy, *c.*1850, of a Meissen yellow ground tea bowl, itself copying Japanese Kakiemon designs of *c.*1830. It is clear that marks cannot be relied on to identify a piece.

▲ **A genuine Xuande mark**
Reign marks were used more frequently in the Xuande period (1426–35).

▲ **A modern forgery of a Xuande mark from Taiwan or South Korea**
The Xuande mark is badly drawn and too large. The stiff decoration should also ring alarm bells.

Reign Marks

The situation as far as Chinese and Japanese porcelains are concerned is quite different. Few pieces of Chinese porcelain or pottery made prior to the 15th century bear reign marks and those that do should be viewed with great circumspection. It was not until the early 15th century that the practice of inscribing the imperial wares of Jingdezhen with the reign mark was adopted.

There is only a small number of pieces with the mark of Yongle (1403–1424); it was during the reign of Xuande (1426–35) that the number increased dramatically. These marks were usually written in underglaze blue enclosed within a double circle or more rarely a double square (the Japanese, incidentally, almost invariably used only a single circle). Towards the end of the 15th century we see retrospective marks for the first time, when a small group of slightly provincial-looking wares were given the mark of Xuande.

During the 16th century the sanctity of the reign mark or *nien hao* was generally observed, although copies of Xuande marks appear during the reign of Zhengde (1506–1521) but the second half of the century saw the advent of non-imperial marks. These include the use of dedicatory inscriptions, so-called "shop" marks, or even an animal such as a hare. In the 17th century the use of previous reign marks was commonplace, particularly the use of the six-character mark of Chenghua (1465–87) during the reign of Kangxi (1662–1722). Ironically it is Kangxi's reign mark that appears most frequently on late 19th- and early 20th-century exportware. The ubiquitous ginger jars painted with prunus blossom on a cracked-ice ground will, if marked at all, nine times out of ten bear his four- or six-reign characters. These are sometimes sold through Liberty & Co. in London.

Another way of writing the reign mark is the use of stylized characters arranged within a square seal. This is rather like using capital letters as opposed to normal handwriting and we are therefore faced with much greater difficulty in ascribing pieces. A thorough understanding of the idiosyncrasies of each reign mark or seal is vital for sorting out the right from the wrong. One of the best guides is the section on marks in Sir Harry Garner's *Oriental Blue and White*.

The Japanese never employed a similar system of reign marks on their own porcelain. Instead they used a series of devices denoting "good luck". They did, however, copy Chinese reign marks from the late 17th to the early 19th centuries, mainly those of the Ming emperors, Chenghua and Xuande. In the latter half of the 19th century any marks on Japanese porcelain will generally refer to the area or the potter but not to the emperor.

Methods of Dating

Every piece of pottery and porcelain possesses certain characteristics which identify it or relate it to a particular group or species. These groups or types have been located and identified by various methods, and each grouping is based on an accumulation of evidence garnered from many sources.

In the first place, crucial archaeological evidence has been produced by excavations of the Imperial Chinese tombs. Certainly until the early Ming dynasty most artefacts discovered in the burial chamber were more or less contemporary with the emperors' reigns.

▼ **A late Ming *kraakporselein* dish, *c*.1640**

The blue is strong.

The decoration is under the glaze.

We have also gained as much in recent years from marine archaeology: for example, from the expedition in 1976 to excavate the wreck of the Dutch East Indiaman, the *Witte Leeuw*, which sank on 3 June 1614 after her powder magazine exploded during an engagement with a Portuguese carrack off the island of St Helena. Among the cargo of this vessel was a consignment of contemporary Chinese export porcelain or *kraakporselein*, as it has been termed since. As this type of porcelain is never marked, the haul gave us an invaluable key to dating.

Many examples of similar *kraakporselein* and also of the "Transitional" family are found in old Dutch still-life paintings; this again helps with dating. Another important source is factory records listing what they manufactured and sold, such as those of Meissen, Sèvres and Chelsea.

Contemporary accounts of visits to factories are for the most part too vague to be of much use in identifying exact forms or objects, but they can give an insight into conditions or current fashion. The visit to the manufactory at St Cloud by Martin Lister, court physician to William III, gives an account of the earliest French porcelain and a comparison with the Chinese variety.

Inscriptions on ceramics can often provide confirmation of origin and date, although it is salutary to remember that the celebrated Percival David Foundation vases had both date (AD 1315) and locality. These were presented to the temple at Hu-Quin-i, just over 100km/60 miles from their place of manufacture, Jingdezhen, but before World War II they were considered by most authorities to be wrong on the grounds of their complexity and sophistication. Now, however, they are accepted for what they are, namely the earliest and most important specimens of Chinese blue and white.

▼ **A 1950s copy of a Chinese *kraakporselein* dish**

The decoration has been produced by a half-tone transfer process – the dots can be clearly seen.

Unlike the original, the reverse has no decoration.

The dish is too heavily potted.

Plain circular rims are never seen on genuine Kraak dishes. Here the rim is very clean and rounded. An original dish will always be chipped.

The blue is too pale and the half-tone to produce washes of colour all too apparent.

The design has been redrawn from an original and is therefore stiff and lacking spontaneity.

Inscriptions

In Urbino, the great maiolica *istoriato* school of painters occasionally signed, dated and located their pieces. In the Wallace Collection in London there is a bowl painted with the descent of Orpheus into Hades and inscribed on the reverse "1152 Alla Carothea Cimba arriva Orpheo" (Orpheus arrives at the boat of Charon); underneath the title is the signature of Francesco Xanto Avelli of Rovigo in the duchy of Urbino, the most important centre for such descriptive or *istoriato* wares. This is written in the distinctive manner of the Renaissance with all the spontaneity one expects from any individual's hand. The Cantagalli or Doccia copyists of the 19th and early 20th centuries were incapable of reproducing this feel and can be exposed from their handwriting alone. There is a lot to be learned from examining maiolica in museums and noting any inscriptions, for it is often on the apparently less important details such as handwriting that the faker comes to grief.

English delftware potters, who on the whole worked for a less aristocratic public than the porcelain manufacturers, inscribed pieces with references to topical events or causes such as the Popish Plot, Admiral Vernon's victory at Portobello or even an election issue. In some cases there are inscriptions of a localized nature which would indicate the probable source, such as the punchbowl painted with the Swedish ship *Wigelantia* and a reference to her docking at Bristol in 1765. But when a piece bears the name of a town, it does not necessarily mean that it was made there, as can be seen from all those little Goss commemorative pieces or the German tourist trinkets with "A present from Brighton" on them. We are on firmer ground, however, when inscribed pieces can be related to shards unearthed at a particular kiln-site.

These identifying features are quite literally and irrevocably baked into the piece. This separates pottery and porcelain from most other materials in that it cannot be altered without seriously affecting its appearance. In contrast, the mahogany from a Georgian linen press can be used to make up an entirely different object. Many years ago I watched a restorer fulfilling an order from a client who had brought in a Hepplewhite dining chair which he wished to have copied in sufficient numbers to complete a set of 12. This same restorer related with some humour how he used to recognize many of his own and other craftsmen's fakes when paying one of his periodic visits to the London auction houses. Similarly with bronzes, oil paintings or silver, it is possible to rework a piece with varying degrees of success.

The greatest difficulty in identification is experienced with the simplest types of unglazed pottery and porcelain, for one has to rely entirely on the appearance of the material and the form of the object. The difference between French biscuit porcelain and Victorian Parian china is not always clear to everyone. Many northern European white tin-glazed wares pose a major problem to experts.

The more complicated a piece, the easier it is to attribute. A glazed and decorated piece says a great deal more about itself than an unglazed one, for it is not just a skeleton, it also has skin colouring and fingerprints. Every factory or type uses a glaze and a range of colours which together serve as this unique fingerprint. To consider solely the appearance of the glaze is extremely hazardous, since certain factories are quite similar. Ludwigsburg and Zurich for example, often have a pronounced smoky ivory appearance, which isolates them from their rivals at Frankenthal and Hochst, but they

▲ **A 19th-century Italian maiolica drug pot, a copy of a 17th- or 18th-century Savona drug jar**
These early wares are noted for the casual but freely drawn animals and flowers on a soft opaque white ground. This later copy is very stiff and unnatural and the glaze has an uncharacteristic glassiness.

▲ **A hard-paste porcelain fake of a Zurich plate, late 19th or early 20th century**
Zurich porcelain of the 1760s is distinguished by the smoky yellowish-grey glaze, often peppered with tiny pinholes. The paste is greyish white with the texture of fine sand which can discolour, rather like early Bow. Infrequently, kiln-grit adheres to the edge of the footrim or base. The flower painting can be extremely fine, the quality akin to Strasbourg *fleurs fines*, but usually pieces are similar to Ludwigsburg bread-and-butter wares. The manufacturer's mark – a "Z" with a horizontal line through it – would date it 1763–92, though the form is not recorded in Zurich porcelain during this period. The creamy, glassy-looking porcelain and slightly warmer enamels indicate its late date.

▲ Identifying marks

The "spur" marks seen here are typical of Chelsea but this technique was not used by other English factories.

can cause some confusion between themselves. One is therefore obliged to use other criteria in order to solve the problem.

The colours or enamels used on most pottery and porcelain are made from different metallic oxides, such as antimony, cobalt, copper, iron or manganese, which one might imagine should produce similar results anywhere, but they don't. For example, William Cookworthy of Plymouth achieved a strange mushroom pink quite unlike any other contemporary pigment. Some factories had enormous difficulties firing or fixing certain colours and as a result only used them sparingly.

Methods of Manufacture

Just as the glaze and colours differ from one place to another or from time to time in the same location, so too the methods of manufacture can help us with classification. Chelsea porcelain wares, for example, are fired on small spurs, usually three, located on the base inside the foot, a method similar to that operated by the Arita potters but not used at other English factories. Factories used different methods of casting; Bow preferred to model by press-moulding, whereas Chelsea and Longton Hall use the slip-casting process. Press-moulding is the use of soft clay pushed by hand or with a tool into the various moulds which form the elements of the figure or group. This process usually means that the figure will be more heavily constructed than one made by the slip-casting method. The latter entails the filling of the main mould which forms the torso (and perhaps a leg or supporting tree-stump) with liquid clay or slip. This watery clay is left to dry out until there is a sufficient thickness of it on the interior wall of the mould to make the figure. The limbs of the figure, however, are still made by press-moulding.

Most Continental hard-paste porcelains are slip-cast, and a Bow model with an anchor and dagger mark which has been made by this method should be treated with much circumspection.

▼ A Sèvres later-decorated dish

This dish is probably a blank Sèvres original *c.*1770 but decorated in England *c.*1850–60. The painting is based on an original by François Boucher and was much copied in England, first by Thomas Askew of Derby and then by other factories. This highly-decorated design is truer to the French original.

▲ Detail of fake Sèvres mark found on dish

Although this piece was an original Sèvres blank, the mark is fake.

▼ **A genuine English delftware bottle with a fake date added later**

A large number of fakes of English delftware were made in the 1920s and '30s. Some were direct copies of rare or early specimens, while others were perfectly genuine pieces "tricked out" or faked to enhance their desirability. This wine bottle is an example of the latter. It is a "right" mid-17th-century vessel which, without a title and date, would be fairly unexceptional. However, the addition of the word "Sack" and the date changes that. After the lettering has been added the piece has been refired. In order to refire a pot successfully, it is necessary to dry it out in a warm oven over an extended period. If this is not done a sudden rise in temperature will cause the long-trapped moisture in or immediately below the glaze to expand too rapidly and explode through the surface as has happened here. This is an extreme case; the usual manifestation of refiring is a speckled or "peppered" effect.

The word "Sack" has been written in a totally unconvincing childlike manner.

The scroll or flourish beneath the date is hesitant and confused.

The numerous craters in the glaze are typical of refired pieces.

Methods of Faking

Among the tricks practised by forgers is the decoration or redecoration of genuine ware. In post-revolutionary France a great quantity of porcelain was sold off from the Sèvres factory to Paris porcelain decorators. They were then painted in the manner of early Sèvres and suitable date letters and artists' marks were added to give them a little more authenticity. These pieces still cause tremendous problems today.

Another method of faking was by "skinning", or removing the enamelled decoration from an ordinary piece of right porcelain and enhancing it with a rarer or more sought-after pattern. A recent case in point was that of a plate apparently from the celebrated Sèvres "Du Barry" service. It was not until this specimen was viewed quite accidentally in a slanting beam of afternoon sunlight that the outline of a previous design could be detected. Instead of realizing several thousand pounds at auction, it was sold for a mere hundred or two. This technique was also used before World War II to great effect by Chinese dealers who redecorated genuine reign-marked period pieces with more interesting or costly designs.

This deception of over-decorating or "clobbering" was used extensively on First Period Worcester porcelain to transmogrify mundane vessels by adding one of the highly desirable coloured grounds, especially claret or apple-green. These faked or "tricked out" pieces can usually be detected by the tell-tale black speckling on the foot or base (see page 180).

In the late 19th century plain white English delftware wine bottles greatly outnumbered inscribed pieces; today the situation is completely reversed. There have been less than a handful on the market within the past 50 years and consequently prices for pure white bottles are very high indeed. It is worth remembering what A. H. Church wrote in *English Earthenware*, published in 1884: "Of the wine jugs a large number of pint and half-pint are extant. Some of these are plain, but many are inscribed not only with the names of the wine they were intended to contain, but also with the date of their manufacture (or possibly the date of bottling) ... However, there are many similar wine-pots of different sizes but perfectly plain." What happened to these "many perfectly plain" bottles is perhaps explained by another quote, this time from G. E. Howard's *Early English Drug Jars*, published in 1931. "... John Hodgkin told me that his father maintained that in his day genuine plain Lambeth jars were exported to France or Holland, where inscriptions, dates or coats-of-arms were painted upon them, after which they were re-fired. He even asserted that he recognized actual specimens, which he had seen bought in sales by a certain individual, in their original, undecorated state, and which, after a short period, reappeared on the market richly decorated." Some authorities, however, held that it would be impossible to reglaze a jar in this manner. According to A. J. B. Kiddell this was precisely the sort of faking carried out by Gautier, the English delftware authority, who may well have been "the certain individual" mentioned by Hodgkin.

Another, but much more unusual, trick is to lute the base of an old but presumably broken vessel to a later vase. Some years ago I was completely taken in by two mirror-black vases which had been treated this way. Fortunately this kind of forgery is rare, as one would have to find vases and bases of similar dimensions in order to perform a convincing transplant. However, it serves to make the point that anything is possible!

ORIENTAL PORCELAIN

Chinese porcelain was probably first produced in identifiable form during the 8th century AD. The earliest pieces are the northern white wares, similar to the Xingyao type which have been excavated at Samarra, together with locally made copies in the Persian Gulf.

During the Northern Song dynasty (960–1127) white wares were further developed in the province of Hopei, where a semi-translucent proto-porcelain called Ding-yao was made. This ware is distinguished by the warm ivory tone of the glaze, which tends to appear a greenish or even honey colour when it pools or dribbles. A characteristic of this ware also shared with the later Yingqing type is that dishes and bowls were fired upside down, leaving an unglazed rim which is then frequently bound with copper.

Both the Ding-yao and Yingqing wares are mainly based on flower forms or lobed seed pods and are either decorated by moulding or with carving. The Yingqing type differs from Ding ware in that the glaze is a soft pale blue-green: the term Yingqing translates as "misty blue". It is from the latter type of porcelain and the closely related Shufu ware that the first blue and

▼ **A late 14th-century dish decorated in underglaze copper red**

The reddishness of the unglazed portion of the dish is characteristic of early Ming porcelain. Qing wares (those from the late 17th century onwards) are generally white or grey, but if they do oxidize a little, it will be to a brown or honey colour rather than this strong russet. Qing wares are also covered in a glaze of uniform depth: the Kangxi period (1662–1722), for example, is noteworthy for its thinness and pure white colour. In porcelains of the late 14th and early 15th centuries such as this dish, the glaze is generally thicker and bubbled, with the result that It looks slightly bluish or greenish and any underglaze decoration can sometimes look blurred or out of focus. The glaze was rarely applied evenly and this led to pooling and dribbling, which can be seen more clearly at an oblique angle under strong light.

▶ **A forgery of a Chinese Song Dynasty Yingqing Dish, *c.*1920s**

Yingqing came to the notice of collectors in the West at the beginning of the 20th century. Small quantities were available but the shortage of material was boosted by forgeries made in China. The key-fret border on this one has an Art Deco feel about it. As with many forgeries the perpetrator has been unable to resist the temptation of over-statement. The bowl is rounded rather than straight-sided and too deep. The most obvious clue, though, is the depth of the relief moulding.

The relief moulding is too clumsy and heavy. The original Song piece, when moulded in this thickness, would be a lot crisper.

Unglazed areas have burned orange in the firing, a more common characteristic of the Yuan porcelain.

The blue-green glaze is too intense in tone.

▶ **An early 15th-century ewer of Islamic metal form.**
Early 15th-century blue and white is epitomized in the perfect balance of design and form in this pear-shaped ewer. Note the blackish areas on the blue decoration. This is where the pigment has been applied thickly and has burnt in firing. The effect is known as "heaped and piled" and was copied with little success by Chinese potters of the 18th century.

▲ **A Ming "Chicken" cup of the Chenghua period (1465–87), painted in *doucai* enamels**
These very rare cups are regarded by many as the finest wares produced during the Ming dynasty.

▲ **A copy of a Chenghua *doucai* "Chicken" cup made during the Kangxi period (1662–1722)**
The Emperor Kangxi encouraged not only the development of new glazes and techniques but also the revival of the classic wares of the Song and Ming dynasties.

white evolved in the early 14th century. The earliest pieces of blue and white – and, for that matter, of copper-red – are composed of exactly similar paste and glaze, and the forms such as cuboid vessels, oil jars and double-gourd pourers and bowls occur in Yingqing, Shufu and in blue and red decorated pieces. This entire group of vessels, although much less sophisticated, is nevertheless akin to the pair of blue-and-white vases dated 1351 in the Percival David Foundation in London.

The David vases are the cornerstone of our understanding of early blue and white and are in turn related to a large number of vessels and dishes in Middle Eastern collections such as those in the Topkapi Sarayi Museum in Istanbul and at the Ardebil Shrine in Iran. The close trading ties between China under the Mongol Yuan dynasty and the Islamic world is underlined by the cross-pollination of form and design in the 14th century. These wares often follow Middle Eastern metal forms and are perhaps slightly more crowded than those of the succeeding Ming dynasty.

The spacious style of the reigns of Yongle (1403–24) and Xuande (1426–35) was developed further and reached its apogee during the reign of Chenghua (1465–87). This period is regarded by many connoisseurs as the finest in Chinese porcelain, and the celebrated "Palace" bowls and the *doucai* (a palette of soft contrasting colours) "Chicken" cups are brilliant examples, which later Chinese potters of the Kangxi period (1662–1722) strove to copy (see left). A characteristic of this reign was the purity of the blue and the definite smoky ivory colour of the glaze, which is impossible to distinguish in an illustration but is quite clear when a piece is juxtaposed with one from any other period.

The 16th century was probably the watershed in the history of Chinese porcelain. The reigns of Hongzhi (1488–1505) and Zhengde (1506–1521) witnessed the changeover from the 15th-century tradition to the looser style which prevailed for most of the 16th century. The most attractive wares of

▲ A Yuan blue-and-white dish
The central theme is painted in a somewhat chaotic manner, with vegetation issuing from all points towards the centre. The idea of an axial arrangement in designs appeared mainly towards the end of the Yuan (c.1360s) period and into the early Ming period.

the Zhengde period are brush-rests and utensils for the scholar's table, bearing either Arabic or Persian inscriptions. These were made for the Muslim eunuchs who effectively controlled the palace bureaucracy until they were themselves ejected by the succeeding Emperor Jiajing (1522–66).

Export Porcelain

In 1514, the Portuguese reached China and the first trade links were formed between China and Western Europe. Thereafter, specific orders for porcelain were placed by Portuguese officials and there are several examples of such ware in the Victoria and Albert Museum with European coats-of-arms or inscriptions. The deterioration in the quality of potting and brushwork can be traced to this period, although there are brilliant exceptions. The use of the vibrant purplish cobalt called "Mohammedan blue", which was mostly imported, is one of the distinguishing features of 16th- and some early 17th-century porcelain.

The increased demand for porcelain in the West led to a further decline in standards. Now, in order to speed up the process, the designs were broken up into compartments so that less skilled craftsmen could cope with the smaller elements of the overall pattern – the beginning of mass production. This ware is typified by poor throwing with much warping, and the undersides were thinly glazed and showed the contour lines. The Japanese copies of this *kraakporselein* made in Arita in the second half of the 17th century are more heavily potted, with no kiln-grit and no tendency to flake on the rim as the Chinese originals do.

▶ Ming Persian blue
The true Persian cobalt blue is deep and runny with a tendency to obliterate, or at least obscure, the design detail. Note that all the elements – the deer, pine, crane and prunus – signify longevity.

▼ **Typical late Ming** *style*
Both these pieces are good examples of
the late Ming compartmentalized style, with
extensive use of panels and geometric motifs.

Late Ming Wares

The late Ming reigns of Tianqi (1621–27) and Chongzhen (1628–44) are
noteworthy for two entirely distinct but attractive groups of porcelain.

The first type, called *kosometsuke* by the Japanese, for whom they were
intended, are freely drawn with sparse landscapes or with scholars meditating
on the bank of a tranquil lake. Others from this group for the Japanese market
are decorated with a combination of repeating diaper or patterns. Both these
types were liberally copied in Japan in the 19th and possibly even the early
20th century as well. As the Chinese wares are very similar in body, glaze
and kiln defects to the *kraakporselein* group, copies should present very little
difficulty.

The second type has been designated "Transitional" ware simply because
it overlaps the decaying Ming dynasty and the incoming Manchu or Qing
dynasty. This group is, in contrast to the slightly abandoned style of the
previous group, painted in a more controlled, academic style with figures in
idyllic cloud-wrapped rocky landscapes. Typical of this group is the use of
plantain and horizontal swirling clouds. The effect of grass is achieved by a
series of small crescent-shaped brush strokes, a method not used elsewhere.
Another characteristic which can easily be overlooked is the use of lightly
incised borders, appropriately termed *anhua* or "secret" decoration by the
Chinese. This group of highly refined export porcelain has been reproduced
within the last 15 or 20 years, using transfer-prints as well as hand-painted
designs. The results are flat and lifeless and should not prove troublesome.

Manchu or Quin Porcelain

The Manchu emperor Kangxi rebuilt the Imperial kilns after their destruction during the civil wars of the 1660s and '70s. As director, he appointed Ts'ang Ying-Hsuan, who proceeded to introduce a number of new monochromes and to revive techniques that had fallen into disuse. The "famille verte" palette was developed from the Ming *wucai,* or five-colour enamel group, in which green dominated. An important sub-division within this group was composed of the black ground wares naturally termed "famille noire", which were highly prized in the 19th century and which as a result were widely faked. There are a number of examples of the forger's art extant where perfectly genuine but commonplace Kangxi pieces have been "skinned", i.e. their glaze has been removed to be replaced by the much more costly "mirror-black" or famille-noire colours.

▶ **A late Ming *wucai* box of the Wanli period (1573–1620)**

Wucai translates as "five-colour". It is a bold palette which uses underglaze blue and several (but not necessarily five) other colours. The designs are generally more loosely drawn and less sophisticated than those executed in the *doucai* palette.

Wucai evolved in the late 17th century into the "famille verte" palette, in which overglaze blue was used rather than underglaze blue.

Comparing an 18th-century Famille-verte Vase with a 19th-century Copy

▶ **Two vases of similar styles**

The vase on the left is a genuine example of Kangxi (1662–1722) porcelain. The one on the right is a Samson copy of an early 18th-century Kangxi exportware original, made in Paris around 1900.

The paste is a good imitation.

The drawing is too crowded and stiff to be an original.

The blue enamel on a 17th- or 18th-century piece produces an halation akin to oil on water on the surrounding glaze which is not normally seen on later examples or copies.

▲ ▶ **English porcelain copying Chinese**
All the European factories copied the Chinese decoration and palette. The Bow dish above is copying the Chinese style seen in these Qianlong "famille-rose" baluster jars.

▲ **A "famille-rose" Nine Peach vase of the Qianlong period (1735–95) decorated in the Chinese taste.**
These wares were made for the domestic market and were not intended for export.

New monochromes appeared, including mirror-black, "clair-de-lune", apple-green and the so-called "peach-bloom". All these monochromes were copied extensively in China during the 19th century but the copies invariably lack the finesse of the original. "Famille rose", a more sophisticated palette which naturally uses pink enamel, was introduced at the end of his reign. Rose pink ("purple of Cassius"), derived from colloidal gold, was originally formulated by Andreas Cassius of Leyden in about 1650. It was first used on German faience in the 1680s before appearing on Chinese porcelain towards the end of Kangxi's reign. By this time Europeans were placing orders not only for conventional blue-and-white and polychrome porcelains but also for services with their own coats-of-arms. These services often included hollow wares based on contemporary European silver or ceramic shapes and copies of such pieces were made in the 19th and early 20th centuries by Samson of Paris.

▲ **Typical monochromes of the Qianlong period, *c.*1736–95.**
Cobalt blue and *Sang du Boeuf* are typical colours.

During the reign of Yongzheng (1723–35) several other glazes were introduced such as "robin's egg", "tea-dust", sapphire blue and a variety of red souffle glazes, but it was the revival of the fine celadon wares of the Song dynasty for which this reign is perhaps most noted.

The following reign of Qianlong (1736–95) at first saw a few new types, but there was still a dominance of retrospective design. It was during both this and the preceding reign that a number of copies and pastiches (see below) of early blue-and-white vases and ewers were made. The Yongzheng examples are possibly more successful, but both fail on the rather laboured brushwork. Towards the end of the reign there is a gradual loss of vitality and direction; this process of decay continued through the 19th century and into the early 20th. Traditional designs continued to be made during this period, but generally the materials are not first-rate and the painting is weak.

◄ **An 18th-century Ming-style blue-and-white vase**
The decoration is derived from early Ming blue and white. Compared to the fluent and more open appearance of earlier pieces (see page 150), it has a relatively stiff design.

Samson's Oriental Reproductions

Emile Samson was certainly the most prolific manufacturer of reproductions, and his repertoire was enormous. He copied French faience, Dutch delftware, Isnik and Persian pottery, German, French and English porcelains as well as Japanese and Chinese exportwares. He used a number of different bodies and glazes which approximated to the type being copied, although the most recognizable is a porcelain with an even bluish glaze and remarkably few flaws found on the ubiquitous "Chinese armorial" wares.

Samson was perhaps most successful in his attempts to replicate the larger Chinese and Japanese polychrome exportwares of the 17th and 18th centuries. These larger jars and vases generally had unglazed bases, which is unfortunate for anyone trying to pass off these French reproductions as "right", since the tell-tale bluish glaze gives them away. The very bold palettes, such as famille verte, famille rose and the sumptuous blue, red and gold of the Imari wares from Arita are particularly good.

The brushwork of old Imari porcelains is generous and sweeping, which is no surprise since most of these patterns were derived from contemporary Japanese textiles. The very free style was presumably intended to mesmerize the eye into disregarding detail. These rich wares were not meant as cabinet or collectors' pieces to be closely studied: they were made to stand as decorative complements to the tapestries and furnishings in the halls, stairways and apartments of grand houses such as Burghley, Longleat and Blenheim.

Since we do not examine the brushwork and tonal subtleties of the Imari palette in the same way as we would those on an early Kakiemon bowl, we can experience some difficulty when we are asked to consider such wares. It is worth remembering that some experts in Japanese porcelain are unacquainted with

▶ **A Samson copy of a "famille-rose" tureen of the Qianlong period, 19th century.**

Casting of the legs and comb are too sharp and the latter too regular.

The painting has a pedantic quality suggesting an attempt at copying rather than spontaneity.

European porcelain or the enamels used on it and are sometimes fooled. The problem is generally solved by peering into the interior of the vessel or the lid. If the glaze is irregular with numerous pinholes or other flaws then the piece might well be old. If it is perfectly smooth and a greyish blue, beware. Samson marked many of his Oriental pieces with either a gibberish Oriental seal or else a square mark (which is in fact a squared "S"), both in red.

Copies of Chinese famille-verte and famille-rose porcelain present fewer problems, even if one cannot examine the glaze and paste, simply because the enamels alone should determine their authenticity. The palette can appear to be quite close at a superficial glance, but a comparison, for example between a Samson famille-verte piece and a genuine Kangxi piece, will show several differences (see page 152). The late pieces never possess the luminosity and iridescence of the green and blue enamels, which invariably develop a crackle. In the areas surrounding the blue on a genuine piece there is a zone of about 3mm/⅛in wide which has a matt appearance. This peculiar characteristic does not occur on 19th-century famille-verte or famille-rose porcelain. The yellow on Kangxi porcelain is very irregular with a dirty or muddy appearance, quite different from the later chrome colour.

▶ **Right, a 19th-century Samson copy of an 18th-century "famille-rose" teapot similar to this rare brocade ball teapot and cover, Yongzheng (above)**
The spherical body is richly enamelled with decoration and the handle and spout are formed by two modelled dogs-of-Fo.

EUROPEAN CERAMICS

Italian Maiolica

A large number of reproductions of early Italian maiolica were made from the middle of the 19th century onwards. Some of these were shown at the major international exhibitions both in England and on the Continent. Many are painted in colours very similar to the Renaissance originals, but they generally fail to pass muster on the brushwork, for it is an extremely difficult task to paint convincingly out of one's time, to capture the spirit of an age or of a movement. Our Victorian forefathers were no exception and invariably rendered the faces of individuals in an idealistic, over-sweet manner. Correct attribution, particularly of the *istoriato* school of maiolica painters, is dependent on the ability to recognize the difference between the treatment afforded to a subject in the 16th century and those of the 19th and 20th centuries.

Cantagalli

The Cantagalli factory was established in Florence in 1878, making reproductions not only of the *istoriato* school and other early Italian maiolica but also of Hispano-Moresque lustreware and the Isnik wares of Turkey. Their reproductions can be quite accomplished; the palette is close enough and there is little difference in the material. The Isnik wares are perhaps a trifle heavier and more slickly potted than the originals, but not always (see page 140). As with many other copies, the most obvious fault is

▲ **A modern tourist copy of a 15th-century maiolica vase**

This piece is not intended to deceive. There has been no attempt to reproduce the rough body of the original, nor the vigour of the painting. The base is inscribed in blue "Deruta, Made in Italy" and with an "AT" monogram.

▶ **A 19th-century copy of a 16th-century lustre Urbino dish, depicting the Judgment of Solomon.**

the failure to recreate the spontaneity. The copyist works in a tentative or groping way, as if trying to follow someone else's footsteps. His situation is analogous, but possibly less obviously so, the efforts of the Bow and Worcester painters trying to copy the reign-marks on the backs of Chinese or Japanese dishes and ending up with nonsensical hieroglypics.

Cantagalli pieces are nearly all marked with the singing cockerel, although it is not always easy to identify as such since it is sometimes rather cursorily or loosely drawn. Occasionally one happens upon a piece of maiolica or Hispano-Moresque where the glaze has been gouged or abraded away – beware, for the bird may have flown. There was probably a cockerel there once. The Doccia factory also produced reproductions of early Faenza and Urbino maiolica, but most are marked and are not in the least troublesome.

▲ **A majolica dish by Francesco Durantino, *c.*1545, Urbino**
This shows Scipio and his troops preparing the force the Roman nobility to swear allegiance to the Republic.

▲ **A Cantagalli tankard base with mark gouged out (see page 140)**
This is an attempt to pass the piece off as a genuine Isnik tankard.

▲ **The Cantagalli factory mark**
The cockerel is found on late 19th- and 20th-century imitation maiolica and Isnik ware, made with no intention to deceive.

▼ **Cantagalli dish**
Ulysse Cantagalli was one of the most prolific manufacturers of late 19th-century reproductions. This Cantagalli two-handled oval bowl painted in the Urbino style with a landscape is typical of the late 19th- and early 20th-century imitations of earlier pieces. Compare it with the Durantino dish above left. However, it does have a value for decorative appeal alone.

Mengaroni

The most convincing faker of all was probably the brilliant Ferruccio Mengaroni of Pesaro, who was born in 1875. Until the time of his death in 1925, when he was accidentally crushed by one of his own monolithic creations, he produced highly deceptive fakes of the early masterpieces from Caffagiolo or Faenza. His work has duped many experts and will probably continue to do so.

Mengaroni took great pains with both the palette and with the detail of the subject, although the former is not quite as accurate as it should be. For anyone who is not well acquainted with his work and style, any of his pieces would be very hard to dismiss with confidence, particularly in a remote saleroom or a shop far from the Victoria and Albert Museum, where it can be checked.

▲ An early 20th-century forgery of an early Caffagiolo roundel (*c.*1510) by Ferrucio Mengaroni
The forgery is so good that for many years this roundel was exhibited in the Oppenheim collection.

The yellow is neither the Urbino orange, nor the Florentine yellow found on original pieces.

The palette has strayed too far to blue spectrum.

The faces betray their late 19th-century origin and are too sweet and sentimental.

The artist has gone to considerable length to create his pastiche by combining the figure of Christ and the soldiers from a woodcut by Albrecht Dürer and shows influences by Andrea Mantegna and Benedetto Montagna.

▶ A "Resurrection" panel after an early 16th-century Faenza original
Probably painted by Ferruccio Mengaroni in about 1900.

Molaroni Copies

Vincenzo Molaroni, also of Pesaro, reproduced the classical wares of Urbino, mainly in the Castel Durante style – typified by an unusual palette of soft blues, greenish-greys and mulberry purple. The flatwares are generally painted with rather sentimental renderings of figure subjects after Raphael, Correggio or Leonardo da Vinci. They are marked on the back with either painted or impressed marks in the form of a "VM" monogram or a plain "M" over "Pesaro", or with the manufacturer's full name in script.

Other notable makers of retrospective or "historismus" maiolica are the factories or studios of Achille Wildi, Bruno Buratti and the partnership of Guido Andreani and Giulio Patrignani, all of whom signed their work, the last using the letters "MAP" for Maiolica Atistica Pesarese.

▶ **Two *istoriato* dishes compared**

The dish near right dates from *c*.1550 and is typical of the highly decorative dishes of Urbino which were treated as a painter's canvas. This illustration is based on an engraving from "Meleager and the Calydonian Bear" by Ovid. The second dish, far right, dates from *c*.1870 and depicts the Old Testament story of Joseph. It is a copy in the 16th-century style by Molaroni of Pesaro. The details below clearly show the differences between the two pieces.

Istoriato **Dish *c*.1550**   *Istoriato* **Dish *c*.1870**

The early pieces have a spontaneity and naïvety that can be lacking in the later copies.

The predominant shades of ochre, yellow, blue, black, and green are typical of this date. A wider palette indicates a later date or a high-quality piece.

Overall the colours on this later piece are much brighter and cleaner than the 16th-century original.

Despite its later date this dish has been skilfully painted and captures the spirit of the original.

Molaroni's pieces are marked on the base with a painted or impressed mark.

▶ **A 19th-century Samson copy of a Moustiers cup and saucer**
The mark is that of Olerys & Laugier, whose factory was established in 1738.

French Faience

The technique for making tin-glazed earthenware was introduced into France by immigrant Italian potters. At first the products of these denizen potters were, quite naturally, very much in their native styles, such as the "Gothic" of Faenza or the *istoriato* tradition of Urbino, and it is sometimes very difficult to differentiate them from their Italian counterparts, particularly in the case of the work of the Lyons maiolica painters.

In the 17th century Nevers and Rouen were the most important potting centres in France. The former used a combination of contemporary Renaissance silver or metal forms but, oddly enough, painted in the Chinese

▲ **A Montagnon copy of a Nevers "bleu persan" sifter, *c*.1900**
Without looking at the base, which is marked "Montagnon" it is easy to see from the fussy painting that it cannot be compared with the bold brushwork of old Nevers. The granular earthenware body on early Nevers is a soft pinkish buff colour; this piece is dense brownish red.

▶ **A 1930 copy of a Rouen cornucopia faience dish, French, *c*.1680**

"Transitional" style with figures in cloud-lapped rocky landscapes. An unusual variation of this was the use of a solid blue ground glaze over-painted in white enamel, vaguely reminiscent of Limoges enamel work, but probably derived from the 17th-century blue ground wares of Persia or late Ming export porcelain (see page 150). This style has been termed *bleu persan*.

The middle years of the 18th century saw the rise of Strasbourg and Marseilles. By this time manufacturers had moved away from the restricted *grand feu* palette to the more sensitive *petit feu* or low-fired colours. This allowed the faience painter greater freedom. He was now able to compete with those who painted on porcelain. In fact, some of the wares of the Sceaux factory are very close to porcelain.

▶ **A Samson reproduction of a Marseilles (Veuve Perrin) jar and cover, probably early 20th century**
This piece is a straightforward reproduction of an early Marseilles jar. The detail of the base shows both the "VP" monogram of the Veuve Perrin factory – which is incidentally the most copied mark on French faience – and the entwined "S" mark of Samson.

▶ **A late 19th-century copy of Marseilles (Veuve Perrin) plate**
The body and glaze are fairly good, but as is usually the case, it is let down by poor draughtsmanship.

The palette is decidedly late autumn, dull and grey. The enamels on genuine Veuve Perrin are fresh-looking and sunny with a dominant milky pink.

The central figures are very stiff.

The trailing flowers on the rim are weed-like and lack detail.

The Marseilles factory of Veuve Perrin is one of the most commonly faked or copied in French faience. It is extremely difficult to sort out the tin-glazed earthenware, since the formula does not vary a great deal from one time to another, or for that matter from place to place. Without the help of decoration the extremely subtle differences between various factories can be almost impossible to detect. This is especially so with Veuve Perrin, which was and is highly prized by collectors and, as a result, has received the unwelcome attention of forgers.

Chantilly, St Cloud and Mennecy

Fakes or reproductions of French soft-paste porcelains are relatively easy to detect. Each factory has distinctive pastes, glazes and palettes unlike the late 18th-century Paris factories, which all produced very similar porcelains. Chantilly used tin in their glaze, which gives an opaque creamy-grey appearance resembling faience or *milchglas* – totally different from Mennecy, St Cloud or Vincennes, which are translucent or glassy.

The silver-mounted "U"-shaped beaker (see page 164) is painted in the Kakiemon style, which was very fashionable in the late 17th and 18th centuries – a fact confirmed by the great collections at Burghley House, Blenheim Palace and Hampton Court and by the collection of Augustus the Strong in the Johanneum. The Prince de Condé, who was patron of the Chantilly concern, was a passionate collector of this type of Japanese porcelain and a large proportion of the factory's production was made in this style. Chantilly Kakiemon wares are painted in a precise manner with the enamels carefully outlined in black, in contrast to the Arita or even the Meissen versions, which do not appear to be so well defined.

▶ **An early 20th-century copy of a Chantilly flower holder**
This is interesting for several reasons. In the first place it is made of an earthenware or *faience fine* very similar to English creamware. The glaze which contains the opacifying tin is remarkably good but fails where it has pooled in the crevices or angles: here the glaze has become quite bluish and is cracked and much like pearlware. The enamelling has effectively captured the original feel and the flowers are well painted and delineated, the only evident weakness being the wheatsheaves and the butterfly which are stiffly drawn. This piece is signed "Lefrond". Compare this decoration with that of the genuine Kakiemon vase on page 179.

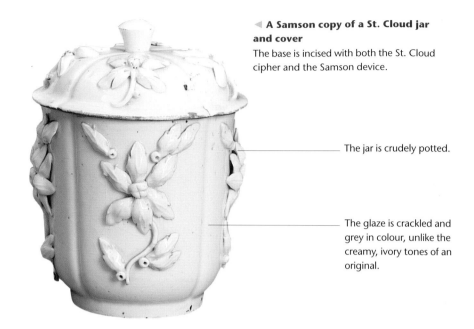

◄ **A Samson copy of a St. Cloud jar and cover**
The base is incised with both the St. Cloud cipher and the Samson device.

The jar is crudely potted.

The glaze is crackled and grey in colour, unlike the creamy, ivory tones of an original.

St. Cloud made a large number of pieces in the white, relying on the form alone for decorative appeal. The shapes were taken from contemporary silver or from oriental ceramics. The body was similar to Chantilly, but the glaze, rather than being opaque, was glassy and of a creamy ivory tone comparable to Chelsea of about 1750. The Samson copies of St. Cloud jars, however, were crudely potted and covered in a dull, widely crackled, greyish glaze on a granular earthenware body.

Small objects such as snuff boxes, scent bottles, étuis, cane handles or other *galantriewaren*, as these objects are designated, are especially difficult to attribute. The unglazed areas are usually impossible to examine because of the metal mounts, and one has therefore to depend solely on the glaze and enamelling (if any).

► **A Samson copy of a Chantilly beaker, late 19th or early 20th century**
The base is marked in red with both the hunting horn of Chantilly and the entwined "S" of Samson. The beaker fails to convince simply because it is composed of hard-paste porcelain which, strangely enough, approaches the mid-18th-century Meissen chalky body. It is covered with a very glassy glaze which is also peppered with small black pinholes, the latter probably contrived to simulate the characteristic fault of Chantilly.

German Stoneware

Stoneware is a high-fired pottery, more often than not composed of clay and ground feldspathic rock. At very high temperatures – somewhere approaching 1400° C/2550° F – the stone vitrifies, rendering it impervious to water and therefore obviating the need for a glaze (although in most cases after the 16th century a glaze was applied).

Stoneware was first made in China, probably during the Han dynasty or a little before, since it has an affinity with Yüeh ware, which is known to have been produced in the third century BC. The early Chinese stonewares were generally covered in a thin translucent olive or sea-green glaze which resembled celadon, but was not as unctuous or opaque.

It is unlikely that the European potters learned the technique from the Orient. They probably discovered it for themselves in the early Middle Ages, perhaps in the Rhineland.

Some medieval stoneware is lead-glazed, but since it could not be fired at very high temperatures, the lead-glazing was not always successful; it stratified and flaked away from the body. The solution was discovered in the 14th century with the introduction of salt-glazing. When the kiln temperature was at its highest, salt (sodium chloride) was thrown into the firing chamber. This immediately vaporized, the chlorine was exhausted from the kiln and the residual sodium combined with mineral elements present in the body to form a thin, close-fitting glaze that is very durable.

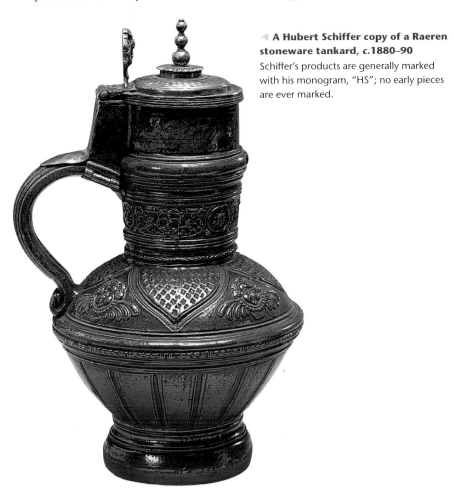

◄ **A Hubert Schiffer copy of a Raeren stoneware tankard, c.1880–90**
Schiffer's products are generally marked with his monogram, "HS"; no early pieces are ever marked.

▲ **A genuine Westerwald jug, c.1668**
The moulded motifs and stamped repeating designs are typical of output at this time and they are detailed in a dark cobalt blue and a patchy manganese. Copies tend to be detailed in a somewhat brighter blue, usually with no additional manganese.

Salt glaze can easily be identified by its pitted, "orange-peel" surface.

Stoneware was produced in the Netherlands, Saxony and, from the 17th century onwards, in Britain, but the most important area of production in Europe was the Rhineland. The leading Rhenish centres were at Siegburg, Raeren, Cologne and Westerwald. Since the wares of all these centres were reproduced in either the 18th or 19th centuries, it is important to give a brief history and description of each type. We can ignore 16th-century coiled wares since very few copies were made of them.

Siegburg

Sixteenth-century Siegburg (production ceased in 1632) is made of a fine greyish-white material. The decoration was invariably of applied oval or rectangular panels depicting the coats-of-arms of principalities or bishoprics; classical figures, perhaps symbolizing the Virtues; or biblical scenes, usually taken from engravings by Virgilius Solis or G. Aldegraver.

The most common form encountered is the tall, slightly tapered cylindrical tankard (*Schnelle*); these were copied at the end of the 19th century, particularly by the firm of C. W. Fleischmann. His products are far too wooden and precise, both in construction and design; they all look machine-made. Other spurious pieces, probably made to deceive, lack the crispness of the original. They are indifferently potted with a flat or nearly flat base (as opposed to a recessed or concave base), which is occasionally scored with grooves in a fairly unconvincing attempt to simulate the thumb-print marks found on some early stonewares. While many of this type were made of stoneware, there is a group which is made of fine earthenware dressed in a thin yellowish-white tin glaze.

Raeren

Brown or very occasionally grey or yellowish brown in colour, Raeren stoneware was produced from the second quarter of the 16th century onwards. Early wares are very similar to Cologne, but those of the late 16th century are quite distinctive. The workshops of Jan and Peter Emens Menniken made fine tankards and jugs with a pronounced central bulge applied with a frieze of dancing peasants or biblical themes, such as Susannah and the Elders or the story of Joseph and his Brothers. The ancillary panels are of small circular medallions or bands of formal scrollwork. Good reproductions of this type were made by Hubert Schiffer (see page 165) and also by the Fleischmann concern during the last third of the 19th century.

Westerwald

The most prolific region is Westerwald, situated between Cologne and Frankfurt-am-Main. Not much of importance was produced here until the arrival of the Knutgen family, the best of the Siegburg potters, in 1590. Their earliest pieces are indistinguishable from those made in Siegburg.

A little later the Mennicken family also migrated from Raeren, and brought their traditional style to Hohr in the Westerwald district. It was here that they developed fully the use of cobalt to enhance or highlight decoration. Towards the middle of the 17th century Westerwald stoneware became more mechanical and the more complex figural subjects were discontinued in favour of small, crudely applied moulded motifs and stamped repeating patterns. In the third quarter of the century manganese was added to the palette.

The most common form is the *Kugelbauchkrug* or, literally, "fat-bellied jug", which later was frequently applied with the device or bust portrait of William III or Queen Anne, or the monogram GR for either George I or II. Other popular forms were the *Humpen*, a short cylindrical tankard or mug, and the taller oviform jug with a narrow neck (*Enghalskrug*). These 17th- or 18th-century vessels were not made with great care and the potter's or workman's hand is usually in evidence.

Late 19th-century reproductions by Reinhold Merkelbach of Hohr-Grenzhausen are characterized by their over-neat potting, the slightly more stylized scratched foliage (even the late 17th-century pieces are fairly abstract) and the rather thin and watery royal blue that was used. The original's cobalt is a darker inky colour. Late pieces are sometimes impressed with numbers; early examples carry no marks at all.

Cologne or Frechen

Cologne or Frechen made stoneware from the Middle Ages. Their most famous products are the brown-glazed globular jugs applied with a bearded mask on the neck, so-called "bellarmines", allegedly named after the notorious and much hated Cardinal Bellarmine. The majority of these vessels are applied with small medallions or an armorial device, which is sometimes the arms of Elizabeth I of England.

Similar but much cruder bellarmines were made in England at Fulham by John Dwight, who took out a patent in 1671. There are no convincing fakes of these wares since those produced by Merkelbach and others are too regular.

▶ **A genuine bellarmine (left) and a fake (right)**
The genuine bellarmine dates from the late 17th to the early 18th century. The fake example purports to be from the late 16th to the early 17th century. The latter has very thick-edged applied medallions and the ends of the beard are too tightly curled and mechanical.

Meissen Figures

Meissen single figures are among the more successful of the many types of porcelain and pottery which were copied by Emile Samson. The Commedia dell'Arte, which originated in the 16th century and was the ancestor of the modern Punch and Judy, was a continuing source of inspiration not only for the Italian porcelain modellers but also for Johann Joachim Kändler of Meissen and Franz Anton Bustelli of Nymphenburg, the finest modellers in German porcelain. From the mid-1730s Kandler began a series of figures and groups based on such characters. Among them are Punchinello, Scaramouche, Dr Boloardo and the Avvocato, which was first modelled in 1748.

▼ **A Samson copy of Tyrolean or Dutch dancers by J. F. Eberlein of Meissen, which was modelled in 1735**
One of the most sought-after models, it was copied in the 1750s by both Chelsea and Bow and, a little surprisingly, by the Chinese potters at Jingdezhen during the reign of the Emperor Qianlong (1736–95).

It has often been said that blue eyes are never found on 18th-century figures. However, Meissen did use a pale grey in both the 18th and 19th centuries, which is deceptively close to blue. Generally, 18th-century figures are painted with brown (often very dark brown) eyes.

The applied rosettes are simply modelled, and unlike those on the original, they have not been worked further with a knife to produce tiny veins.

▲ **Meissen figures by Kändler**
A Commedia dell'Arte Harlequin modelled by Johann Joachim Kändler, c.1744. Kändler was undoubtedly the finest modeller at Meissen, and his figures epitomize the vigour and movement of the late Baroque. The strong enamel colours were typical of the 1730s and '40s.

▶ **A late 19th-century copy of an early 18th-century Augsburg Hausmaler-decorated Meissen tea bowl and saucer**

German Hausmaler

Large numbers of Meissen blanks were decorated outside the factory in the second quarter of the 18th century in the painting studios of Hausmaler ("house-painters"). Some of the finest work was done in these studios by painters such as Johanna Aufenwerth, Ignaz Bottengruber, J. G. Heintze or J. F. Metzch, who mainly used coloured enamels. Elias Adam, the brothers Bartholomaus and Abraham Seuter worked principally in silver or gold. They were the most prominent of the Augsburg Hausmaler and specialized in chinoiserie subjects. Their method was painstaking and the results lacked spontaneity, but they were nevertheless a great deal more lively than subsequent fakes of their work.

Figure subjects on genuine Augsburg decorated pieces have a naturally fluid posture, whereas the graceless forms on the fakes resemble shapeless sacks. Beneath each chinoiserie vignette the pendant scrollwork or *ferronnerie* on the copy is crude and amorphous when compared with the controlled cursive ornamentation of the original. The gold on Böttger Meissen porcelains has a subtle coppery appearance with slight iridescence, unlike the gilding on the copy, which is dull and brassy. Differences between the glazes are also quite marked – Böttger Meissen is a warm smoky ivory or cream colour, in contrast to the hard glassy grey Thuringian porcelain of the late 19th century.

▲ **A late 19th-century copy of an early 18th-century Augsburg lid**

This was possibly made as a replacment after an original decorated in the manner of Abraham Seuter.

Nineteeth-century Copies

The increasing numbers and the growing wealth of the new bourgeouise meant that by the middle of the 19th century more people could spend more money on more than the bare essentials. The new dynasts required that their houses be filled with fashionable artefacts and ornaments, which resembled – superficially at least – those in the houses of the aristocracy and the landed gentry.

The demand for decorative items in porcelain and pottery led to the foundation of a large number of factories. But from the end of the Neo-Rococo period, in about 1840, the greater proportion of this ceramic output was a re-hash of the porcelains made at the leading European factories, particularly Meissen and Sèvres.

The Neo-classical period, which included the so-called Empire style, gave way to a debased revival of the Rococo and with it ever increasing elaboration. This can be seen on vases, inkstands and other ornamental wares which were heavily encrusted with applied flowers. Figures took on a more sickly hue, all exposed parts of the body were painted in flesh tones and the faces were given an overall yellowish tone, in contrast to the more obviously rouged but more pleasing faces on most 18th-century figures (with the exception of some Italian and Thuringian factories, whose figures were often quite gaudily painted).

The greatest difference between, say, an 18th-century Meissen figure and a 19th-century copy is in the detail. Just a casual glance, for example, at the hair will immediately distinguish early from late. On the former it seems that every strand is picked out with an ultra-fine brushstroke, whereas

Compare the detail of the hair with the 19th-century group opposite.

There is more movement and liveliness in the modelling of this earlier group that typifies the late Baroque style.

▶ **A Meissen Commedia dell'Arte figure group of Colombine and Pantalone, *c.*1740** on the latter the hair appears widely-spaced like the teeth of a comb.

Both Thuringian and Saxon factories in the second half of the 19th century followed the over-elaborate style which had developed in the second quarter of that century. The prolific Thuringian factories, most notably the Voigt Brothers of Sitzendorf and Schierholz of Plaue-am-Havel, used an insipid range of pastel enamels which included a pale pink and dull turquoise. The porcelain itself has a hard greyish appearance. Both these factories used parallel line marks crossed by either one or two diagonals, perhaps to simulate the crossed swords of Meissen.

Other German factories were even less scrupulous and blatantly copied both the models and the crossed swords of Meissen; and even if purists regard 19th-century Meissen as decadent, it is nevertheless superior to all other factories, with the possible exception of its neighbour at Potschappel. This factory produced some fine-quality work in a palette similar to that employed at Meissen. Carl Thieme, the proprietor, used a "T" between crossed batons as his early factory mark, again causing confusion to the uninitiated.

Copying in France

In France a similar situation prevailed vis-a-vis Sèvres and other lesser concerns. Many Parisian factories freely copied the interlaced "L"s of the Vincennes and early Sèvres factories. It would not be exaggerating to say that over 95 per cent of pieces thus marked are later copies or forgeries. Apart from the usual differences in technical skill and the enamels used, the most obvious mistake is the use of a mark only found on early soft-paste when almost all later French porcelain was hard-paste.

Compare the flesh tones with the 18th-century group opposite.

The applied flowers and overall fussy elaborate style of the modelling and painting are typical of the Rococo Revival.

▶ **A Meissen group, "The Test of Love", after a model by Michel Victor Acier and Johann Carl Schonheit, _c._1870**
Note that the formal Neo-classical base jars with the essential Rococo feel of the figures, which are clearly 18th-century in style. Such a marriage only took place in the Rococo Revival period.

▶ **A fake Japanese Imari delftware vase**
This type of Japanese Imari delftware first appeared in the early 18th century but the painting, although crowded, is much more flowing than in this stiff copy from Holland. Copies were made throughout the 19th and into the 20th century.

Dutch Delftware

The technique of making tin-glazed earthenware in the Netherlands was introduced by immigrant Italian maiolica potters early in the 16th century. With continued persecution in the southern Netherlands, they were forced to move from Antwerp northwards to Rotterdam, Haarlem, Delft and even across the North Sea to England. Delft became the largest centre for the production of tin-glazed pottery during the 17th and 18th centuries.

The major portion of the output was blue and white, loosely based on Chinese exportware, but polychrome wares in imitation of the fashionable Japanese or Chinese Imari wares were also made. It was the advent of Josiah Wedgwood's creamware at the end of the 18th century that signalled the demise of the tin-glaze industry, including Delft, not only in Britain but throughout Europe. Production, except for tiles and industrial wares, virtually ceased in the 19th century.

English Delftware

A great deal can be learned by comparing a late 19th-century forgery of an English delftware wine bottle with a genuine bottle. In the first place the genuine bottle is made of a buff-coloured clay, whereas forgeries are often made of a dryish-looking, white to chalky clay. A genuine bottle should show no concentric throwing rings on the base, but a fake will. The glaze on the fake is often dull and speckled with minute and barely visible spots of cobalt – no right bottle is every similarly marked. Early pieces have a thick, creamy, undulating glaze, which, if cracked at all, is a more obvious brown or buff colour. The fake's glaze, on the other hand, is often covered in a regular network of fine but pale, almost quadrangular crackle. It is very hard for the forger to recreate the correct crazing of glaze.

Always check the handle of any item carefully – does it serve its function and stand up to repeated ware? The handles of authentic delftware bottles are connected to the neck at a downward sloping angle in a natural manner, whereas the handle of the forgery is joined to the neck at a right angle and appears to have been pushed hard enough to form an awkward kink close to the body. Don't forget the genuine piece would have been made by a potter turning out dozens of these items. Shaping and attaching the handles would have been second nature to him and this gives the handle a sense of "rightness" that is very hard for any forger to achieve.

As a postscript, it is worth quoting again from Geoffrey Eliot Howard's *Early English Drug Jars*. In his note on fakes he writes, "Next come the commonest kind, which were made in France, probably about 50 years ago. [He was writing in 1931.] The whole jar is a clever imitation, made of 'white ware' in the exact shape of the Jacobean vessels, and with a perfect imitation of a Jacobean inscription. Two clues should guide the collector in detecting these. The body of the jar is composed of a much whiter clay than was used in Lambeth and very often rectangular cracks appear in the glaze such as are seldom found in genuine specimens."

▼ A genuine and a fake Whit delftware bottle

Despite its misleading date, the fake Whit (white wine) bottle on the right probably dates from the late 19th or early 20th century. However, the potting is convincing. The clay is a grainy biscuit colour.

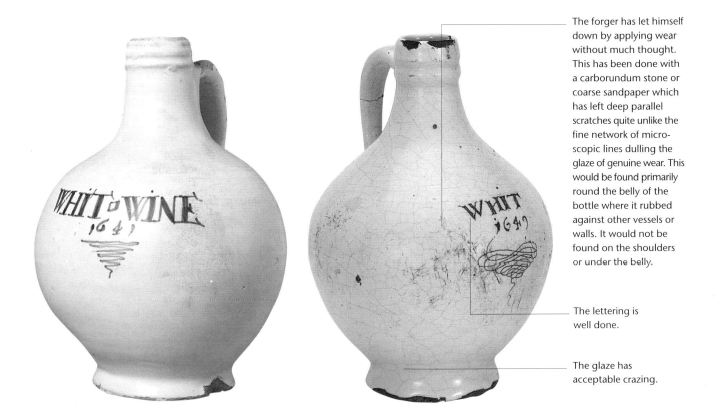

The forger has let himself down by applying wear without much thought. This has been done with a carborundum stone or coarse sandpaper which has left deep parallel scratches quite unlike the fine network of microscopic lines dulling the glaze of genuine wear. This would be found primarily round the belly of the bottle where it rubbed against other vessels or walls. It would not be found on the shoulders or under the belly.

The lettering is well done.

The glaze has acceptable crazing.

▲ **Reproduction Leeds candlesticks**
These elaborate pierced candlesticks are reproductions of early Leeds creamware, probably using the original moulds, which were acquired by Slee's Modern Pottery in 1888. They differ only slightly from the originals. The later body is a fraction lighter in weight, and the crackled glaze is more thinly and evenly applied, allowing the yellowish grey body to show through and giving an overall dull impression. In comparison, the early piece is an ivory-cream colour with a more lustrous appearance and with an "orange-skin" texture which can be seen when it is looked at in a raking light.

Creamware and Related Wares

Creamware is a fine, lightweight pottery covered in a clear lead glaze. It involves the use of flint and gradually evolved from other Staffordshire earthenwares in the first half of the 18th century. The credit for its invention in the 1740s belongs to Enoch Booth, although it was Josiah Wedgwood who completed the process. Booth's formula enabled him to produce an attractive, creamy-looking, thin and crisply moulded ware at relatively low cost, and this allowed Wedgwood to compete with the more expensive and vulnerable delftwares. The success of this earthenware eventually led to the demise of the tin-glaze industry in Europe. By the end of the century, for example, all the delftware factories in England except Lambeth had closed, and even Lambeth had discontinued the manufacture of decorative ware in favour of more utilitarian and industrial items.

Creamware manufacture was also started not only by other Staffordshire potters but also at Bristol and at Leeds. Apart from flatware, which was made in all these areas, the Wedgwood and Leeds potteries made more ambitious pieces including centrepieces, cake stands and candlesticks, which were pierced to resemble lace-work.

Another form of creamware, also invented by Wedgwood, is "pearlware". This is fundamentally the same material, but it has a greater proportion of white clay and flint in the paste. It has a decidedly bluish appearance to the glaze, doubtless contrived to emulate the glaze on contemporary Chinese blue-and-white exportware. Much pearlware is decorated in underglaze blue, either by hand painting or by transfer-printing. Examples of the former can be deceptively close in look to the less accomplished porcelain from Liverpool, since they are nearly as finely potted as porcelain. Pearlware, however, is completely opaque, unlike porcelain. The traditional "willow-pattern" almost certainly began life on this type of earthernware.

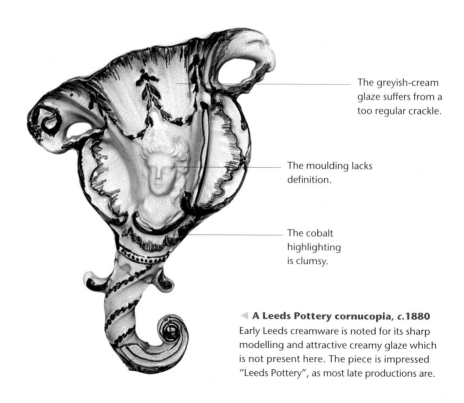

The greyish-cream glaze suffers from a too regular crackle.

The moulding lacks definition.

The cobalt highlighting is clumsy.

◀ **A Leeds Pottery cornucopia, c.1880**
Early Leeds creamware is noted for its sharp modelling and attractive creamy glaze which is not present here. The piece is impressed "Leeds Pottery", as most late productions are.

▼ **A copy of a Staffordshire tea canister**
This is a perfect example of a copy taken from a genuine piece and not from the original mould. In the first place it is a fraction smaller than the original. Secondly, there is a serious loss of definition, caused by taking a mould from an already glazed piece. This has effectively disguised the "message" of the late 18th-century original, which was in effect a broadside against current fashion, being modelled in shallow relief with "Macaroni" figures sporting preposterous wigs. All this is missed in the slovenly potting and careless application of these rather bright overglaze enamels. Compare the quality of the figures with the genuine item on the right.

◄ **A genuine Prattware jug with typical palette of subdued high-temperature blue, green, ochre, and brown on a bluish pearlware glaze**

▶ **An early 20th-century forgery of a Wedgwood Whieldon teapot**
This teapot is thickly constructed and covered in a green and cream glaze. Both these colours differ from the original in that they are definitely greyish and hard-looking. The green on an 18th-century piece has a warm yellowish tone and a fine network of crackle, unlike this later piece, on which the uncrackled green is dull and tends towards the blue end of the spectrum. The modelling of the flower part of the vegetable on the early piece is very realistic, whereas on the late piece it is clear that the modeller has never examined his subject in nature. It looks more like the magnified surface of an orange. The intended deception is revealed when one examines the interior of this "teapot". The eight strainer holes are very small and all but two of them are blocked by glaze, rendering the vessel useless.

Prattware

Prattware is associated with the creamware group in that it is made of the same material, although it is additionally decorated in high-fired enamel colours, such as ochre, blue, green and manganese. The name derives from Felix Pratt, a potter from Delph Lane (Tunstall), Staffordshire, who produced classical figures, wall plaques and utilitarian items, including a tea-caddy moulded with so-called "Macaroni" figures, all decorated in this range of colours. This type of ware was not only made in Staffordshire but in north-east England by Dixon and Austin of Sunderland, and in Scotland.

There have been few reproductions of any of the creamware group, other than the more elaborate Leeds pottery, presumably for the obvious reason that although it has a simple charm it is not much sought after.

Teawares

The Staffordshire potters of the 1750s and '60s, among them Josiah Wedgwood and his former partner Thomas Whieldon, produced a number of teawares semi-naturalistically modelled after fruit or vegetables. The most common forms were the pineapple and the cauliflower. Generally speaking, the Wedgwood versions are superior since they are more carefully and thinly potted and have sharper detail.

▲ **A modern forgery of a Staffordshire model of Stanfield Hall, c.1970**
Copies of originals have often been moulded from a larger original and are smaller than they should be. The second generation casting results in a loss of definition. After firing, and while still hot, many of these figures or models are dropped into cold coffee. The glaze immediately crazes and produces the brown appearance of age but it is very unlike the true crazing which is much more open and more irregular.

Staffordshire Portrait and Flat-back Figures

Before World War II it would have been inconceivable for anyone to produce a forgery of a Victorian Staffordshire portrait or flat-back figure. The serious collector of pottery regarded little that was made after 1800 as worth considering, and there was no general interest in such primitive and relatively recent "fictile abominations" as they were called by one late Victorian *Punch* cartoonist. Nevertheless, reproductions of the more common types have been made more or less continuously up to the present day. These have been sold legitimately as reproductions with no intention on the part of the manufacturer to deceive. But once they have been circulated or passed through the original outlet, unscrupulous or ignorant people may well sell them again as genuine. This is when the reproduction becomes a forgery. These modern copies of Staffordshire pottery include cottages such as Stanfield Hall, money boxes, and figures and groups such as Dick Turpin, Grace Darling and the prize fighters, Heenan and Sayers.

What distinguishes them for the originals? In the first place, the originals were press-moulded, i.e. the clay was pushed into the mould by hand, which gave an uneven look to the interior of the figure, and the finger-prints were mainly obscured by the slightly greyish lead glaze. It was a process that required some skill and could be quite time-consuming to the uninitiated. Most reproductions, however, were made by the slip-casting method, which needs little skill. The technique uses liquid clay or slip, which is poured through a small vent hole in each mould and allowed to dry. The longer the liquid clay is left in the mould, the thicker the walls of the object become, and with very, very few exceptions these slip figures are much lighter than genuine 19th-century examples.

The moulds for these pieces are not themselves taken from the early moulds but from a genuine group or figure. There is obviously a great loss of detail, as the genuine figure is glazed and therefore less well defined than the mould cast.

Comparing Two Staffordshire Agateware Cats

▷ **Left, a genuine 18th-century original Staffordshire "Solid Agate" figure of a seated cat. Right, an early 20th-century copy**
Low-fired lead-glazed pottery presents fewer technical problems to the faker, particularly if the piece to be copied is primitive ware such as this. One is forced to rely on more subtle clues in order to uncover the fake. There is little difference between the form or the general appearance of this figure and the original, although it must be said that the late piece is marginally thicker in construction, a fault that may not necessarily always apply. On almost all recognized "right" pieces, however, the simulated agate is defined by thin, "combed" striae, which are the same on the inside as on the outside, unlike the amorphous marbling on this fake. Inside the painted lines tail off where the brush cannot reach.

▲ A late 20th-century "Piper"
Many of the fakes that have come on to the market since the mid-1990s are unknown in genuine Staffordshire. These reproductions are made in porcelain and do not have genuine earthenware bodies.

When a figure is fired in the kiln it shrinks by approximately ten per cent. If taken from a Victorian figure, a reproduction will therefore be smaller by the same degree. The glaze on reproduction pieces is frequently given an artificially induced network of pronounced, fine, very regular crackle. This characteristic is often quite erroneously considered by the layman to be a symptom of antiquity and therefore of authenticity. The greyish but translucent lead glaze of Victorian Staffordshire pottery is crackled but not nearly as obtrusively; it runs erratically and is widely spaced. The dry wiped or brushed look of the clay on the unglazed foot is also a feature unknown on true Victorian pottery, which is usually partially glazed and with traces of kiln-grit.

Longton Hall

Porcelain and pottery tea- and flat-wares based on vegetables or fruit forms were popular in England in the middle of the 18th century. Chelsea, Bow, Derby and Longton Hall all produced these wares, but it is the later Staffordshire factory which is most closely identified with naturalistic forms. At their best they have a primitive charm, but more frequently they are clumsy or awkward. As the factory only ran for a period of ten years between 1750 and 1760, these wares are rare and command high prices, and therefore encourage forgeries.

Comparing Staffordshire Slipware Dishes

▽ ▷ Right, a genuine slipware dish; below, a modern copy
The tradition of making lead-glazed earthenware decorated in slip in England probably began at Wrotham in Kent early in the 17th century. The finest pieces, however, were made in the second half of the century in Staffordshire by Thomas, Ralph, and James Toft and George and William Taylor. Favourite themes included the Pelican in her Piety, Adam and Eve, mermaids, cockerels, and royal portraits such as this one of King Charles II and Queen Catherine of Braganza by Thomas Toft, c.1662–85. A number of fairly accurate copies were made early in the 20th century, employing similar materials.

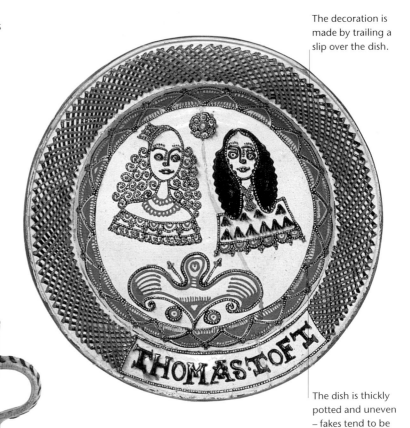

The decoration is made by trailing a slip over the dish.

The dish is thickly potted and uneven – fakes tend to be thinner and more regular in finish.

EUROPEAN PORCELAIN

Bow

A large proportion of the production of the early Bow factory was utilitarian blue and white. The designs on these early wares were either fanciful chinoiseries or copied directly from the Chinese or Japanese export blue-and-white porcelains that were shipped in vast quantities, virtually as ballast. The painters even when so far as to simulate oriental reign-marks with amusing results.

The dish immediately below is painted in the beautifully spare Kakiemon style with its distinctive palette of iron-red, cerulean, turquoise, gilding and black for outline. This palette was introduced in Japan by the legendary Sakaida Kakiemon in the third quarter of the 17th century. It soon became extremely popular among European aristocratic collectors, most notably Augustus the Strong of Saxony, the Prince de Condé and Queen Mary, whose collection was inventoried at Kensington Palace in 1697. The style was copied at Chantilly, St Cloud, Mennecy, Meissen, Chelsea, Worcester and Bow, the latter particularly favouring "Quail" pattern.

The fake is copying a Bow plate of about 1755 painted after a Chinese original of the Yongzheng (1732–35) or early Qianlong (1736–95) period. Bow porcelain of this date can be very heavily potted and opaque, even when

▶ **A genuine Bow dish with the Quail pattern, _c._1755.**

The glaze on Bow pieces is never crackled.

The Kakiemon palette is very distinctive.

▶ **A French hard-paste copy of a Bow Kakiemon dish, late 19th or early 20th century**
The forger has added a Chelsea red anchor mark – a typical example of a forger making a simple mistake. The base is unglazed unlike a genuine example.

held against a strong electric light. The glaze is thickly applied and suffused with air bubbles, which frequently give a slightly blurred effect on the blue decoration. Another characteristic is the bluish appearance of the glaze where it has gathered or "pooled" in the footrim. Finally, the unglazed paste tends to discolour to a brownish buff colour.

The copyist on this plate has attempted to emulate these idiosyncracies, and, apart from some inept handling of the border, the plate only fails with the glaze itself, which has a thick, crackled, dull grey tone resembling pearlware. Bow is rarely crackled like this.

A useful comparison can be made between the fake dish, which incongruously bears the red anchor mark of Chelsea, and a genuine Bow dish of about 1755, above. The French dish has a deep glaze of greyish glassy appearance covering a white smooth paste with slight impressions left by kiln-grit on the unglazed base. Its colours are generally much more intense than those of the original, which is delicately but fluently executed in thinly washed colours. On the genuine Bow piece the glaze has been very lightly applied, giving a creamier softer look.

Worcester

The Worcester porcelain factory was established in 1751. Its earliest products were predominantly blue and white and a hybrid palette synthesized from Japanese Kakiemon and Chinese famille-verte porcelains. Unlike their contemporaries at Chelsea, Bow and Derby, who were most strongly influenced by Meissen, Arita and *Blanc-de-Chine* porcelains, Worcester designers based their work on a fanciful vision of China as an exotic country composed of pavilions and pagodas set among idyllic islands. Their delightful chinoiseries have an almost folksy appeal, in contrast to the more stylish and sophisticated efforts of their rivals.

The Kakiemon Style and its Imitators

The Kakiemon palette and style were widely copied among all the European factories, as can be seen here. Note the similarity of colours and the variation in the painting of the phoenix.

▲ **A rare Kakiemon vase, Edo period, late 17th century**

▲ **A Chelsea baluster vase and cover, c.1752–55, with red anchor mark**

▲ **One of a pair of Bow vases decorated in Kakiemon style, c.1755**

By 1760, however, events on the Continent had had a profound effect on their output. In Germany the Seven Years' War had seriously disrupted production at Meissen and, perhaps as a consequence, the factory had lost its initiative in the markets of Europe. The leader of fashion was now the Sèvres factory under the patronage of the French king. Its sumptuous porcelains proved irresistible to the rest of Europe, and as a result almost all the leading factories adopted the Sèvres style. Worcester was among them, introducing an assortment of coloured grounds, including yellow, green, claret and the very popular blue scale.

Copies of First Period Worcester (late 1760s and early 1770s), dating from the early 20th century, are found. While the overall impression of these is pleasing, they differ from the originals in several respects. First, a Worcester example is entirely hand-painted in rich enamel colours which, in spite of a tendency to sink into the glaze, as they do on most soft-paste porcelains, nonetheless give a sense of depth. The copies are decorated using transfer prints which are then painted over in thin enamel, giving a dull, flat appearance. The black outline of the print can also be seen. Second, the gilding, which also follows a printed matrix, lacks dimension and has a somewhat brassy glitter to it, a characteristic of most mass-produced gilded porcelain or pottery from the end of the 19th century onwards. Third, they are opaque, which is not surprising since they are made of earthenware, whereas a Worcester specimen would be translucent, having a greenish tint in transmitted light. Fourth, the glaze on the original has a slightly bluish or greenish look and is generally "pegged" (i.e. a narrow band of glaze is wiped away from the interior of the footrim leaving the body exposed). The copies

▼ ▶ **A Worcester ribbed cup and saucer**
A bone-china copy or replacement for a Worcester original, probably painted in the studio of James Giles around 1770. This pure glassy white type of porcelain was only invented in the 19th century and contrasts with a greenish steatitic original. The palette is also incorrect: the Brunswick green was never used on early Worcester.

Note that both pieces are speckled and blackened on the foot, indicating that they have themselves been later decorated.

▶ **A Samson copy of an early Worcester silver-shape sauce boat, late 19th or early 20th century**
Among the most appealing of English porcelains are the early chinoiserie blue-and-white wares made at Worcester in its first ten years. They are painted in a greyish under-glaze cobalt blue which fuses perfectly with the body under an off-white slightly greenish glaze that is often speckled with minute black grains. The painting on this copy is tentative and slightly wooden, and the cobalt has a purplish hue under the very glassy bluish glaze.

are a dead white, and are not pegged but glazed all over. Finally, the shape lacks the more sinuous, elegant lines of the original, and the handles, which are formed from one thick piece of rolled clay, lack the groove which is found in the original.

Lowestoft

The Lowestoft factory, which was established in 1757, is noteworthy for a considerable number of commemorative or inscribed pieces. These wares date from the early 1760s and are often painted in underglaze blue (enamels were introduced at Lowestoft in 1770).

The mug below is inscribed and dated on the base "Abrm. Moore, August 29th 1756" and is a fake, probably produced in France at the end of the 19th or the beginning of the present century. The original was from a set of three and it is worth quoting Geoffrey Godden on the appearance of these early wares: "The 1764 and later pieces are normally of a new lighter body, which I describe as 'floury' as it appears open rather than compact, but the reliefs are now not so sharply defined as those made from the earlier compact body, often being quite blunt. The covering glaze is now almost perfect and clear, not blued, and the early tendency to bubbling has been corrected. This

▶ **A forgery of a Lowestoft Abraham Moore mug, late 19th century**
The forgery has been painted in a runny under-glaze cobalt blue, exaggerating the slightly blurred appearance found on some of the earlier Lowestoft wares. The glaze on this hard-paste copy is also crackled, a characteristic never found on phospatic soft-paste porcelain.

new body and glaze would seem to have been first introduced in about 1764 and was universally employed from about 1768."

After 1770 coloured or enamel decoration was introduced at Lowestoft and the factory continued to supply inscribed pieces. The cylindrical form of tankard superseded the bell shape from around 1775, the shape and restrained decoration being more in keeping with the Neo-classical style current in the last quarter of the 18th century.

The interest shown by late Victorian and Edwardian collectors encouraged a number of French factories to copy these porcelains. Godden cites an advertisement of 1914 by Paul Bocquillon, the Parish manufacturer, which includes a plate bearing the inscription, "A Trifle from Lowestoft".

Plymouth

William Cookworthy, a Plymouth chemist, spent many years searching for the right materials to produce true or hard-paste porcelain in England. He eventually obtained the correct ingredients, and his experiments proved satisfactory enough for him to take out a patent in 1768, a year before the French were able to produce hard-paste at Sèvres.

▶ **A copy of a Plymouth tankard made c.1900 in France, almost certainly by Emile Samson**

These bell-shaped tankards were copied in some quantity, probably because the originals were extremely scarce collectors' items. It is painted in the late French Rococo style in the manner of the mysterious Monsieur Soqui, who was employed as a painter at the Plymouth factory. However, it is painted with the copyist's usual hesitancy and in a palette which differs from the Plymouth colours. The colours are generally too bright and the puce is too "clean".

▼ **Another forgery of a Plymouth tankard, even less convincing than the one above**

The glaze has a fine "orange-skin" texture, but the Plymouth glaze is quite smooth. In transmitted light, the original appears white, whereas the copy is a dull orange.

The shape is not correct: it lacks the elegant curves and good proportions of the original.

The brushwork is far too clumsy and insensitive compared to an original.

The mark on the base is poorly written. The footrim is too neat and with no adherent grit or dribbled glaze.

His earliest efforts were not particularly successful, largely because of the intractability of the clay and its tendency to warp in the extreme heat of the kiln. And he also encountered difficulty with smoke staining from his coal-fired kiln, which gave some pieces a decidedly burnt ivory patina.

Richard Champion, a fellow Quaker (who was to take over the factory when it had moved to Bristol), notes in a letter to Caleb Lloyd dated 7 November 1765 during the period of experiment that preceded the official opening of the Plymouth factory "... But in burning there is a deficiency; though the body is perfectly white within, but not without, which is always smoky."

Characteristically of Plymouth – and for that matter Champion's Bristol and Newhall factories, which were all related in their use of very similar material – is a tendency to show the potter's throwing contours, known as "wreathing". This is most noticeable when looking at a vase or bowl held at a slight angle to the light.

Nineteeth-century Chelsea and Derby Copies

Samson's rabbit (below right) is a late 19th- or early 20th-century copy of an 18th-century Chelsea tureen (below left). The Chelsea red anchor tureen was described in the sale catalogue of the Chelsea factory for 22 March 1755 as "A very fine tureen, in the form of a RABBIT BIG AS LIFE, in a fine oval dish." As is often the case, the Samson copy is smaller than the original at 22.9cm/9in in length, it is 12.7cm/5in shorter. Details on both examples are fairly close, the most noticeable difference being the very fine brushwork on the fur of the Chelsea piece.

The Samson tureen is made of hard-paste porcelain which gives a definite metallic ring when tapped, unlike the somewhat duller sound of Chelsea. The base has the entwined "S" mark (see page 162 for an example), and it is also die-stamped with the number 23. Chelsea porcelains are never impressed with numerals in such a manner. Samson figures can often be identified by mould seams which have not been smoothed off. These are never evident on Chelsea or indeed on most 18th-century figures.

▲ **A Chelsea red anchor rabbit tureen,** *c.***1755**

▲ **A late 19th- or early 20th-century Samson copy of the Chelsea tureen**

◀ **A Samson hard-paste figure of a sheep**

Twentieth-century Chelsea and Derby Copies

Samson's sheep above, thinly potted by the slip-casting method, is after a Derby model, itself based on a Meissen original which was probably made by Kändler in the 1750s. Both the Meissen and Derby examples would be much heavier, modelled by press-moulding with unglazed bases, the former being flat with a small vent hole, the latter probably hollow with an irregular interior surface.

The interesting pair of birds below, reproducing 18th-century Derby originals, was made in Torquay around 1950. One is very lightly slip-cast, but the other is much heavier although taken from the same mould. The forger, perhaps realizing that the first was too light to pass as an early figure, allowed the second to stay longer in the mould, thereby making the sides much thicker and heavier and the whole figure consequently more convincing. The glaze is glassy and quite milky, not too dissimilar to early Chelsea, but the pastel pink flowers are too weak. On the base there are incised numerals, just like the ones that can be found on the right figures.

▶ **Torquay soft-paste porcelain finches, *c.*1950**

► **A Torquay porcellaneous model hare, c.1950**

These copies of English figures were made by Reginald Newland at Union Street, Torquay from the 1950s until his death in 1971. These hares, which sold for £3 ($4.50), were sold in large quantities, unlike the squirrel (below) which cost £50–100 ($70–145). They capture the naïve charm and the thick, crazed greenish glaze of the originals. When these first appeared on the market in the late 1950s everyone was fooled initially and they were making four-figure sums on the market.

▼ **A Torquay forgery of an early English porcelain squirrel, c.1950**

This figure has a long genealogy. The original was probably modelled by J. J. Kändler around 1735, since there are teapots of very similar form recorded by him in May of that year. This was subsequently copied at Chelsea during the incised triangle period (1745–49) and then a little later at Derby, for which there is an entry in William Duesbury's London Account Book for 22nd May 1751. This piece can easily be identified as Torquay by the dried-out fissured paste, the poor glaze and careless painting.

The Torquay hare is the last in a long line of figures stretching back to the Meissen original modelled by Johann Joachim Kändler in about 1745. It was copied at Chelsea during the red anchor period, i.e. between 1752 and 1757, contemporaneously in Staffordshire salt-glaze and finally at Torquay. The Torquay model is attempting to copy the Chelsea version, since the detailing is less sharply defined than one would expect on Meissen. The Torquay paste has a quite primitive look which goes a long way to explaining its success in beguiling one into thinking that it is very early and experimental soft-paste porcelain from either Chelsea, Bow or Derby. It is open-grained, grey and dry, most closely resembling either Bow of the 1750s or perhaps even early 19th-century Derby. The slightly dirty crackled glaze adds to the confusion. However, a careful examination, when the hare is compared to his earlier colleagues, will highlight his inadequacies, the most obvious being the absence of applied flowers and the poor modelling of the paws.

The dirty-looking crackled glaze is not typical of the originals.

The rather careless streaky painting of the fur identifies it as a fake. The earlier models, if coloured at all, are all very finely brindled.

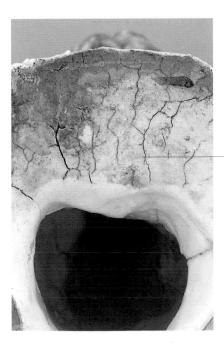

The base shows dried-out fissures which make it look like the early and faulty efforts of a newly established 18th-century factory.

▲ **A London-decorated piece of Welsh porcelain, *c.*1820**

Welsh Porcelain

Arguably the finest porcelains produced in the first half of the 19th century in the British Isles were from the Welsh factories at Swansea and the closely related works at Nantgarw.

Nantgarw was founded by William Billingsley, the celebrated flower painter, in 1813, but the entire concern was moved to Swansea in the following year. It is therefore not surprising that the early porcelain from Swansea is very similar to that from Nantgarw. The Swansea formula was changed, however, since the Nantgarw body was prone to vitrify suddenly, causing the silicate to fuse with the kiln-furniture and resulting in considerable loss (90 per cent in one record firing).

Early Nantgarw porcelain is slightly thicker than the succeeding Swansea porcelain. It is translucent and appears a pure white in transmitted light. Features of Nantgarw porcelain are the patches of iridescence noticeable on the base inside the foot. The glaze is thick and silky with no obvious rippling, such as can be found on thinner glazed porcelain of later Swansea.

Later Swansea variations are the so-called "duck-egg", "trident" and "glassy" porcelains. The first and probably the most famous of the three is highly translucent and very thinly potted with a slight suggestion of green, which is obvious in transmitted light.

The great majority of the output of both factories was composed of dishes, plates and shallow wares. More ambitious pieces such as ice pails and vases were made only in small numbers, almost certainly because of their extreme vulnerability in the kiln. Much Welsh porcelain was sent "in the white" to be decorated in London. When Nantgarw or Swansea wares were not available, the London enamellers used wares from other factories such as Coalport, Davenport or even some of the Paris factories. In the past this had led to some quite erroneous attributions, since it is quite easy, for example, to assume mistakenly that an ice pail surrounded by Nantgarw plates decorated in the same hand is also another Welsh piece.

▶ **A collection of Swansea porcelain**

▼ **A Martin Brothers grotesque bird with incised marks, 1880**

Martinware has enjoyed huge popularity and fakes do appear. These can normally be identified by their lack of subtlety in decoration and moulding. Fakes are sometimes made from taking a mould of an original piece; hence the marks are also moulded. This should indicate to any prospective buyer that the piece is a fake.

Closest to the Welsh is contemporary Spode porcelain, but there is often confusion also with Grainger's Worcester, Davenport and Coalport. It should be noted that plates moulded with floral cartouches similar to those at Nantgarw and Swansea were also made at Derby, Davenport and Coalport around 1820. The Welsh plates with this decoration can be recognized quite simply – literally with one's eyes shut. It is easy to feel the contours of the mould on the backs of the Welsh pieces but not on the English versions.

Modern Studio Pottery

At the time of writing the author is unaware of any forgeries of Studio pottery except the now celebrated attempts by inmates of Featherstone prison near Wolverhampton to copy the works of Bernard Leach. These fakes first appeared on the market in 1980 and fooled both auction houses and dealers alike, and it is worth quoting from an article which appeared in *The Sunday Times* on 10 January 1981. "By last summer there was a notable rise in the number of 'rare' Leaches on the London art market. A London dealer and ceramic specialist, Richard Dennis, was one of the first to spot that there was something 'rather wrong' with a number he had bought. For example, at Bonham's last October he successfully bid £600 ($900) for one, a stoneware bottle vase".

Dennis finally became suspicious after buying a handsome and unusual green-glazed dish at Christie's. "When I went over to Phillips I saw two more and they, too, had the same peculiar green glaze", he said. "When I saw so many dishes like that I thought there was something wrong."

This illustrates perfectly the common mistake of putting too many objects on the market in a short space of time. If the "master-potters" of Featherstone Prison had been as sophisticated in their marketing as in their potting, they would probably still be enjoying the revenue from their efforts during occupational therapy hours.

The work of Shoji Hamada, Hans Coper, Lucie Rie, William Staite Murray, Michael Cardew and other leading 20th-century potters has to my knowledge not yet received similar flattery, but doubtless it will in future.

Netsuke & Okimono

The netsuke is a small object, usually in wood or ivory, designed to suspend a pouch, pipe case, and/or *inro* (set of miniature boxes) from the *obi* (sash), holding together the pocketless kimono formerly worn by Japanese men and women. To fulfil its function, it could not be too large or it would be uncomfortable to wear, nor could it have projections that might get caught up in the kimono. This sorts out a true netsuke from the later *okimono* (standing figures) or groups carved by the same *netsuke-shi* (carver), either for indigenous collectors or more often for export. Okimono started to be produced when Japan was opened up to Western influence after Commander Perry of the US Navy sailed into Yokahama Harbour in 1853. Okimono continued the netsuke tradition of two holes (*himotoshi*) in the base but were obviously too large to be worn.

The Materials

To tell fake from genuine netsuke you need some familiarity with the materials from which authentic pieces were made. The numbers of original netsuke carved in ivory and wood were about equal, but there are more forged ivory carvings on the market. There are several reasons for this. First, up until about five years ago, ivory netsuke were more highly regarded and more expensive. Second, the patina of wooden examples, both that put on by the original carver and that developed through age, is a great deal more subtle than on an ivory of comparable date and therefore harder to recreate. Third, the availability of plastic to simulate ivory.

Ivory is not indigenous to Japan and elephants were introduced only in the 19th century. Strictly speaking, the term should be applied only to the tusks of elephants (either those we know today or mammoths), though a wider

► **Two okimono compared**
The Japanese okimono of rice sellers on the far right dates from *c*.1900 and is made of ivory. The okimono of the peasant is about the same date and moulded in plastic (see the base of this piece opposite on page 189). Seen side-by-side the differences are apparent. The carving on the ivory okimono is sharp and expressive – particularly on the faces – compared to the soft, blurred features of the plastic figure. The modern figure lacks detail in the basket and clothing. It is also much whiter and a more even colour overall. The original ivory piece has a good patina and dirt has caught in all the places you might expect.

definition includes the teeth of the hippopotamus, narwhal and walrus, of which only the third is a consideration here. Tusks are incisors from the upper jaw and are entirely formed of dentine. This is composed of innumerable minute longitudinal tubes which are, when fresh, filled with oil. This oil enables ivory to take on its characteristic polish and is slowly lost with age. It is a fallacy that ivory goes brown with age; in most cases it does not. Netsuke were stained by the carver.

Faint longitudinal stripes are a sure guide to identifying the simulated ivories that appeared at the turn of the century with the stripes built into them. If the suspect ivory is held near a light source so that the stripes are visible and then revolved slowly horizontally through 90 degrees, the light and dark stripes on genuine ivory will become less pronounced or disappear. On the simulation, they will be visible at any angle; they also tend to be wider and more regular than on the genuine article. This test takes some learning but once learned is invaluable. The colour of these simulations is also revealing: they are not stained but an even white all over – too white. The forgeries made about 1900 are in casein (made from milk), celluloid and other plastics and occasionally have the "signature" of the "carver" moulded into the base. The base also displays the same striping as the sides, whereas a cross section of ivory shows concentric lozenges.

Another substitute for elephant ivory is walrus tusk, which can be distinguished from true ivory by its core of granular dentine, though this is often disguised by cross-hatching or similar patterning. Walrus ivory is formed of different layers and so is less stable than ivory and more prone to cracking.

A cheaper and readily available material which is often passed off as ivory is bone, and netsuke in this material are at large to trap the unwary. Bone, unlike ivory, is provided with a blood source and, therefore, even in small pieces, has minute pores and channels though which the bone is kept alive. They appear on a carving as small brown or black spots or channels.

▲ **Manju netsuke with silver metal purse attachment**
This netsuke displays light and dark stripes simulating ivory, but they do not disappear when the piece is revolved. It is early 20th century, made from similar plastic to the peasant okimono on the previous page.

Characteristic parallel lines of simulated ivory, and the moulded signature can be seen. Note the piece is on its side so the top of the signature is on the right.

The radiating, intersecting lines form minute lozenges and the concentric rings of lighter and darker colour are visible.

The slight darkening at the edges is typical of the walrus. Note this signature in the centre panel is also on its side.

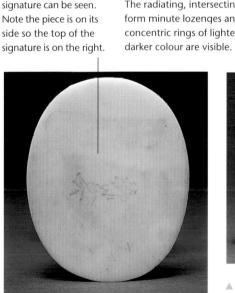

▲ **The base of the plastic figure opposite**

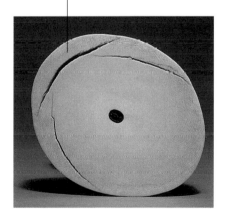

▲ **The base of an elephant ivory figure**
The cracking is not uncommonly found on a large cross-section. The nerve canal has been inset with a black lacquer panel signed "Sei".

▲ **The base of a walrus ivory**
The granular, translucent appearance of the core has been disguised by lotus leaf carving. It is signed "Tamayuki" on a lacquer reserve.

Casting in Plastic Resin

Since the mid-1970s large numbers of deceptive netsuke and figures have been produced by casting in plastic resin using a flexible mould. These are extremely difficult to detect as they are taken directly from originals, usually those of the okimono type from the second half of the 19th century, and the process is so sensitive that it picks up every detail of the original, including undercutting. After casting they are stained in a deep sepia, which is thinner on the proud surfaces and gives a realistic impression of wear. They can be found in antiques shops, antiques fairs and country auctions, frequently with the deeper portions retaining quantities of dust, suggesting that they have come from an old, neglected collection. In fact, dust is blown into the interstices from the wrong end of a vacuum-cleaner as part of the finishing. Turn-of-the-century plastic netsuke and okimono are lighter in weight than the originals but this problem has been overcome with the modern copies.

There are two ways of distinguishing the modern products. A chip on a genuine ivory shows an irregular new surface of similar colour but perhaps slightly paler in tone. The modern resin chip is more akin to glass, with a shiny white surface. The other aid to identifying the plastic forgery is temperature. Ivory feels much colder than the reproduction as it conducts heat away from the skin far more readily.

The definitive temperature test is burning. If you have ever had a tooth drilled you will know the characteristic smell of a burning tooth. Hold a pin in a pair of pliers and heat it glowing hot and then stick it in some inconspicuous part of the carving. On ivory the pin will barely mark the surface but there will be a burnt-tooth smell; on the plastic it will enter readily with a puff of smoke and throw up a burr at the edges of the hole. There will be a strong smell of burning plastic. Some experts with a very good sense of smell say that it is enough to rub a plastic reproduction vigorously on a piece of fabric or clothing – this warms it enough to release volatile oils and therefore the smell of plastic.

The brown-black flecks, pin holes and a larger brown canal have had leaves and a floret carved over them in an attempt to disguise them.

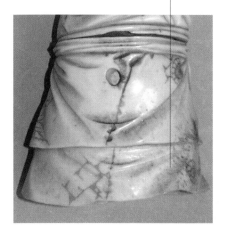

▲ **Section of a figure composed of carved bone parts**

▼ **A modern resin netsuke (4.5cm/1¾ in), made in flexible rubber mould from a poor original with the underneath shown right**

The colour is not the sepia-brown of an original but a nasty gingery hue.

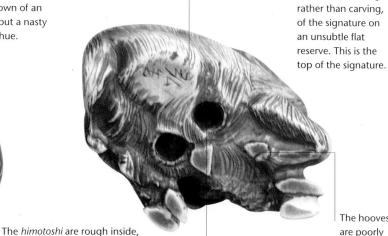

Note the moulding, rather than carving, of the signature on an unsubtle flat reserve. This is the top of the signature.

The *himotoshi* are rough inside, they should be smooth.

The hooves are poorly defined.

▶ **A modern resin netsuke with a view of underside below**

The whole is stained a deep sepia, "worn" on the extremities.

There is considerable dirt in the recesses.

The chip on the prow has exposed the white, glass-like material.

The age cracks of the original.

The moulded (rather than carved) signature "Tomochika". (The signature begins here, on the right.)

The wear to the original himotoshi is visible.

IDENTIFYING RECENT RESTORATION

Recent restoration, invisible to the eye, can sometimes be detected by the nose. Many modern adhesives have a lingering smell; smoke may have been used to darken a part and this too is detectable for quite a while afterwards. And the acidic, vinegary miasma that accompanies chemical staining can drift around a piece long after it has left the workshop.

Signatures and Attributions

Once the material has been established as ivory it may still be necessary to consider the matter of attribution in some detail before deciding that a carving is altogether genuine.

East is East and West is West and the twain certainly do not meet over their attitude to imitation. The 18th- and 19th-century netsuke-shi were not regarded as artists but as craftsmen of a very lowly order; only rarely did they achieve any recognition for their skills. As such, they frequently did not sign their work, particularly in the 18th century. Those that achieved a degree of fame were unashamedly copied by their contemporaries, with or without the originator's or their own signatures. The successful carver would be unable to supply the demand for his work and would employ pupils who would copy the master's work as closely as possible, starting by roughing out the shapes until skilled enough to undertake the whole carving on their own. Occasionally a pupil would subsequently set up on his own, but many continued to work in a master's studio. As a result, there were not only a great many unsigned pieces, but pieces were originally signed in ways that can now be confusing.

The Japanese, as in the West, have a surname (written first) and a given name, but these are only infrequently their working names. It was much more common to adopt a professional name (*go*) which could be changed several times throughout a craftsman's life: Kaigyokudo Masatsugu, for example, signed variously: Masatsugu, Kaigyokudo, Kaigyoku and Kaigyokusai; he also used an adoptive family name. A pupil would adopt

▲ An ivory sleeping boar netsuke by Kaigyokusai Masatsuga
Note the high-quality carving which gives such character to the piece, and the fine detail.

▼ Another genuine sleeping boar by Kaigyokusai with a very good copy
The smaller boar (left) is a genuine carving by Kaigyokusai. The carving on the copy next to it is highly skilled and only the over-large (but not impossible) size and the less careful handling of the hair marking suggest at first sight something may be wrong. The false signature seen on the underside, far right, supplies a further clue. The first character is badly engraved and hesitantly formed, the second slightly better, the third better still and the fourth is carved with considerable bravura, probably indicating the trepidation with which the forger embarked upon his work and his increasing confidence. It must be said, however, that the first character in Kaigyokusai's signature is never as well formed as the rest.

one character of his master's name, which aids the tracing of a particular school, but overall it is difficult to attribute all but the greatest carving with certainty.

The matter is complicated by the Japanese love of travel within their own country – the carvers would have been influenced by work from other centres that they passed through. Attributing netsuke to a particular artist working in a particular centre is therefore fraught with difficulties. All that we can do is propose likelihoods.

There is a trend in connoisseurship to make the mistake of believing that a netsuke carved in the style of a master and bearing his signature but which is in some way less powerful or inventive than one might expect must perforce be either the work of a pupil, partly worked by a pupil, the work of a follower, or an out-and-out forgery. But great artists do not always turn out masterpieces. One only has to look at some of the inferior work turned out by Picasso to see the truth of this, but no one doubts his standing as the major artist of the 20th century.

There seems to be a preference for signed netsuke over unsigned, although the quality may be no better. But the preference is sufficient to tempt fakers to indulge in a little "attribution" and sign an unsigned piece. This may spoil a good piece as most collectors, when told that their perfectly genuine Tomatada bore a later signature, would rate it less highly. It goes without saying that only the signatures of major artists are liable to be forged.

Modern Copies

Now that a netsuke has fetched over £200,000 ($300,000) at auction, the urge to copy pieces in a quasi-authentic manner is irresistible to the unscrupulous. There are two levels at which forgery may appear. One is in the rarefied atmosphere at the high end of the market, say over £5,000/$7,500. Here the forger must provide his highly skilled carver with a model which is uncommon, or better still unknown, give him as much time as is necessary to carve one or two meticulous copies and then sell them to collectors long on money and short on experience. Such an operation is both expensive – the money invested in the genuine example is tied up for a long period and the carver will not come cheap – and risky – the dud piece

Seen side by side with the copy, this genuine piece is smaller.

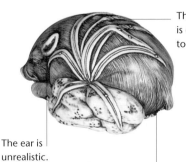

The ear is unrealistic.

The hair is less well-carved on the forgery.

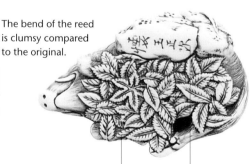

The bend of the reed is clumsy compared to the original.

The leaves are too pronounced.

The signature is badly engraved – particularly the first character, which is on the right.

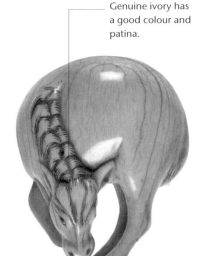

Genuine ivory has a good colour and patina.

▲ An ivory netsuke of a grazing horse, 18th century

This ivory netsuke is standing in a typical attitude and has an excellent patina that has built up naturally over the years and is much more irregular than a faker could ever produce. It also has slight age cracks. The eye pupils are inlaid with pale horn.

Signs of wear should always correspond to function – as here.

▲ A rare ivory netsuke of a winged dragon, 18th century

There is visible signs of wear to the right of the himotoshi where the cord has rubbed over time – an encouraging sign of authenticity.

cannot be released via a major auction house but must wait for passing trade. With this in mind, exercise the utmost caution in buying from galleries and shops on the tourist routes, including that most expensive of operations, the hotel shop.

There is a safeguard, however: a copyist is not a creative artist; were he so he would have no need to copy and run the risk of prosecution. He therefore takes a borrowed model from a bent collector or dealer and in reproducing it almost always loses the vitality and often the attention to detail of the original. In one noted case, a forger copied an instantly recognizable rabbit and its young by Okatomo from Bushell's *Collectors' Netsuke*, but not having an illustration of the reverse he left the back of the carving almost flat (see overleaf). A knowledge of reference books is therefore of great value when a rare netsuke is being sold for what appears to be a bargain price.

At the other end of the scale is the tyro collector, the tourist after a souvenir or the small-time dealer hoping for a snip. To satisfy this demand, China is supplying quantities of "hand-carved" netsuke, in ivory, but produced in very large numbers. They make no pretence to having any antiquity or pedigree, although some are artificially stained. I have not encountered any with signatures that could lead to confusion with a collectable carver. They can be found in profusion at airports, hotel shops, fairs and small dealers and are remarkably cheap. They are, however, carved from new tusks (old ivory becomes too hard to work) and in numbers too great to be supplied from the strict quotas now in force to protect elephants. Purchasing them can only lead to further slaughter.

Signs of Wear

The old netsuke, those made in the golden age between the late 18th century and the middle of the 19th, show over a century of natural ageing and wear to their surfaces. This will include, as the pieces were in everyday use, wear to raised portions and particularly to the cord holes, the *himotoshi*. This wear is almost impossible to reproduce realistically and the forger, if he considers it at all, fails to make the smaller cord exit hole display more wear than the larger hole which accommodated the knot. If the holes were originally of a similar size, one will display more wear than the other. In addition, a patina builds up from constant handling and exposure to the air, which is never perfectly reproduced. As ivory ages it darkens, but in a haphazard fashion. The staining with sepia dye on modern reproductions is consistent, unrealistic and generally with an unpleasant pinkish tinge.

General characteristics of these modern netsuke are the crudeness of the carving and the use of black staining to emphasize details such as facial features to cut down on carving time. They frequently bear signatures in crude characters, albeit finely engraved. The subjects are usually those that can be carved with the minimum expenditure of material and time and include human figures and simple animals such as snakes and birds.

Despite the fact that the netsuke is no longer a useful object, honest examples are still being made and there are a number of superb modern carvers whose pieces are avidly collected. As their work is very expensive and obtainable only through particular galleries, the chance of forgeries of their work being offered for sale is small, but no doubt they will come with time.

▼ Wood netsuke of a rabbit
This netsuke was copied from an illustration in
Collectors' Netsuke by Raymond Bushell, 1971,
p.32, no.24 (5½cm/2¼in).

The copyist has
engraved the hair
markings very crudely
and the reverse side,
which was not
illustrated in the book,
is still less well carved.

The original by
Okatomo has a fine
patina which the
forger has imitated
with a stain of almost
black colour, now
worn off in patches
to expose a much
paler body.

The only advice that can be offered here is the same as with early netsuke – be familiar with the carvings of the artists that interest you. One of the greatest of these modern artists, Masatoshi, has written a biography with the aid of his mentor Raymond Bushell, and amongst the wealth of pertinent information is the astonishing fact that a satisfactory polish can take up to twelve hours' work and six different materials. While it is unlikely that all earlier carvings had that amount of time expended on them, it is a fact that modern forgeries do not have the deep patina obtained through hard work. In fact, so rapidly have many of them been produced that fragments of ivory scrapings and dust can often be found in the crevices.

 The genuine netsuke sits comfortably at the waist and presents itself logically. A horse, for example, should hang in an upright position (see page 193). This is rarely considered by the faker, who places the *himotoshi* without thought. A little time spent working out how the netsuke would sit is time well spent. The placing of the signature can also be used as a guide. On a genuine example it was never placed where it could be seen when in use and if the netsuke is viewed head on and then turned up to view the underside the signature should appear the right way up. The forger is frequently unaware of this.

 The larger Japanese carvings in walrus and elephant ivory made after the market for indigenous netsuke collapsed in the 1860s have not been reproduced in resin to any great extent although it is difficult to say why this should be so. Large Chinese "carvings" of Immortals and the Emperor and Empress abound, so there can be no technical reason for reproductions to be limited to netsuke or small okimono size. Only one large piece has come to notice, purchased in an auction by someone who had not viewed the piece, which was added to the lot at the last moment.

Inlaid Carvings

So far we have looked only at okimono carved from single pieces of ivory. There was however a long-established tradition of netsuke with small details such as the eyes inlaid in a different material – tortoiseshell into wood, for example. Over the years, wood will shrink in one direction and ivory may in many; this, or degradation of the glue or a knock, may be enough to release an eye or a stud. With the former, always check that both pupil and iris have the same amount of wear and patination. The smart restorer replaces both pupils and if this is done well there is unlikely to be any great loss of value. Later netsuke, figures and works of art could have considerable amounts of inlay in coral, mother-of-pearl, amber, coconut, tortoiseshell and stained ivory. Again, these may have been lost over time and replaced. A careful comparison with the colour and tone of remaining inlay may reveal discrepancies. Inlays into lacquer grounds are particularly difficult to replace accurately and usually show a gap between the ground and the inset; when they were first made the ground was applied up to already fixed inlays. The resetting, as opposed to replacement, of loose pieces is not in any way a detraction if it is properly done. Of all the techniques used on netsuke and okimono, the most easily damaged is lacquer. Only the Japanese have conquered it fully and where it has been damaged a "restorer" might have found it easier to remove the area rather than repaint. A matt shadow will usually remain.

Sectional Figures

Towards the end of the 19th century, as the market for ivories exported to the West increased, sectional figures were produced, made from separate pieces, many of which were offcuts sold by the makers of large carvings. These figures often mixed walrus and bone and there are two distinct grades of them. The first is of exceptionally finely carved groups which had to be constructed from several pieces as no single tusk would be large enough to accommodate them. What should be watched for here is the replacement of a lost part by one newly carved. The most obviously delicate sections such as pipes, tools, arrows, small boxes, etc, should be examined for changes in colour or texture of the ivory, a downgrading of quality or slight changes in scale. A substitution of a lost piece by something appropriate from a group too damaged to be of use but of comparable quality is undetectable and as such will not affect the value.

Many of these sectional groups were signed on a small red lacquer panel let into the base, and the belief seems to have arisen that a lacquer reserve indicates quality. Alas, both the best and the junk can have this feature, so look for the care with which the signature has been engraved and beware of the thin, spidery hand. New lacquer signatures have also been noted on originally unsigned groups.

The Tokyo School carvings produced from the end of the last century up until the First World War, usually from a single large tusk, have risen in value dramatically over the last few years. The major carvers, such as Ishikawa Komei and Yoshida Homei, are now becoming recognized. There is no likelihood of reproductions of their work ever being made as the skills are no longer around to produce them, but carvings bearing Ishikawa's name (though too poor to be by his hand) were produced contemporaneously. These are on the market and have deceived people who paid too much attention to the signature and not enough to·the quality of the piece.

Note the carefully undercut strings which would be likely to be damaged.

There is a fabulous rhythmic movement to the draperies.

◀ **Ishikawa Komei okimono**
A superb carving by a major carver in which he has, through brilliant technique, made the width of the tusk appear impossibly large. Typically for Komei, the ivory is unstained and very white. Such work is uncopyable today. Its height is 26cm/10¼in.

Quilts

▲ **20th-century quilts**
Relatively recent quilts like this Lattice Baskets quilt, made in Pennsylvania *c.*1930, are seldom faked. The scalloped border is usually an indication of early 20th century origin. At present there are plenty of originals available and at reasonable prices. However, this type of quilt is being reproduced in China and sold as new. While these are not fakes, collectors should be aware that there are contemporary versions of this type of quilt around.

Interest in quilt collecting developed in the United States over 40 years ago and spread gradually to Japan, West Germany, France, Britain and Scandinavia, where there are now major collections. In the past 30 years collectors from these areas have had a major impact on the market, driving prices for better examples to new highs.

The major source of period quilts is the United States, where they have been made since at least the 18th century, although few of these exist. It is very rare to find a quilt made before the first quarter of the 19th century. Canadian quilts, which closely resemble American examples, are of similar vintage. The earliest documented English quilt dates to 1718 with some fabrics in it nearly 100 years older.

Collectors' interests are very clearly differentiated. Early and fine examples are treated as folk art or paintings and displayed on walls beneath protective glass. Demand for the finest pieces outstrips the supply, but ordinary or damaged examples raise little interest and remain abundant. It is only the best examples that are liable to be faked: the amount of time and degree of skill required ensure that only a piece that will bring a substantial price will be altered or reproduced.

The Valuation of Quilts

Several elements go into the valuation of a quilt, and the importance of each varies according to a collector's attitude. For a small but highly sophisticated group the important thing is the quilting – that is, the stitching that holds the back of the piece together and supports the inner batting. Connoisseurs look for elaborately designed quiltings: hearts, vines, floral groupings and, in rare cases, human and animal forms. They will also pay a premium for the closest stitching. The more stitches per inch a seamstress achieved the more highly thought of her work is. Solid white quilts, of little interest to most enthusiasts, are snapped up by this group if the stitchwork is of the finest. Since quilting of this quality is time-consuming and beyond the ability of all but a very few people, it is not likely to be faked.

A major group of collectors seeks strongly graphic quilts with bright colours and bold designs. Many of these resemble abstract paintings and they are displayed as such by their owners, who often have no interest at all in other antiques. Some of the major problems with faking and reproduction occur in this area. Because they are often of geometric pattern these quilts are not hard to put together, and since would-be purchasers frequently have little knowledge of or interest in quilting or early fabrics they are more easily gulled than individuals in the previous groups. Moreover, as the time and skill involved in faking are modest and the prices that can be obtained for the more spectacular examples are quite high, the fakers are naturally drawn to this area.

While there are collectors most interested in extremely early quilts or those that are dated, signed or have some authentic historical association, these pieces form such a tiny proportion of all existing quilts that they offer little inducement to the faker. However, all names and dates should be regarded with suspicion and examined closely to make sure that they are of an age and style appropriate to the quilt on which they appear.

▶ **A genuine Ohio Amish Railroad Crossing quilt,** *c.*1920

The Types Most Likely to be Faked or Reproduced

Robert Bishop, the late Director of New York's Museum of American Folk Art and the author of a leading book in this field, *America's Quilts and Coverlets*, notes that the three major problem areas today are Amish quilts and similar graphic geometrics; crib quilts; and Baltimore "album" quilts.

The Amish quilts are a particularly difficult area because Amish women were among the first to use sewing machines, not only to bind the edges of a quilt but also to piece it. Consequently, the general guideline that machine stitching in a 19th century quilt is a danger sign might not apply. Remember, however, that the Amish always hand-stitched their quilting, which was often quite complex. But Amish quilts are so sought after at present because they are composed of relatively large, geometric units of bold colour, and this type of construction is much more easily and quickly duplicated than that of a detailed quilt such as the Postage Stamp variety or a complex appliquéd quilt.

▲ **A Pennsylvania crib quilt, *c*.1870**
This is a true miniature with a design in proportion to scale and is typically square – 91.5cm/36in – rather than rectangular. Crib quilts are rare and can command high prices, therefore beware of "knock-offs" made from a full-sized or damaged quilt. Ideally a crib quilt should have a border indicating that it is not made up from a full-sized quilt, but not all genuine crib quilts have borders so identification is not always clear cut. Misrepresentation by a dealer is not always deliberate, but more often it reflects a lack of knowledge of the particular piece.

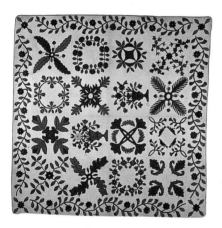

▲ **"Baltimore Album" quilt, *c*.1850**
Among the most valued of textiles, quilts such as this one command high prices. If the elements of the design have been appliquéd to a single solid ground, repairs and alterations can be spotted readily. Beware, though, of album quilts made from individual blocks, as was often the case. The size and fabrics of each block was not necessarily uniform to begin with. Take particular care to determine whether the inconsistencies are original or indicate that the quilt was tampered with to increase its desirability.

It should also be borne in mind that many women of the Amish sect are still making quilts in the traditional manner. Some of these are done in synthetic fibres and can therefore be quickly recognized as contemporary, but a quilt in traditional wool or cotton may be very hard to recognize as recent.

Age is not usually regarded as important in Amish quilts, since the look is what sells them. In fact, many of the most spectacular period examples date only from the 1920s and '30s. On the other hand, no one wants to pay $2,000/£1,350 for an Amish quilt in the belief that it was made 50 years ago, when in fact it was produced only last year.

Crib and doll quilts are smaller versions of full-size bed coverings. The former are usually about 1m/3ft square, while the latter can be as small as 30 x 45cm/12 x 18in. Both types may be faked. The usual procedure is to cut an appropriate section out of a damaged full-size quilt. Some crib quilts are completely made up or reproduced, but Bishop notes that "the modest prices to be realized in this field have served as a brake to any major faking". Nevertheless, the convenient wall hanging or display size of these fabrics makes it likely that they will continue to be made.

Remember that a crib quilt is a true miniature, not a piece of something else. That means that the same balance and symmetry that are to be expected in a full-size quilt should be evident here. Borders should run all round the quilt: missing borders on two sides usually means that the smaller quilt was cut from a corner of a larger one. A central motif or medallion should be in the centre and it should be properly balanced on all sides by design elements. Always check the border and binding. A new binding or elements of new binding on some sides may indicate recent cutting. Patterned quilting should terminate within the body of the quilt – a quilted rose, for example, that runs to the binding with some of the leaves missing is almost a guarantee of reworking.

During the past few years prices paid for album quilts, particularly those made around Baltimore, Maryland, during the mid-19th century, have increased sharply. A fine example will now bring upwards of $50,000/£35,000 and charlatans have been quick to note this. An album quilt consists in most cases of many separate quilt blocks, each of which is carefully appliquéd in a different design. Flowers, hearts, human figures, buildings, trees and animals are among the favourite devices, which are usually done by appliqué on a solid piece of fabric. These bed coverings were usually made as gifts and frequently bear signatures, dates and other mementoes.

Bishop says that skilled seamstresses are taking known Baltimore quilt patterns and either duplicating them or altering them slightly, employing old fabrics appropriate to the period. Such deceptions are particularly hard to spot. One thing to look for, Bishop suggests, is new thread. Even if the faker has dyed the thread with tea or some other stain, a knowledgeable conservator can recognize modern thread used in the stitchwork. Conservators and others familiar with the textiles used in a given historical period can also provide information about whether or not the cloth in a quilt is appropriate to its design and suggested date. However, one must bear in mind that textile remnants for use in quilts were often kept for years or even decades before being incorporated into a bed covering. It is entirely possible for a legitimate quilt to be made from fabrics or to incorporate fabrics dating from 20 or 30 years before it was worked.

IS IT GENUINE?

Nothing can replace the experience of handling a large number of quilts but it is useful to run through the following checklist when you are considering a purchase:

• Does the quilting show the skill and technical sophistication appropriate to the period of the textiles used?
• Does the stitching look new? New quilting and batting might indicate a recently quilted top.
• Sewing machines were commonly used by quilters by the 1870s but machine stitching might indicate that a piece lacks age.
• With combination appliqué and patchwork quilts check that the appliqué, particularly if it is a border, has not been added recently to enhance value. Look for differences in colour, fading and stitchwork.
• Do the front and back appear to be originally joined?
• Does a stain that appears on the front also show on the back?
• Look for repairs that might have involved simple patching and replacement of an entire block.

None of these points on their own necessarily mean a piece is not genuine but these are the type of clues that help to form an opinion of a piece. Quilts were used and it is inevitable that many have been restored and repaired but it is important that the price reflects the true condition and that you, as the purchaser, are aware of it.

Restoration and Repair

The earlier and the more valuable a quilt is, the more likely that it has been restored. Damage from tears, insects, the dissolution of fabric due to certain dyes used to colour it – all these as well as stains can seriously affect the appearance and value of a bed covering. There are many skilled conservators capable of repairing damage, and there is, of course, nothing wrong with buying a restored fabric as long as you know that work has been done on it and the price reflects this fact. Depending on its nature and extent, restoration can decrease the value of a quilt by between 30 and 70 per cent.

When considering a purchase always look a quilt over with minute attention. Do all sections or blocks show equal wear, fading or discolouration? Is the stitchwork essentially identical throughout? Is the same thread used and in the same way? Any sections made from cloth of a different pattern or period from the majority should be closely scrutinized. The quilter may just have run out of fabric, but the odd section may also be a later repair. A stain that ends abruptly at the edge of a square may mean that a more seriously stained adjacent square has been replaced. Does the pattern maintain its original symmetry? If the design seems less developed in one direction or the quilt seems lopsided that may be because a worn end has been removed. Checking the binding for uniformity of wear and material may verify this suspicion.

It is unlikely that all these points will be found on one piece, but if several apply it is likely that it has been restored.

Buying

The field of quilts is a subtle one, and all but the most expert may be fooled by some fakes or some repairs. Your best protection against an unfortunate purchase is to deal only with reputable sellers who are knowledgeable in the field and who will guarantee their merchandise.

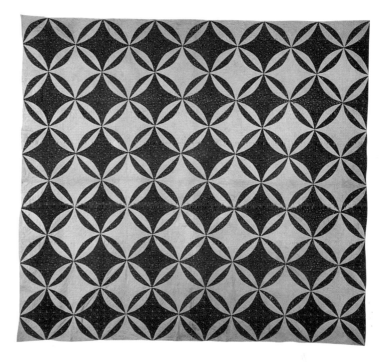

▶ **"Robbing Peter to Pay Paul" quilt, origin unknown, c.1830**
This quilt is soiled, and damage to the red fabric can be seen, but it is probably too fragile to survive washing.

Decoys

▲ Decorative carving
This Bobwhite quail is a decorative carving made in Illinois during the 1970s. It was designed as a piece of sculpture, not as a working decoy, and such pieces are attractive in their own right. But with faked wear and paint loss they may be passed off as much older than they really are. Always check painted wood closely for signs of age.

The decoy, a more or less realistic representation of a bird designed to lure wildfowl within gunshot, is collected primarily within the United States, though European examples will be encountered and Canadian decoys form an important separate classification. While many birds have been imitated as decoys, including crows, owls and doves, the majority of forms fall within two categories – ducks and shore birds. In each of these enthusiasts distinguish between working decoys, which were actually used or "hunted over", and purely decorative wildfowl carvings. Many well-known carvers produced both types. Collectors include duck hunters and folk art enthusiasts.

The value of a decoy is primarily dependent upon the reputation of the carver, the rarity of the individual work and, to a lesser extent, aesthetic considerations. The last are of most concern to those who pursue decoys as a form of folk sculpture. Since a connection with a particular maker is so important the faking of either makers' marks or their styles is the customary avenue of fraud.

The Prevalence of Fakes and Reproductions

Jeff Waingrow, author of *American Wildfowl Decoys* and a leading authority in the field, notes that "generally speaking, faking of famous makers' work is uncommon". This is due to a great extent to the fact that those who seek such pieces are usually extremely knowledgeable sportsmen and carvers, familiar with the styles of the carvers whose work they seek and thus very difficult to fool. Shorebirds may bring as much as $50,000 (£35,000) at auction, and a pair of Merganser ducks have sold for over $90,000 (£60,000). With this kind of money at stake the market for the best decoys is small and most trading is done among a small group of experts.

On the other hand, there are many fakes and reproductions among birds selling for $1,000 (£700) or less, especially those retailing for a few hundred dollars, which are often bought by people knowing little or nothing of the field and seeking only a certain "look". The commonest kind of fake is the

One trick is to build a new body to go with an old head, since the latter were often made up in quantity and may be found in old shops or among hunters' stores.

The crackled paint on this canvas body indicates clearly that this is not a recent reproduction.

▶ A genuine Canada goose decoy
Since they are both interesting in appearance and popular with collectors, Canada geese are often faked.

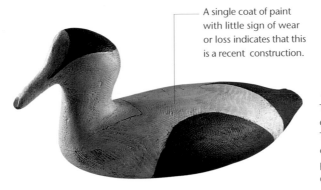

▼ A modern eider duck decoy
Eider decoys are among the more spectacular of wildfowl lures and among those most often faked.

A single coat of paint with little sign of wear or loss indicates that this is a recent construction.

▲ Tin shorebird decoy
Tin shorebird decoys were made in factories during the second half of the 19th century. They are popular with collectors but be sure to check the paint to see if it is original. Since the paint is frequently lost and the body rusts, such decoys are liable to have been repainted.

outright reproduction, in which both body and paint are new. In most cases the paint will be distressed to create an illusion of age and use. The makers of such reproductions tend to focus on the more spectacular and hence more saleable types such as swans, Canada geese and Mergansers. New heads may be joined to old bodies, lost beaks might be replaced or an older body embellished with carved feathering. Most such work is relatively crude as the amount to be gained in this price range does not justify fine work.

Points to Watch For

Always be aware of prices and be suspicious of a good-looking bird that is well under the normal market value. Familiarize yourself with current market prices for different types – if you are offered something that appears to be a bargain, it probably has problems.

Working decoys were repainted each year and should show several coats of paint with worn spots, small chips and cracks from wear and age. Shot holes can occasionally be seen, though they are not common as most sportsmen do not shoot birds on the water. Wear is usually simulated with sandpaper or steel wool. Examine worn areas under a magnifying glass. If deep, rough ridges or gouges appear, the wear is artificial. True, old wear produces smooth, spiderweb-like crazing with softened edges.

Few makers marked their birds, though many owners did. Familiarize yourself with the marks of well-known carvers. Always compare a mark with an example of the carver's signature in a book or on an authenticated example. Like other parts of the decoy, the mark should show proper wear. It is also important to familiarize yourself with the carving and painting techniques used by the makers whose work you seek, since most attribution is based on a particular carver's style. Never buy a bird simply because it is said to "look like a Nathan Cobb", or "resemble a Joe Lincoln goose".

Decoys can be bought in many places, but if you want to buy quality, go to a reputable dealer with long experience in the field. Most of these will warrant their attribution of a bird, and, equally importantly, they will still be in business if you have reason to make a complaint. One of the characteristics of the faker is his rapid disappearance once the sale is made.

▲ These fine shorebird decoys all date from the early 20th century
The Greater Yellowlegs in the centre is by the famous carver, A. Elmer Crowell. Learn to recognize the style and carving techniques employed by a craftsman like Crowell, as few such makers ever marked their work.

Scientific Instruments

Note the "S" with the serif – Lloyd Williams' trademark signature.

▲ A Lloyd Williams fake silver universal ring dial, c.1750
Signed "Narcy à Paris", with full North/South latitude scale, subdivided hour ring, bridge with solar declination/Zodiacal/calendrical scales, twin pinhole sights, 0-90 degree solar altitude scale and sliding suspension mount, 1.6cm/4in in diameter.

Fakes and Reproductions

The first thing that a collector needs to be aware of is the difference between a fake and a reproduction: a reproduction is simply a copy, while a fake is deliberately intended to deceive. You cannot always rely on what the seller tells you, and it can be hard to know what to look for when trying to determine whether a piece you are interested in buying is a fake or not. A good place to begin is to find out which items are most often faked. Some are just too difficult or costly to fake – musical boxes, for example. However, reproductions of items such as phonographs, which are made from casts of an original, have a value in their own right. Deliberate fakes do exist, though, and they can range in quality from those that fool even the most experienced to those which are only going to deceive the novice collector. The following are examples from both these categories which began trickling onto the market in the late 1970s and '80s. Oddly enough, they came from two distinct parts of the world and both ends of the value spectrum.

Lloyd Williams' Fakes

First of all, from France came beautiful and rare instruments in brass and silver. They spanned a number of centuries and were of excellent quality, which was reflected in the prices realized. Some were sold to dealers, others went through the major London auction houses. At first, few people noticed anything out of the ordinary. One well-regarded American curator was known to feel something was wrong, as were other academics. It took two Paris dealers to take stock of items they had recently purchased to realize all was not well. First they asked themselves how it was so many rare instruments, not in the styles of any known makers, had come on the market in such a short period of time. Closer examination revealed that the faker had not rolled his own brass, but used stock brass which was generally too thick. They then compared the engraving on the different instruments. Although done beautifully, and in different styles and from different periods (medieval, Renaissance, etc) they all had similar characteristics, the chief being the serif on the letter "S", which proved to be the "signature" of the forger who was later identified as an Englishman gunsmith by the name of Lloyd Williams. The matter was pursued in the courts and eventually Williams was successfully prosecuted and sent to prison.

Fakes from India

A few years later came instruments of another sort from the workshops of India: bad copies of not-so rare or valuable instruments. India is known for its brassware so it was hardly surprising when cheap copies of such common instruments as level finders, marching compasses and horn gramophones began surfacing. A walk down Portobello Road market in London today will still yield a number of these. Also from the same source were slightly rarer items such as kaleidoscopes and pocket sextants. At first a few people were fooled, but only because it had never occurred to anyone that someone would

▲ A recent, probably Indian, fake brass three-circle pattern sextant
Tell-tale signs are the overly shiny surface (usually black), badly divided scale, poor-fitting telescope and shades, new screws and still-sharp edges. The case is also too new-looking.

▲ A fake Renaissance portable globe sundial, c.1980
The globe is of stained resin instead of ivory (see page 189 for identifying the difference) and is moulded instead of engraved. Portable dials usually have adjustable gnomons but this one is fixed at 90 degrees, which is of very limited use. The pillar is attached to the base by a machine-made thread. This piece is of no value at all.

even bother to fake items such as these. But soon it became obvious to all but the least seasoned. Sadly, however, these less seasoned buyers are still fooled, and will pick these items up for reasonable prices only to find out they are fakes. They are, thankfully, very easy to spot if you know what to look for. One initial giveaway is that many of the instruments are signed "Stanley, London". The Stanley company was very proficient and made many such items, but of far better quality. The ones being faked, however, usually have a brand new appearance, which any experienced collector knows rarely happens. Also, they are badly made. The castings are crude, the gearing is sharp from its newness, and finally, the signature is either stamped or cast into the piece, rather than engraved as would be expected on an original. More recently, fake sextants and Leica cameras have appeared from the same area and these are usually identifiable from the same characteristics.

What to Look For

Even top-quality fakes and reproductions have tell-tale signs. For instance, if every single screw in a supposedly early 18th-century piece is machine-made, alarm bells should ring. One or two screws might have been replaced in an original, but if all of them are of a much later date, something is wrong. A piece that looks like new but which the seller claims is unrestored should also be a cause for concern. Anything that is more than a couple of years old is going to show signs of wear – and the older it is, the more wear you should expect. The wear should always correspond to the function of the object and its parts. The place where you find an item can also give clues to its authenticity.

Astonishing items do occasionally show up in out-of-the-way places, but it does not happen very often. A genuine medieval French quadrant is really most unlikely to have found its way to an antiques fair in Little Rock, Arkansas. Of course, if the seller is willing to attest it in writing, then you do not need to worry. But if the seller is not as forthcoming as you would wish, you should walk away. Good sellers should always be able to tell you something about pieces. If they honestly don't know, and even the experts don't always have all the answers, then they should say so.

The key to spotting fakes is practice. Get to know what items should look like. Handle as many as you can, open them up, look underneath, even smell them. It does not take long to train your instinct. And use other people's expertise: get to know fellow collectors and dealers and ask their advice. More experienced collectors may come across something they didn't know existed. Occasionally this is something to get excited about, but more often it is something to be suspicious of. For instance, a brass kaleidoscope was recently advertised online as being signed "Ross, London". Ross was a very fine instrument maker but he is not associated with kaleidoscopes. A check through his original catalogues confirms that indeed he never listed them. The moral is, if a piece doesn't seem to fit with what you know, be very wary.

Scrimshaw

The collector of scrimshaw runs into an immediate problem: exactly what is it that he or she is collecting? The word defies accurate definition and can cover as narrow a group of objects as those produced by North American sailors from whale teeth during the first three-quarters of the 19th century to anything made by sailors from whale, fish or other sea animals and stretching as far as prisoner-of-war work in bone, engravings on ostrich eggs and elephant ivory.

We are concerned here with forgeries produced on whale bones, walrus tusks, turtleshells and baleen (the fibres in the mouth of the baleen whale, often referred to as whalebone but actually keratin, the same material as fingernails).

Whalers were away on voyages that lasted three or four years – on occasion, eight. One of the most serious dangers came not from storm and tempest or a harpooned whale wrecking the boat, but from the utter boredom of waiting for weeks on end for a whale to appear. Scrimshawing (or scrimshandering in the United States) filled in time for all hands from the captain down. It was executed with the most primitive tools – the seaman's knife and sail needles figuring prominently.

Subjects and Sources

Subjects tend to reflect the daily life of the whaler, the life he left behind on dry land (or an idealized version of it) and contemporary events. Thus ships

▶ **A modern fake scrimshaw made of plastic**

The most obvious clue here is the poor quality of the "engraving". On an original, the lines are very fine and, as tooth is a very hard substance, there is an economy in their use. On the fake, the design is too complex, the lines are wide and are filled with too black a paint.

The ends of plastic scrimshaw are the best give-away. The interior is usually black-stained, unlike the originals, and they terminate in rounded bobbles rather than the quite sharp angles of the originals, the holes of which penetrate further into the tooth.

Note the gum end where the irregularity has been brown stained.

the whalers themselves, anchors, ladies dressed in finery or less commonly without it, homesick doggerel verses, political figures, flags and American eagles were common. Occasionally the recipient's name appears, more rarely the name of the carver and exceptionally a date, a ship's name, or a record of whales caught on the voyage. A combination of two of these themes is not uncommon, three is unusual and more rare indeed. And herein lies the downfall of the scrimshammer, as we shall refer to this forger of sailors' items. In an attempt to generate the maximum from his effort he goes too far.

The scrimshammer is also let down by poor research. His sailing ships have faults to the rigging that no sailor could possibly conceive; he engraves lettering from one period while his style is of another.

The sailor, while he had endless time to concentrate on his work, was rarely an artist. Had he been, he would have been unlikely to sign on for the poor rewards usually accruing from a whaling trip. He therefore turned to images he knew at first hand or used illustrations in books or magazines as reference material. Until the 1840s and '50s these would have been copper or steel engravings, which make up the image from numerous finely engraved lines and dots. Thus genuine early scrimshaw reflects this source material and is finely engraved. From the 1850s to the '80s and '90s wood engraving was the common method of reproduction. The picture here is made up of heavier, blacker lines of varying thickness. Still later examples would reflect the photomechanical processes that reproduced pen drawings. By the end of the century a great deal of the charm had been lost and later scrimshaw lacks invention, merely reproducing blindly someone else's work.

Prior to the turn of the 19th century, inscriptions would be in flowing script or with copies of printed letters, which at that time all had serifs. At the beginning of the 19th century, "fat face" letters, with exaggerated thick and thin strokes, were prevalent. Capitals without serifs are extremely unlikely before 1880. Naturally, styles afloat continued long after changes had taken place ashore, but they do provide a way of discounting some fakes.

The human figure is the downfall of even the most skilled scrimshammer, even when copying an illustration. He therefore frequently resorted to pricking around the figure in one of two ways; either through onto the tooth, joining up the pin pricks (which can still sometimes be distinguished), or pencilling through the holes. The scrimshammer may ape these pin pricks but will probably not be able to resist the temptation to overdo them. There is also a world of difference between an untutored hand striving to make the best possible reproduction of an illustration and a third party attempting to reproduce a naïve reproduction. Anyone doubting this should try copying a child's drawing.

The majority of forged engravings on whale teeth of modern origin are in the style of the very late 19th century and have been copied skilfully from books of the period. The collectors should be extremely hesitant about buying any work in which the design is a very dense black and in a naturalistic, pictorial style. Perspective is rare and limited to seascapes with ships and whales, but even here there is a childlike, cut-out or theatrical quality in the genuine article that is very hard to recreate. What is often apparent is a natural skill at pattern making, zig-zags, diamonds, hearts and borders. These, particularly in the American examples, bear an affinity to quilts and are instinctively well balanced.

▲ **A genuine 19th-century piece**
There are several clues here to the rightness of this scrimshaw. Firstly, the unselfconscious combination of the beloved and the ship; secondly, the two-tone effect of the colouring which rarely appears on copies; thirdly, the mottling of the tooth itself with considerable depth of translucency; and, fourthly, the crack. Cracks are possible in plastic but they rarely penetrate too far into the body of the piece.

Good signs of authenticity

Here, again, there is a good feeling of depth between the ship (in a darker colour) in the foreground and the mountain. The lines are engraved extremely finely. Curiously, the dart border at the bottom would, simple though it seems, be very difficult to fake today. The lettering is entirely right for the time and perfectly irregular.

The faker (as distinct from the forger, the former altering a piece, the latter making something new in imitation of the old) has been at work on scrimshaw. Take a tooth with a perfectly genuine but somewhat unexciting ship, add an American flag or a date and, hey presto, you double your money in minutes. The collector has to be on his guard and examine every detail of the engraving, looking for variations in depth, width of line, staining, hesitancy (the faker has a lot at stake and the result is often an unsure line) and plausibility.

A warning might be added here of the distinct possibility of producing on a blank tooth an exact reproduction of a genuine design by photocopying an original, sensitizing the tooth and etching the line. While this is entirely possible, an examination of the line through a magnifying glass should reveal irregularities where the acid bit inconsistently.

A raw whale tooth is ridged and rough and considerable time must be spent in smoothing and polishing before engraving can begin (the polishing instrument was sharkskin stuck to a wooden handle). An exposed surface of tooth, be it elephant, whale or walrus, develops a patina which is impossible to reproduce (see page 193 for some examples of genuine pieces). The new tooth – not that there is much likelihood of new teeth appearing on the market as most countries now respect the ban on whaling – is fresh white with irregular staining. The overall creamy colour appears with age and no amount of heating or staining can simulate it.

Reproductions are available on the market from such respectable retailers as the shops in British and North American museums in moulded plastic taken from flexible rubber moulds and picking up every minute detail of engraving, pitting and cracking. They are extremely well coloured to reproduce the original and the weight is realistic. While there is no suggestion that such sources are in any way irresponsible, the fact is that these reproductions are appearing in auctions, trade fairs and antiques shops all over the country. In some cases the auctioneer or dealer may be ignorant of the fact that he is handling a reproduction, but in most cases this must be a generous assessment. In the case of the auctioneer, check that the catalogue states the material – remember, any information that is left out can be just as significant as what is included (see page 194). In the case of the dealer, always ask for a written receipt stating the material and the date of the piece.

Another source of modern copies is an American manufacturer who has an enormous variety of plastic scrimshaw – whale bone, tortoiseshell, walrus tusks – on offer, but, presumably through ignorance, has chosen to reproduce nothing but forgeries. There is also a continuing tradition of scrimshawing in the Azores on new teeth engraved with traditional motifs. These are let down by the newness of the tooth and the poor, rather than naïve, quality of the workmanship.

Toys

▲ **A modern reproduction of the first of many toy robots made in the 1950s**
This is clearly a shiny new reproduction toy with no intention to deceive but with a few years of wear it would be harder to distinguish. Collectors need to be aware that modern reproductions are in the marketplace. Compare with the original on page 214.

It is understandable – indeed, to be expected – that forgeries should exist in the long-established collecting fields such as silver, furniture and porcelain, where prices have been high for many years. It may come as a surprise to many, however, to learn that the collector of toys must be just as rigorous in his or her assessments as a collector of drawings trying to decide whether the Samuel Palmer pen-and-ink he is considering is as original as a Keating pastiche.

Across the wide field of toy collecting the production of modern copies, designed to deceive, is being encouraged by the high prices at which toys change hands in shops, at auctions and privately. Since most collectable toys are constructed from either pressed tinplate or cast-iron, both expensive methods to recreate, copies are either produced in large quantities by a process parallel to the original manufacturing process, spreading the high cost of "tooling-up", or alternatively they may be handmade to simulate the work of a machine. The latter method is obviously much more laborious and is used only to construct highly desirable and correspondingly expensive toys, with which a good return can be made on the time invested in production.

Today some highly skilled craftsmen construct their own interpretations of early toys. These are sold as reproductions by the manufacturers, but in years to come, when they have acquired a patina of age, it is possible that the unscrupulous or the unknowing will pass these on as authentic vintage toys.

Restoration

Restoration can be as detrimental to the desirability and value of a toy as a repair to a piece of porcelain, since any restoration undertaken removes the toy further from its original state of manufacture. Most collectors dream of finding a toy in mint condition within its original box, and restored acquisitions tend to stay in an established collection only until an unrestored example can be obtained. Restoration includes repainting, the manufacture of missing pieces and the marriage of original and non-original sections to recreate a complete toy. In some cases a maker's trademark or label is added to a toy which is either wholly unoriginal or is one which would be worth considerably more if it could be identified as the product of a particular manufacturer. A trademark on a toy may also mislead amateur enthusiasts by persuading them to buy a piece about which, in other respects, they might have been doubtful.

▶ **Toys with original boxes are always more collectable**
Always check the box as carefully as the toy itself to determine both are as they should be.

Identifying Repaints & Recasts

A Dinky pre-war tractor, English

The red wheels and yellow parts are all repainted. They are slightly the wrong colour and the wear does not match the rest of the toy.

Mass-produced die-cast model vehicles and toy soldiers are now worth so much that people spend considerable time faking and repainting them. Generally the basic vehicle or figure is standard, it is just the finish that can make the model rare. A Dinky car in an unusual colour can make that vehicle worth £2,000/$2,900 rather than £50/$73. This means it is tempting to repaint the toy. You can check for repainting by scratching with a thumbnail somewhere which is not too noticeable. Original paint finish is baked on and hard; on repaints the paint will flake off. Also look for signs of the rivet on the underside or the axles and wheels being removed during repainting.

A Dinky post-war car, English
The base has been removed and pale blue hubs have been added from another vehicle to make it a much rarer toy. The rivets and the tyres have also been replaced.

A Dinky French Factory Citroën Light 15, English
This is a recast in white metal and is much heavier than the original.

Britain's Toy Soldiers

ORIGINAL PACKAGING
Many toys came originally in boxes. These in some cases can be worth ten times more than the toy itself, consequently they also are being reproduced. The collector needs to learn to distinguish the difference between printed and photocopied cardboard when examining boxes.

Britain's toy soldiers are commonly repainted or given head swaps to create valuable rare and unique regiments. They are stripped down to the basic casting, and a head from another figure is soldered on and then repainted. You can identify resoldering by poking a pin in the air hole in the top of the head; if it stops at the neck it is a fake. Check the base: once stripped, a brighter-coloured metal, which has not oxidized from exposure to the air, can emerge where the paint was originally overlapping the bottom. A "dirty" brown finish can be added as an artificial sign of age.

An original rare Britain's Royal Engineers Pontoon Section, in Active Service Order

This is one of the most copied types of toy soldier. These steel-helmet troops were only issued for a short period at the start of World War II, and a copy would look no different to this. A standard Pontoon Section and the heads of standard World War II soldiers in tin helmets would be married together, and it would be almost impossible to tell it has been done.

▼ Pair of fake bears

A pair of typical fake bears that appear on the market. These bodies are not the right shape, and wrong proportions can be a clue to a fake. Old knitted clothing is often added to fake bears – accompanied by a story about a "little old lady" who has had the bear since childhood! Stall holders at antiques fairs and even auctioneers are not always experts and they can be deceived by fakes.

Always get a receipt if you are buying from a dealer, but if you buy at auction, remember you are buying "as described". However, descriptions can be purposely very vague.

Teddy Bears

The media has expressed its astonishment at the prices realized by discarded teddy bears at auction. Prices exceeding £5,000/$7,250 are now commonplace, and it was to be expected that fakers would cash in on this bonanza. Modern manufacturers now produce limited editions of replica bears which are identical copies of the originals. They are produced as collectables in their own right with distinctive labels and numbering, but potentially could be passed on in the secondary market as originals by the unscrupulous.

It is unusual to find a muzzle bald but no other signs of wear on the head.

The fabric on a fake can be a type of cotton velour which has been made really dirty in an attempt at ageing.

Steiff never used leather on its bears' paws. Suede paw pads are not found on original Steiff bears.

▶ "Freddie Farnell"

This bear made by Alpha Farnell c.1930 and first appeared on the BBC's *Antiques Roadshow* in 1999. He had been wrapped up for many years in a wardrobe, but when his true value was revealed his owner decided to sell him at auction.

▲ **Detail of the original Farnell label**

The blue-and-white embroidered label was used 1925–45. It was often sewn lengthways onto the bear's foot.

Merrythought acquired the right to use the name of Alpha Farnell on replica bears in 1996.

▲ **Replica of "Freddie Farnell" by Merrythought, limited edition of 250**

He is an exact copy even down to his size of 66cm/26in. Under the left arm is a tag giving the number of the bear as well as a guarantee of quality. Beware of fraudsters attempting to pass off replicas as genuine.

A white centre-seam Steiff bear, c.1907

Only every seventh bear made had this feature as it enabled fabric to be joined and one extra head to be cut out of each length of cloth.

The prominent long-shaved muzzle and cupped ears are typical of Steiff

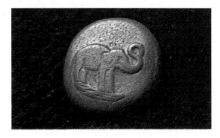

Trademark Steiff "Elephant" Button, used c.1904–5 on the left ear

Buyer beware – buttons are not a guarantee of authenticity. Fake buttons are added to fake bears, genuine buttons can be removed from less expensive Steiff dolls or worn-out bears and added to replica or fake bears, and holes are made in fake bears to give the impression of a lost button.

Teddy bears were made by a number of factories, but the best and most sought-after examples come from the German company of Steiff. The Steiff company was established in 1882 as a family firm and the original plush bear was designed by the nephew of the founder in 1902. It is believed that these bears were used as table decorations at the wedding of Theodore Roosevelt's daughter, Alice. Theodore Roosevelt had refused in 1902 to kill a young captive bear cub when a hunting expedition had proved fruitless. Cartoonists rapidly represented him as a friend to bears and the plush toy bears that adorned the tables at his daughter's wedding were nicknamed "Teddy's Bears" after this hunting incident.

The Steiff trademark is a small nickled or steel rivet found in the left ears of their bears. Since the mid-1980s these original metal rivets have been found in the ears of bears that are modern fabrications. The bear illustrated middle left is an original by Steiff; the muzzle is stitched down either side, rather than having a seam running down the centre – however, the other Steiff bear (c.1907) shown above left does have a centre seam. Every seventh bear made had this feature, because for bears of 41cm/16in or more Steiff joined the bear fabric together, which enabled one extra head to be cut out of each length of cloth. This illustrates the danger of jumping to conclusions about whether a toy is either genuine or a fake.

If a bear is genuine you would expect the fur to be worn, but in the places where you would expect the fur to have been eroded by many years of affection. There are some bears on the market that have been worn in the most unlikely places – they are obviously reconstructed from the pelts of cannibalized toys of the correct date. Other points to look for are the shapes of the ears and facial features such as the muzzle, the nose and eyes. Early Steiff bears should have a prominent, long, shaved muzzle and cupped ears. The pile of the fabric on authentic bears should run downwards . The limbs of authentic teddy bears should be swivel jointed, with the flat edge of the shoulder and hip joints butting against a flattened body surface. In the case of copies, the limbs may be simply stitched to the body with thread without this swivel facility. The Steiff button is considered a sign of authenticity but these are often copies of originals and are only there to persuade the dubious collector that a bear is an authentic example.

Trains

Toy trains are not widely copied but, with prices inflated to the £113, 750 ($165,000) realized by a 1906 toy train at Christie's in 2001, reproduction trains will surely appear in greater numbers. Quality of manufacture is one important guideline when judging the authenticity of a piece; although toys were mass produced by machine, the complexity of the machining and tooling as well as the finish of the paintwork are useful indications as to the date of manufacture. If you were to compare an original c.1905 Plank train with a reproduction, the latter's cruder construction should instantly set off alarm bells. The originals were made by Ernst Plank of Nürnberg, a company founded in 1866 and renowned particularly for its locomotives, steam accessories, cars and boats until production ceased in the 1930s. The trains have spoked wheels of cast metal, a painted oscillating cylinder driving the wheels, delicately modelled smoke stack, buffers and shaped cab.

▶ **Schönner South East & Chatham Railway 4-4-0 locomotive and tender, late 19th century**
This train has been repainted and restored. Originally it was made using a finish that consisted of applying large printed transfers over a hand-enamelled finish. Even with this restoration because of the rarity of Schönner trains, this is still a sought-after toy.

The copies that turn up are of entirely different construction, with drilled brass wheels, a brass oscillating cylinder and crudely modelled details; in addition, the brass boilers are very poorly constructed and roughly soldered and would not be steam-proof under pressure. The locomotive should also have a spirit burner to heat the boiler from below. Reproduction trains sometimes have a reproduction maker's trade label applied to the body, so marks are no guarantee of authenticity.

Steam Cars

One of the most convincing fake toys produced during the last twenty years has been a copy of a 1902 steam-driven toy car, originally produced by the Nuremberg company of Gebr der Bing. The authentic toy has been highly rated by collectors for many years, and as early as 1978 an example in almost mint condition, and with its original box, was sold for £3,400 ($5,100) at Sotheby's.

Modelled on a full-sized vehicle of the same period, the toy is of pressed and hand-painted tinplate. After application the paint was baked on a low heat to give the finish a hardened enamel-like quality which is difficult to reproduce today. With a padded front seat, delicate suspension and large headlamps the vehicle is powered by a simple, spirit-fired, single-cylindered steam engine at the back, linked to the rear axle and propelling the toy forward on its delicately spoked rubber-tyred wheels. The copy is almost identical, making it extremely difficult for a knowledgeable collector, let alone an enthusiastic amateur, to recognize the slight differences without the benefit of direct comparison with the original.

Particular attention should be given to the quality and texture of the paint to judge whether it has the enamel-like finish of the original. In the case of a toy driven by steam (unless in absolutely unused condition in its original cardboard box), one would anticipate some signs of use: bubbling or blistering of the paint where it has been affected by heat from the steam engine, slight rust where steam or water from the tank regularly dampened the paint surface and, most difficult to recognize, wear to the propulsion cylinder. It would be extremely expensive to reproduce accurately the complex tooling required to mass produce the headlamps as made for the original toy; those on the copy are constructed from turned brass and nickel-plated. This is a case where the price that such toys can realize makesit financially viable to produce the pieces almost entirely by hand.

Cast-iron Toys

The production of cast-iron toys involves separate casting of a number of different pieces that fit together to make the finished toy. This is an expensive process for the manufacture of a small number of toys, but highly profitable when many thousands are produced. The original cast-iron toys were made largely in America from the 1870s. Here manufacturers of cast-iron farming, commercial and household equipment, such as J. & E. Stevens Co. of Cromwell, Connecticut, and H. L. Judd Co. of Wallingford, Connecticut, soon learned that a smaller amount of raw material could reap greater profits for the company if made into a toy or a money bank.

In the 19th century these toys were painstakingly cast and assembled so that each piece aligned exactly against the next; the crack at the join of

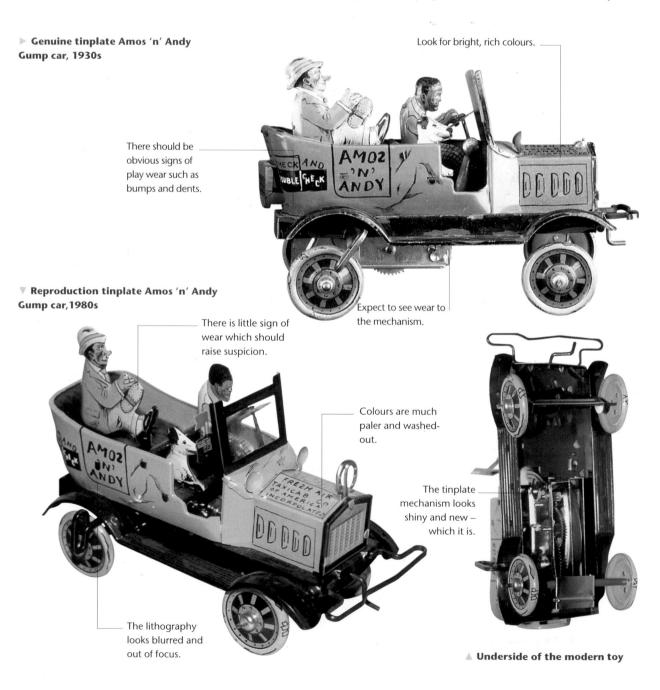

▷ **Genuine tinplate Amos 'n' Andy Gump car, 1930s**

Look for bright, rich colours.

There should be obvious signs of play wear such as bumps and dents.

Expect to see wear to the mechanism.

▽ **Reproduction tinplate Amos 'n' Andy Gump car, 1980s**

There is little sign of wear which should raise suspicion.

Colours are much paler and washed-out.

The tinplate mechanism looks shiny and new – which it is.

The lithography looks blurred and out of focus.

▲ **Underside of the modern toy**

the two sections is practically unnoticeable on the original examples. The surface was smoothly finished and colours were applied and baked, creating a hard enamel-like finish which chips rather than peels if damaged. Each of the different designs was registered at the American Patent Office and cast-iron toys and money banks generally have the patent-granted date stamped clearly on the underside. The mechanisms in original money banks are well finished and operate smoothly when a lever is pressed down – any stickiness in the action can normally be remedied by the application of a little oil.

Reproduction Money Banks

In the 1970s and '80s, cast-iron money banks were reproduced in enormous quantities in Taiwan and were exported worldwide. These banks were not originally made to deceive, however, and all examples were stamped with the name of the country of origin in capital letters on the underside. It has only been in recent years that the unscrupulous have either ground out the name or filled it in to mislead the public.

These reproduction money banks are usually roughly cast rather than smoothly finished and are crudely painted in bright, harsh colours without detail. The original hues should be mellow with a dulling patina of age. To try and reproduce this patination modern banks are often buried under-ground for a period. This certainly makes them dirty and encourages rust, but cannot really mislead if the collector is aware that this practice exists. The Taiwanese do not reproduce clearly the patent date stamped on the under-side of a bank and often this may be the only way to judge the authenticity of a toy which in every other respect may appear to be of the correct date.

Originally sold in shops as reproductions for a few pounds, banks such as that illustrated now often appear on market stalls and in general auctions, realizing prices of £100 to £150/$145–220, albeit probably believed by the traders to be authentic examples. Each design of bank has a different name stamped clearly on the front of the toy. Certain banks, such as the "Trick Dog", "Uncle Sam" and "Punch and Judy", were originally made in large numbers; others such as "Dentist", "Magician", "Jonah and the Whale", "Indian and Bear" and "Boy Scout" are scarcely seen as original examples outside the United States; if one is found it is most probably Taiwanese.

Check for smooth casting and that seams match up closely.

Colours should be muted.

There should be no signs of file marks on the toy.

▲ **Genuine Paddy and Pig Bank, 1885**

Colours are likely to be over-bright.

Look for uneven seams and bumpy or grainy casting – all a sign of reproductions.

▲ **Reproduction Paddy and Pig Bank, 1940s**

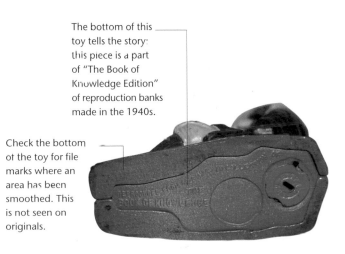

The bottom of this toy tells the story: this piece is a part of "The Book of Knowledge Edition" of reproduction banks made in the 1940s.

Check the bottom of the toy for file marks where an area has been smoothed. This is not seen on originals.

Dating Modern Toys

▼ **Genuine Atomic Robot Man with original box – although flaps replaced**
Compare with the reproduction on page 207.

▼ **Modern copy of an old German toy**
This toy turns up often at antiques and collectors' fairs. Many a person has thought it an old toy. The lithography is not good and plastic is used for the legs. Many toys like this appear on the market.

▶ **A Nomura Earth Man made in Japan, c.1957 and, far right, its modern copy**

Advertisements now appear regularly in specialist magazines from companies selling modern copies of old toys. In some instances these copies have been produced from the original moulds and presses and have no features to distinguish them from the originals, with their gleaming tinplate and bright lithographed colours. But in 20 years' time when their tinplate is dulled and their clockwork motors have rusted, will the toy collectors of the next century be fooled into buying a fake?

A selection of clockwork tinplate toys are now being made in Eastern European countries, India, China and other Far Eastern countries. These are often purchased by unsuspecting novice collectors as original, although they are not being sold as such. The reproductions generally have a very pale and indistinct printed finish, with the printing pixels clearly visible. They often use modern types of plastic and metals, which collectors should familiarize themselves with. Priced at usually no more than £5–20/\$7–30, they are obviously far too cheap for an old toy and are not the bargain they might seem.

Toy collecting has now expanded to more recently produced items, and consequently these are now also being copied and reproduced.

Robots and space toys has for a number of years been a popular toy collecting field, with some robots fetching five-figure sums. Some of these models have now been reproduced. They are not done to deceive, and are clearly marked as reissues. But again, the unscrupulous could easily remove these marks and dupe a new robot collector. As the original items are so rare, not many people have had the experience of handling them to know what they should be like. These include Mr. Atomic and Robby Space Patrol, both produced by M. T. H. Mike's Toy House.

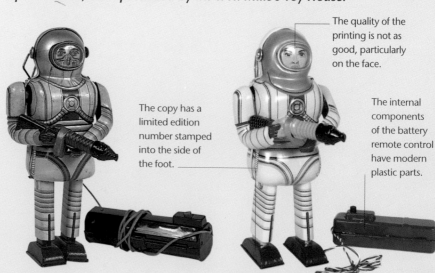

The quality of the printing is not as good, particularly on the face.

The copy has a limited edition number stamped into the side of the foot.

The internal components of the battery remote control have modern plastic parts.

BIBLIOGRAPHY

CONTINENTAL FURNITURE

HAYWARD, Helena (ed.), *World Furniture*, Hamlyn, London, 1965
KREISEL, H., *Die Kunst des Deutschen Mobels*, C. H. Beck, Munich, 1973
LEDOUX-LEBARD, Denise, *Les Ébenistes du XIXe Siècle*, Éditions de l'Amateur, Paris, revised edition 1985
PAYNE, Christopher, *19th Century European Furniture*, Antique Collectors' Club, Woodbridge, 1985

ENGLISH FURNITURE

BLY, John, *Discovering English Furniture*, Shire, Aylesbury, 1976
CHINNERY, Victor, *Oak Furniture: The British Tradition*, Antique Collectors' Club, Woodbridge, 1979
EDWARDS, Ralph, *The Dictionary of English Furniture* (3 volumes), Country Life, London, revised edition 1953
SYMONDS, R. W., *English Furniture from Charles II to George II*, The Connoisseur, London, 1929
SYMONDS, R. W., *Furniture Making in 17th and 18th Century England*, The Connoisseur, London, 1955
The Journal of the Furniture History Society, The Department of Furniture and Interior Design, The Victoria and Albert Museum, London, 1965-

AMERICAN FURNITURE

HECKSCHER, Morrison, *American Furniture in the Metropolitan Museum of Art*, Knopf, New York, 1972
KIRK, John, *American Chairs, Queen Anne and Chippendale*, Knopf, New York, 1972
MONTGOMERY, Charles F., *American Furniture, The Federal Period*, Viking, New York, 1966
MOSES, Michael, *Master Craftsmen of Newport*, MMI Americana, New York, 1984
NUTTING, Wallace, *Furniture Treasury* volumes 1, 2 and 3, Macmillan, New York, 1928
SACK, Albert, *Fine Points of Furniture*, Crown, New York, 1950
STONEMAN, Vernon C., *John and Thomas Seymour and Supplement*, Special Publications, Boston, 1959

CLOCKS

ALLIX, Charles and BONNERT, Peter, *Carriage Clocks: Their History and Development*, Antique Collectors' Club, Woodbridge, 1974
BAILLIE, G. H., *Watchmakers and Clockmakers of the World*, volume 1, NAG Press, London, 1974
BRITTEN, Frederick James, *Old Clocks and Watches and Their Makers*, Spon, London, 1933
CESKINSKY, Herbert C. and WEBSTER, Malcolm R., *English Domestic Clocks*, Spring Books/Hamlyn, London, 1969
DAWSON, P. G., DROVER, C. B., PARKES, D. W., *Early English Clocks*, Antique Collectors' Club, Woodbridge, 1982.
LOOMES, Brian, *Watchmakers and Clockmakers of the World*, volume 2, NAG Press, London, 1976
ROYER-COLLARD, F. Bernard, *Skeleton Clocks*, NAG Press, London, 1969

GLASS

BICKERTON, L. M., *English Drinking Glasses*, Barrie and Jenkins, London, 1971
BROOKS, John, *The Arthur Negus Guide to British Glass*, Hamlyn, London, 1981
CHARLESTON, Robert J., *English Glass and the Glass used in England c.400–1940*, George Allen and Unwin, London, 1984
KLEIN, Dan and LLOYD, Ward, *The History of Glass*, Orbis, London, 1984
NEWMAN, Harold, *An Illustrated Dictionary of Glass*, Thames and Hudson, London, 1977
SPIEGL, Walter, *Glas des Historismus*, Klinkhardt and Biermann, Braunschweig, 1980

BASE METALS

COTTERELL, Howard, *Old Pewter: Its Makers and Marks*, Batsford, London, 1968
FEILD, Rachael and GENTLE, Rupert, *English Domestic Brass*, Elek, London, 1985
HORNSBY, P. R. G., *Pewter of the Western World*, Schiffer, Exton PA and Moorland, Ashbourne, 1983
LAUGHLIN, L. I., *Pewter in America*, Crown, New York, 1981
LINDSAY, J. Seymour, *Iron and Brass Implements of the English House*, Tiranti, London, 1970
LISTER, Raymond, *Decorative Cast Ironwork in Great Britain*, George Bell, London, 1960
MARSDEN, B. M., *The Shadwell Shams – The Story of "Billy and Charley" Forgeries*, Coins and Antiquities, March 1999
MICHAELIS, Ronald Frederick, *Old Domestic Brass Candlesticks*, Antique Collectors' Club, Woodbridge, 1978
PEAL, Christopher Arthur (ed.), *More Pewter Marks*, Norwich Print Brokers, Norwich, 1979
WILLS, Geoffrey, *Collecting Copper and Brass*, Mayflower, London, 1970

SHEFFIELD PLATE

BRADBURY, F., *History of Old Sheffield Plate*, Northend Press, Sheffield, 1968
FROST, T. W., *The Price Guide to Old Sheffield Plate*, Antique Collectors' Club, Woodbridge, 1971
HUGHES, G. B., *Antique Sheffield Plate*, Batsford, London, 1970
VEITCH, H. M., *Sheffield Plate, Its History, Manufacture and Art*, George Bell, London, 1908
WALDRON, Peter, *Price Guide to Antique Silver*, Antique Collectors' Club, Woodbridge, 1985

ENGLISH SILVER

BARR, Elaine, *George Wickes, Royal Goldsmith*, Studio Vista/Christie's, London, 1980
CLAYTON, Michael, *The Collector's Dictionary of the Silver and Gold of Great Britain and South America*, Antique Collectors' Club, Woodbridge, 1985
CULME, John, *Nineteenth Century Silver*, Antique Collectors' Club, Woodbridge, 1985
JACKSON, Sir Charles James, *An Illustrated History of English Plate*, Macmillan, London, 1905
JACKSON, Sir Charles James, *English Goldsmiths and Their Marks*, Dover, New York, revised edition 1965

AMERICAN SILVER

BOHAN, Peter and HAMMERSLOUGH, P., *Early Connecticut Silver, 1700–1840*, Wesleyan University Press, Middletown, 1970
BUHLER, Kathryn C., *American Silver in the Museum of Fine Arts*, Boston, New York Graphic Society, New York, 1982
BUHLER, Kathryn C. and HOOD, Graham, *American Silver in the Yale University Art Gallery*, Yale University Press, New Haven and London, 1970
CARPENTER, Charles H., Jr., *Gorham Silver 1831–1981*, Dodd, Mead, New York, 1982
ENSKO, Stephen, *American Silversmiths and their Marks* (3 volumes), Ensko, New York, 1937
FALES, Martha G., *Joseph Richardson and Family, Philadelphia Silversmiths*, Wesleyan University Press, Middletown, 1974
PLEASANTS, Jacob Hall and SILL, Howard, *Maryland Silversmiths, 1715–1830*, Lord Baltimore Press, Baltimore, 1930
RAINWATER, Dorothy T., *Encyclopedia of American Silver Manufacturers*, Crown, New York, 1975

POTTERY AND PORCELAIN

ATTERBURY, Paul (ed.), *The History of Porcelain*, Orbis, London, 1982
BRITTON, Frank, *English Delftware in the Bristol Collection*, Sotheby's, London, 1982
BRUNET, Marcelle and PREAUD, Tamara, *Sèvres, Des Origines a Nos Jours*, Office du Livre, Paris, 1978
CHARLESTON, Robert (ed.), *World Ceramics*, Hamlyn, London, 1968
FOUREST, Henry-Pierre, *Delftware: Faience Production at Delft*, Thames and Hudson, London, 1980
GARNER, Sir Harry, *Oriental Blue and White*, Faber, London, third edition 1973
GIACOMOTTI, Jeanne, *French Faience*, Oldbourne Press, London, 1963
GODDEN, Geoffrey, *British Porcelain*, Barrie and Jenkins, London, 1974
GOMPERTZ, G. St G. M., *Chinese Celadon Wares*, Faber, London, 1958
JENYNS, Soame, *Japanese Porcelain*, Faber, London, 1965
LUNSINGH SCEURLEER, D. F., *Chinese Export Porcelain, Chine de Commande*, Faber, London, 1974
RACKHAM, Bernard, *Catalogue of Italian Maiolica in the Victoria and Albert Museum*, HMSO, London, 1940
WALCHA, Otto, *Meissen Porcelain*, Studio Vista/Christie's, London, 1973

NETSUKE

BUSHELL, Raymond, *Collectors' Netsuke*, Walker/Weatherhill, New York, 1971
BUSHELL, Raymond, *Netsuke Familiar and Unfamiliar*, Weatherhill, New York, 1975
DAVEY, Neil K., *Netsuke*, Sotheby's, London, 1974, revised edition 1982
KINSEY, Mirian, *Living Masters of Netsuke*, Kodansha, Tokyo, New York, San Francisco, 1983
MASATOSHI, *The Art of Netsuke Carving*, Kodansha, Tokyo, New York, San Francisco, 1981

QUILTS

BISHOP, Robert and SAFFORD, Carleton, *America's Quilts and Coverlets*, Dutton, New York, 1972
GREENSTEIN, Blanche and WOODARD, Thomas K., *Crib Quilts and Other Small Wonders*, Dutton, New York, 1981
KHIN, Yvonne M., *The Collector's Dictionary of Quilt Names and Patterns*, Acropolis, Washington D. C., 1980

DECOYS

EARNEST, Adele, *The Art of the Decoy*, Schiffer, Exton PA, 1982
MACKEY, William J., *American Bird Decoys*, Dutton, New York, 1965
STARR, George Ross, Jr., *Decoys of the Atlantic Flyway*, Winchester, New York, 1974

SCIENTIFIC INSTRUMENTS

PETERSON, Harold L., *How Do You Know It's Old?*, George Allen and Unwin, London, 1977
TAYLOR, E. G. R., *Bostock, Hurt and Hurt. An Index to the Mathematical Practitioners of Hanoverian England*, Harriet Wynter, London, 1980
TURNER, Gerard L'E., *Collecting Microscopes*, Studio Vista, London, 1981
TURNER, Gerard L'E., *19th Century Scientific Instruments*, Sotheby's, California, 1983
TURNER, Gerard L'E. and WYNTER, Harriet, *Scientific Instruments*, Studio Vista, London, 1975

SCRIMSHAW

FLAYDERMAN, E. Norman, *Scrimshaw and Scrimshanders*, Flayderman, New Milford CT, 1972
FRERE-COOK, Gervais (ed.), *The Decorative Arts of the Mariner*, Jupiter, London, 1974
RANDIER, Jean, *Nautical Antiques for the Collector*, Barrie and Jenkins, London, 1976

TOYS

HILLIER, Mary, *Teddy Bears: A Celebration*, Ebury, London, 1985
LEVY, Alan, *A Century of Model Trains*, New Cavendish, London, 1984
NORMAN, Bill, *The Bank Book*, Accent Studios, San Diego, 1985
PRESSLAND, David, *Art of the Tin Toy*, New Cavendish, London, 1976

Index

ACKNOWLEDGMENTS

Front jacket:
tl Amos 'n' Andy toy, Christie's; **tr** silver bowl with fake mark, Octopus Publishing Group/Christie's South Kensington/Premier Photography; **bl** George III mahogany side table *c*.1745, Sotheby's; **bc** copy of decanter, Octopus Publishing Group/Steve Tanner/Mark West; **br** copy of Staffordshire figure group *c*.1920, Octopus Publishing Group

Back jacket:
l George III giltwood mirror, Christie's Images; **r** reproduction gateleg table *c*.1930, Octopus Publishing Group/Ian Booth

Key:
a above, **b** below, **c** centre, **l** left, **r** right

AB Angela Bowey's Online Glass Museum (http://www.glass.co.nz/ysart.htm) Images by Kevin Holt, first published in the article "Identifying Paul Ysart Paperweights" **AJP** A. J. Photographics **BAL** Bridgeman Art Library **BBR** BBR Auctions, Elsecar Heritage Centre, Barnsley, S. Yorks S74 8HJ (tel: 01226 745156) **BHGM** Broadfield House Glass Museum, Compton Drive, Kingswinford, W. Midlands, DY6 9NS **Bon** Bonhams **C** Christie's **CH** Chris Halton **CI** Christie's Images **CP** Christopher Payne **DB** David Battie **DR** Derek Roberts Antiques, 25 Shipbourne Road, Tonbridge, Kent TN10 3DN (tel: 01732 358986) **ESTO** ESTO Photographics **FITZ** Fitzwilliam Museum, University of Cambridge **GL** Gordon Lang **IB** Ian Booth **JB** John Bly **KH** Kevin Holt **OPG** Octopus Publishing Group **P** Phillips **P/B** Phillips/Bonhams **PA** Peter Anderson **PC** Private Collection **PS** The Pewter Society, c/o Worshipful Company of Pewterers (see below) **RMN** Réunion des Musées Nationaux **S** Sotheby's **SG** Sweetbriar Gallery, Sweetbriar House, 106 Robin Hood Lane, Helsby, Cheshire WA6 9NY **SIA** Sotheby's Institute of Art, 30 Oxford Street, London W1D 1AU **SK** Skinner Inc, Auctioneers and Appraisers of Antiques and Fine Art, Boston, MA, USA **SNY** Sotheby's New York **SP** Sue Pearson, 131/2 Prince Albert Street, Brighton, BN1 1HE **SPL** Sotheby's Picture Library **SR** Stella Rubin, 12300 Glen Road, Potomac, Maryland 20854, USA **ST** Steve Tanner **T** Tennants Auctioneers, The Auction Centre, Leyburn, N. Yorks DL8 5SG

TOB Tobar, St Margaret, Harleston, Norfolk, IP20 0TB **TQA** Treasure Quest Auction Galleries, Inc, 2581 Jupiter Park, Drive, Suite E-5, Jupiter, FL 33458 **TR** Tim Ridley **V&A** Victoria & Albert Museum **WCG** Worshipful Company of Goldsmiths, Goldsmiths Hall, 13 Foster Lane, London EC2V 6BN **WCP** Worshipful Company of Pewterers, Pewterers Hall, Oat Lane, London EC2V 7DE **WD** West Dean College, West Dean, Chichester, PO18 0QZ

1 DB; **3** OPG/ST/SIA; **5** OPG/ST/BHGM; **6** SIA; **7a** OPG/IB/S **bl & br** OPG/IB; **8** CP; **9a & c** CI **b** P/B; **10** CI; **11** V&A; The Wallace Collection, London; **13** CI; **14** RMN; **15** OPG/IB; **16** SPL; **17** CI; **19** V&A; **20** SPL; **21** CP; **23r** CP **c & l** OPG/IB; **24** OPG/S; **25–26** CI; **27 from tl** OPG/S, OPG/Pro-Photo, OPG/TR/Bon, CI, OPG/Pro-Photo/Bon x2, OPG/Pro-Photo x2, OPG/Pro-Photo/S x 2, CI, OPG/Pro-Photo/S x 2, OPG/TR/Bon x 2, CI, SPL; **28a** SPL **b** OPG/IB; **29a** JB **b** SPL; **30–32** JB; **33** OPG; **35** JB; **36tl & tc** OPG/IB; **36c & cr** CI **bl & cbl** OPG/William Bedford plc **br** SPL; **37–38** JB; **39** CI; **40** OPG/IB; **42** SPL; **43** CI; **44** JB; **45al** SPL **all others** OPG/IB; **46–49a** JB; **49b** CI; **50** JB; **52–3** SPL; **54–61** JB; **62–64** Israel Sack, Inc; **65** CI; **66–8** Israel Sack, Inc.; **70** DR; **71–73** WD; **73ar** DR; **74** CI; **75–76** DR; **77** WD; **78–79** OPG/ST/BHGM; **80a** SIA; **80bl–86** OPG/ST/BHGM; **87al** Toledo Museum of Art; **87ar–89** OPG/ST/GHGM; **90a** OPG **b** BHGM; **92–93a** OPG/ST/BHGM; **93b** OPG; **94–95b** OPG/ST/BHGM; **96** BHGM; **97** OPG/ST/D. & P. Atkinson; **98–99** OPG/ST/BHGM; **100l** BHGM **r** OPG/ST/BHGM; **102a & ac** SG **all others** AB/KH; **103** SG; **105–107** OPG/ST/PS; **108–109cr** OPG/ST/WCP; **109bl–110a** OPG/ST/PS; **110b** OPG/ST/WCP; **110bl** OPG/ST/PS; **111c** OPG/ST/WCP; **111b** OPG/ST/PS; **112** CI **bl** PC/BAL **br** CI; **113a** PC/BAL **b** SPL; **114a** CI **b** Haslam & Whiteway Ltd, London/BAL; **115** CI; **116a** C **b** V&A; **117a** OPG/Pro-Photo/CSK **b** OPG /AJP/CSK; **118–119a** WCG; **119c, b & bl** OPG/AJP/CSK; **120a & c** WCG; **120bl** OPG/AJP; **bc** OPG/AJP; **121** T; **122l & a** OPG/AJP/CSK; **122b** OPG/IB/S; **123** CI; **124** Cotehele House, Cornwall, UK/BAL; **125al** CI **ar** V&A **b** OPG/Pro-Photo/CSK. **126l** OPG/IB/S; **126b–127** CI; **128** OPG/AJP/CSK; **129al & ar** CI **b** OPG/IB/S; **130** OPG/AJP/CSK; **132a** OPG/AJP/CSK **b**

SPL; **133bl** SIA **br** OPG/ST/SIA; **135a** OPG/Brand Inglis **b** SNY; **136t** CI **b** Museum of Fine Arts, Boston: the Philip Leffingwell Spalding Coll, given in his memory by Katherine Ames Spalding and Philip Spalding, Oakes Ames Spalding, Hobart Ames Spalding 42.242; **137a** SNY/S **137bl–138l** CI; **138r** SNY/S; **140l** CI; **140r–141a** SIA; **141b** OPG/ST/SIA; **142l & al** SIA **ar** CI; **143a** OPG/CH/P **ac** OPG/ST/SIA; **143cb–144** GL; **145** SIA; **146a** OPG/CH/P; **146bl–147** OPG/ST/SIA; **148al & cl** GL **cb** SIA **b** OPG/ST/SIA; **149a** SIA; **149cl & b** GL; **150a** SIA; **150bl–151** GL/S; **152a & bl** GL; **br** OPG/ST/SIA; **153a** P **ar** CI **b** GL/S; **154a** GL **b** CI; **155** OPG/ST/SIA; **156** SIA; **157a** OPG/ST/SIA **b** OPG; **158al** SPL **cl** OPG/ST/SIA **cr** GL **b** CI; **159** OPG/ST/SIA; **160al & bl** CI **ar & br** OPG/P; **161al & ar** OPG/ST/SIA **161bl–162tl** SIA; **162ar** OPG/ST/SIA; **162b** SIA; **163–164bl** SIA; **164 br** OPG/ST/SIA; **165** SIA; **166** GL; **167l** OPG/ST/BBR **r** OPG/ST/SIA; **168l** CI **r** OPG/ST/SIA; **169a & c** SIA **b** OPG/ST/SIA **170–171** CI; **172** GL; **173l** V&A **r** SIA; **174a** OPG/ST/SIA **174b & 175l** SIA; **175a** CI **b** SIA; **176a** OPG/ST/SIA **bl** BAL **br** SIA; **177a** OPG/CH/Donna Thynne **bl** OPG/ST/SIA **br** FITZ/BAL; **178a** GL **bl & br** OPG/ST/SIA; **179l & c** CI **r** Bon/BAL; **180l–182** OPG/ST/SIA; **183l** V&A **r** GL; **184a & b** SIA; **185a & bl** SIA **br** OPG/ST/SIA; **186a** OPG/CH/P **b** GL; **187** CI; **188l** DB **r** PC/BAL; **189–191** DB; **192a** V&A **bl, bc & br** DB; **193** SPL; **194** DB; **195** PC/BAL; **196–198** SR/ESTO; **199** SR/Harriet Wise/Collection of Polly Mello; **200** ESTO/Schecter Lee; **201al** ESTO/Chun Lai **ar & b** ESTO/Schecter Lee; **202** SK/Dr David Coffeen/Tesseract; **203** SK; **204** DB; **206** SPL; **207a** TOB; **b** OPG/IB/CSK; **208** CI; **209** OPG/SP **bc** SP; **210** OPG/PA/Chuck Steffes; **211–212a** CI; **212b–213** TQA; **214a** SK **bl & br** TOB **bc** OPG/IB/CSK